Special Populations in Gifted Education

Working with Diverse Gifted Learners

Jaime A. Castellano

Gifted Education Program Administrator
School District of Palm Beach County, Florida

Boston   New York   San Francisco
Mexico City   Montreal   Toronto   London   Madrid   Munich   Paris
Hong Kong   Singapore   Tokyo   Cape Town   Sydney

Executive Editor: *Virginia Lanigan*
Editorial Assistant: *Robert Champagne*
Executive Marketing Manager: *Amy Cronin*
Editorial-Production Service: *Omegatype Typography, Inc.*
Manufacturing Buyer: *Andrew Turso*
Composition Buyer: *Linda Cox*
Cover Administrator: *Kristina Mose-Libon*
Electronic Composition: *Omegatype Typography, Inc.*

For related titles and support materials, visit our online catalog at www.ablongman.com.

Library of Congress Cataloging-in-Publication Data

Castellano, Jaime A.
    Special populations in gifted education : working with diverse gifted learners / Jaime A. Castellano.
        p. cm.
    Includes bibliographical references and index.
    ISBN 0-205-35958-2
        1. Gifted children—Education.   2. Gifted children—Identification.   I. Title.
LC3993.2 .C39 2003
    371.95—dc21

                                                                                2002074378

Printed in the United States of America
10 9 8 7 6 5 4 3 2 1   07 06 05 04 03 02

This book is dedicated to my wife, Lillian Castellano, whom I love very much and who for the past 18 years has gone above and beyond in order that I may pursue my career as an educator, administrator, university professor, consultant, and writer. Her passion, frankness, and understanding are respected and appreciated. To my children Jaime Jr., Alejandro, Gabriel, and Gisell who amaze, challenge, and inspire me. They are my proudest accomplishment. To my mother-in-law and father-in-law, Ismael and Delia Torres, who never doubted me for a moment. To my brother and sisters and their spouses (Frank and Yolanda Corona, Sergio and Cynthia Barerra, Olympia Salas, and Michael and Kelly Castellano) and their children who will always be a part of my heart and my life despite our geographical separation. Finally, to my childhood friends, Laura and Cynthia Robles, sisters, who taught me about life, friendship, believing in myself, how to dream, how to challenge myself, and who emphasized that an education was the key to my future. Thank you from the bottom of my heart.

CONTENTS

PREFACE

Since their inception, gifted education programs have been filled primarily with white middle-class boys and girls. Not much has changed over the past 30 years, despite the fact that the United States is as diverse as it has ever been in its more than 225-year history. Culturally and linguistically diverse students have impacted virtually every school-based program that exists, with the exception, arguably, of gifted education. Poverty rates of public school students are at an all-time high. And special interest groups who strongly advocate for a specific group of students have filled the past 30 years with court battles. The research also validates that African Americans continue to be identified as an underrepresented group in gifted education programs.

Over the years, however, we have become much wiser and more accepting. As a result, the number of special populations of diverse learners in gifted education has grown. For the first time in modern times, for example, researchers and practitioners in bilingual/ESL and gifted education are formally interacting to ensure the equal participation of students who speak a language other than English. Advocates of gay and lesbian students also argue that as a group these students are not receiving the social and emotional support they require in any school program, including gifted education. Those who possess a handicapping condition, regardless of what it might be, are not getting a fair share either.

This book is intended to provide a desperately needed update to reflect today's rendition of who the special populations are in gifted education. It is not only African Americans, Hispanics, and females any more. Today's special populations include a complex cross-section of students. From the gay or lesbian student to the one who is biracial and bicultural; and from the indigenous to the dual labeled. Certainly, there are more special populations than could be covered in one book. The intent is not to exclude any student group. On the contrary, the focus is inclusionary in nature. This book on special populations in gifted education includes any combination of the following areas of interest, among others: characteristics; curriculum and instruction; identification, assessment, and evaluation; nurturing; and meeting unique social, emotional, academic, and cognitive needs.

This book is also intended to reflect a paradigm with deep roots that acknowledges that gifted and talented students transcend cultural, ethnic, and linguistic ties; conditions that are disabling; sexual orientation; poverty; and geography. In every possible subgroup of students there are those who are deserving, by right, not privilege, of those benefits typically associated with gifted education programming. This book helps shed light in this regard. It reflects today's student demographics and serves as a valuable resource tool for educators, parents, and administrators who choose to promote access, equity, and excellence to the special populations of students targeted here.

Acknowledgments

I would like to first acknowledge the contributing writers to this project for helping make this book a reality. Without their passion, commitment, and professionalism, this book would not have been possible. A special thanks goes to Mr. Robert Woltman whose two wonderful poems, "The Gift" and "The Lesson," help capture the message we are trying to send. His creative gift and talent is evidenced in his poems for all to read and share. I would also like to thank the following reviewers: Norma E. Hernandez, Modern Language Services–Baton Rouge; Beverly J. Irby, Sam Houston State University–Huntsville; Hui Fang Huang Su, Nova Southeastern University–Boca Raton. Additional thanks to Virginia Lanigan, executive editor, and Erin Liedel for believing in the potential and value of this book, and for their professionalism, patience, and collaborative work style.

ABOUT THE CONTRIBUTORS

Nilda Aguirre is the gifted education program supervisor in the East Baton Rouge Parish School System in Baton Rouge, Louisiana. Aguirre's particular areas of expertise include gifted education, English as a second language, bilingual education, and the interface of these disciplines. She presents regularly for the National Association for Gifted Children and the National Association for Bilingual Education, where she serves as co-chair of the Special Interest Group in Gifted Education. As a national staff development consultant, Aguirre has helped train hundreds of teachers throughout the United States in identifying and serving culturally and linguistically diverse students in gifted education. As national project disseminator of project GOTCHA (Galaxies of Thinking and Creative Heights of Achievement), she has implemented programs in six states.

Clar Baldus is the administrator for the Rural Schools Programs and Inventiveness Programs at the Belin–Blank Center and the state coordinator for Invent Iowa, an invention program that serves kindergarten through twelfth grade. As administrator for Rural Schools, Baldus is implementing a grant that will provide all Iowa students with access to advanced placement courses. She received her B.A. in art education from Mount Mercy College, Cedar Rapids, Iowa, and her M.A. in education for applied research from Marycrest College, Davenport, Iowa. She completed a Ph.D. in educational psychology (with emphasis in visual–spatial abilities) at the University of Iowa. Her research has been guided by her passion for art, interest in creative processes, and commitment to talent development. Before joining the Belin–Blank Center, Baldus was a resources specialist and assessment facilitator for elementary gifted and talented students in Cedar Rapids Community Schools. Baldus's extensive teaching experience includes many years working with students at the secondary, postsecondary, and professional development levels. Her professional affiliations include Iowa Talented and Gifted Association, National Association for Gifted Education, National Rural Education Association, American Council on Rural Special Education, and Phi Delta Kappa.

Ernesto Bernal, Ph.D, is an educational consultant who specializes in dual language education, gifted education, psychometrics, and program evaluation. He is also vice president of the San Antonio, Texas, Gifted Education Foundation. Bernal conducted the first study of gifted Mexican American children and continues to work with innovative school programs that seek to improve assessment practices and educational opportunities for all students, with a focus on students from culturally and linguistically diverse groups.

Jaime A. Castellano is one of the leading national figures in gifted education in the identification, assessment, and education of culturally and linguistically diverse and low-socioeconomic status students. He has assumed leadership responsibilities with the National Association for Gifted Children (NAGC), where he currently serves as the secretary of the Special Populations Division; and the National Association for Bilingual Education (NABE), where he serves as the chair of the Special Interest Group in Gifted Education. Castellano also serves on the staffs of Florida Atlantic University and Lynn University, both in Boca Raton, Florida, where he is a graduate school adjunct professor, teaching courses in English to speakers of other languages (ESOL). During his career in the public schools of Illinois and Florida, he has served as a special education teacher, bilingual education teacher, assistant principal, principal, director of gifted programs, Title VII director, and administrative assistant to the superintendent. He has written numerous articles on gifted and bilingual education and continues to consult with school districts throughout the United States on the identification of historically underrepresented students for gifted education programming. Castellano currently serves as a gifted education program administrator for the school district of Palm Beach County, Florida.

Sandy Cohn is currently associate professor in the Division of Curriculum and Instruction at Arizona State University in Tempe, Arizona. He has been involved in the field of gifted education for almost 30 years and has written numerous articles on the gay gifted learner. In addition, for the past 11 years he has been an advocate for the education of gifted migrant students, coordinating a program to meet their unique needs. His professional affiliations include the National Association for Gifted Children, American Psychological Association, and the Council for Exceptional Children/The Association for the Gifted. His advocacy and writing on behalf of gay gifted students in facing the challenge of homophobia and antihomosexual bias in schools have received national acclaim.

Ken Dickson has experience that includes teaching, educational administration, advocacy, and consulting. His professional career began in 1973 in Arkansas as a fine arts teacher and administrator of gifted program services. He continued serving as a gifted program administrator in Wisconsin and, later, in interdisciplinary services in Kentucky. Dickson has served as a consultant with the U.S. Department of Education's Office of Educational Research and Improvement (OERI), Colorado Office. Dickson earned a B.A. in education, an M.A. in education, and certification in special programs supervision. Currently, Dickson is involved in action research with school districts and educational agencies through Educational Solutions & Consulting Network (ESCN), Upper Marlboro, and a consulting service he established. He is a member of the board of directors of the National Association for Gifted Children and is on the executive board for the Division for Culturally and Linguistically Diverse Exceptional Learners of the Council for Exceptional Children.

Anne Faivus has worked in the field of gifted education for more than 15 years as a teacher of gifted students or administrator of gifted programs. She received her master's degree in gifted education from the University of Southern Mississippi. Faivus has implemented an innovative middle school curriculum for gifted students on the Holocaust and African American studies. She currently is employed as a gifted education specialist with the school district of Palm Beach County, Florida.

Kevin Foley serves as a high school teacher in the school district of Palm Beach County, Florida. He coaches swimming and sponsors the high school yearbook. His particular interests include working with culturally and linguistically diverse students. Prior to that, he taught psychology, journalism, and English in Fairfax County, Virginia. He received his B.A. in American literature and psychology from James Madison University and his M.S. in industrial/organizational psychology from George Mason University in Fairfax, Virginia. Foley is currently taking graduate-level course work from Florida Atlantic University.

Virginia Gonzalez has an interdisciplinary professional and academic background, with a Ph.D. in educational psychology from the University of Texas, Austin, in 1991. She is a native speaker of Spanish, having been born and raised in Lima, Peru. Her major area of expertise is the development of innovative models and educational applications for the assessment and instruction of both child and adult English as a second language (ESL) learners. She has published extensively and is recognized for her scholarly commitment, having received national honors and awards from major national and international associations for her contributions to second-language learning, bilingual education, and cognitive and language development. Gonzalez was recently appointed as a visiting scholar for the College Board during the 2000–2001 academic year, under the sponsorship of the board's Division of Education and Academic Initiatives.

Jim Granada is director of the Department of Advanced Academic Services for the Austin Independent School District in Austin, Texas. Granada has worked extensively in the field of gifted education for many years, specializing in the areas of gifted Hispanic students, creativity, and gifted program design. Granada has served as the chair of the Creativity Division of the National Association for Gifted Children (NAGC) and has presented on numerous topics in gifted education across the United States. He has taught in the public school system for 17 years; served on the faculty of Willamette University in Salem, Oregon, and the University of Texas at San Antonio; and was a gifted education specialist at the Education Service Center, Region 20, in San Antonio, Texas.

Valentina Kloosterman serves as a research associate at the Center for Children and Families at the Education Development Center, Inc. in Newton, Massachusetts. Her research and practice focus on bilingualism, talent development, diversity, and child development. She has traveled extensively across the United States and Latin America, conducting workshops and providing professional development for researchers and practitioners. She regularly contributes to many educational associations as editorial reviewer, translator, consultant, and mentor. One of her primary areas of interest is the provision of appropriate and meaningful education for high-ability culturally and linguistically diverse children. She is committed to bridging the gap between diversity and talent development in gifted education. Kloosterman is currently co-editing the forthcoming book, *A Historical and Contemporary View of Hispanic Students in American Schools.*

Terry Neu is currently an assistant professor of education at Sacred Heart University in Fairfield, Connecticut. He served as the codirector of project High Hopes, an educational research grant funded under the Jacob K. Javitz legislation, from 1993 to 1996. This program focused on developing the talents of high-ability learning-disabled, hearing-impaired, or emotionally- or behaviorally-disordered students in the arts and sciences. Neu trains and consults nationally in using the multiple intelligences approach in the classroom and specifically meeting the needs of students with learning disabilities in science education. Neu also serves on the board of the Association for the Education of Gifted Underachieving Students (AEGUS) and heads the Special Populations Division of the National Association for Gifted Children. He has also been a classroom teacher of biology, gifted education, and special education for seven years in Arkansas.

Olivia Skenandore has been an award-winning gifted education teacher in New Mexico for more than 15 years. She is presently a doctoral student at the University of New Mexico and has served as chair of the Special Populations Division for the National Association for Gifted Children. As a national advocate for the inclusion of Native Americans in programs for the gifted, Skenandore has conducted workshops and training across the United States. Her gifted characteristics checklist for Native Americans is used by school districts throughout the Southwest to assist them in identifying this student population.

Keith Suranna, Ph.D., serves as a research associate at the Center for Science Education at the Education Development Center, Inc. in Newton, Massachusetts. He has served as an assistant professor of education at Endicott College and as an adjunct professor and student teacher supervisor at the University of Connecticut. He has also taught kindergarten in New York City and third grade in Connecticut. Suranna is currently writing a book tentatively titled *Conceptualizing Teacher Leadership for American Schools.* His professional interests include teacher leadership, preservice teacher education, and qualitative research. He earned his B.F.A. in dramatic arts and his M.A. in early childhood and elementary education, both from New York University. Saranna earned his Ph.D. in curriculum and instruction from the University of Connecticut.

Will White earned his doctorate degree in gifted education at the University of Connecticut and has experience as a classroom teacher, school administrator, and university instructor. White has presented at state and national conferences and has served as a consultant to school districts in the areas of program development and curriculum development for gifted and high-performing students. He is currently employed as program planner for gifted education with the school district of Palm Beach County, Florida, which serves almost 9,000 gifted students.

Robert Woltman has spent most of his career as an artist, commercial graphic designer, and museum curator/exhibition designer. As the exhibit curator for the Albuquerque Museum in Albuquerque, New Mexico, Woltman is responsible for designing and constructing the exhibit sets. In recent years, he has directed his attention to writing short fiction, nonfiction, and poetry. As one of Albuquerque's rising poets, his work has been published at the local, state, and national level. Two of his poems, "The Gift" and "The Lesson," can be found in this publication. He has also recited for the National Association for Gifted Children and the National Association for Bilingual Education. Woltman lives with his wife, Janet, in Albuquerque, New Mexico.

THE GIFT

For Rachel Carson
By Robert Woltman

See those kids sprawled
In the summer grass,
A shower's first raindrop
Falling softly on their faces?

That girl is wondering,
Her eyes open to the clouds,
How these raindrops were born
Before their trip to the sky.

This boy giggles,
Deciding how he'd say
"Raindrops are like wet kisses
Tiny hummingbirds give you."

These kids clumped together,
Arms and legs in a starburst,
Sing an improvised round,
As each drop splats a note.

Now, we can discuss the four modalities,
Study analyticals and globals,
Gardner's nine intelligences,
And learning styles and models

Rows of penciled in ovals
Wait in line to be tabulated.
We check, measure, and classify,
Write up and file reports.

But stop and consider something remarkable:
How raindrops, all the same,
Can water imagination
In infinite ways.

Because all children are gifted
With a "sense of wonder."
Each uniquely fascinated
By everything everywhere.

It lets them first feel
Before wanting to know
Answers to questions
They still haven't formed.

Yes, of course all kids are different
But they're still all alike in their needs:
Encouragement, recognition
And lots of chances to dream

Given these, the sense of wonder
Will stay with them throughout their lives.
And they'll always remember what can be learned
By just lying out in the rain.

THE LESSON

By Robert Woltman

Where I went to school,
the flag we pledged to had forty-eight stars
and hung with pictures
Of Ike, Jesus Christ, and the Pope.
Being a "W" I always sat in the back
at creaky desks that smelled of oil
    and ammonia.
I looked out the big windows
and spent a lot of time drawing.
I was good enough at it so that when I
    drew people,
the arms were attached to their shoulders
and not sticking straight out from their sides.
Kids who could draw seemed almost
    special somehow,
and maybe I was gifted in my own goofy ways.
But programs for me?
There were none I recall;
with fifty plus baby boom kids in a class,
those nuns had no time for the bottom or top.
But the sisters always encouraged my talents,
and never let me forget they were gifts
    from God.
Mom and Dad did too, though they considered
    my art as
"something to fall back on,"
growing up as they did in tough,
falling-back-on-times.
Blessed and lucky I was, but of course I still
    wonder
what going to school would be like today.

Maybe, for instance, I'd finally comprehend
even just the basics of rudimentary math.
We know so much more now about how
    people learn,
so many differences in the way things are
    taught.
But there's so much still dependent
on one absolute constant:
the need for a teacher devoted to these kids.
A catalytic teacher, fanning imagination's
    embers
until they flare,
then burn steady and bright
A teacher courageous enough to believe in
the power she has
to change a young life.
A teacher to recognize what makes each child
    unique,
to celebrate and enrich every child's
    distinctions.
A teacher whose vision
scans past the horizons familiar,
leading kids to a place beyond what can
    be learned
out to somewhere further
than what they can know
to where they can dream
of what they can do.

1

Casting a Wider Net

Linking Bilingual and Gifted Education

JIM GRANADA

In this diverse U.S. society, educators must recognize the educational challenges and make reflective decisions that positively impact the unique needs of students that a diverse population generates. As gifted education and the many variables that impact the delivery of gifted educational services in schools and school districts are considered, special attention must be given to the complexities that impact students who are gifted and potentially gifted and also bilingual and bicultural. In this chapter, the relationship between bilingual and gifted education is examined; the nature and needs of students who are bilingual/bicultural gifted are explored; and methods of identification, programming, and instruction are presented. The chapter concludes with general recommendations for the development of sound gifted bilingual/bicultural programs.

A Brief History of Gifted Education for Bilingual Students

Various forms of bilingual education may have been implemented in the United States since its infancy, but federal legislation addressing bilingual education was not passed until the late 1960s. In a political examination of bilingual education, Crawford (1998) reviews significant issues that resulted from the Bilingual Education Act of 1968 and addresses the different perspectives of bilingual education emphasis. Crawford compares a language-as-problem emphasis with that of language-as-resource. In the former, a quick-exit pedagogy focuses on rapid acquisition of English as a priority goal. In the latter, a late-exit enrichment model results from a combination of native-language instruction and English acquisition. The implications of which perspective is adopted by an educational community are extremely significant. Students who are in the "fast lane" toward acquiring a second language may be consistently overlooked for consideration as gifted, particularly if the gifts are not in the area of language acquisition. Those in bilingual programs that emphasize language as resource would appear more likely to have a context in which giftedness in many forms could be identified and nurtured. Bilingual programs with either perspective can connect with gifted education, but they must be approached in very different ways.

Gifted education in the United States has a long history, dating at least back to studies of gifted children in the 1920s. However, gifted education has not received the same level of recognition and funding as have both special education and bilingual education. A national definition of giftedness was outlined in the early 1970s (Marland, 1972), but a gifted education act has proven elusive to advocates of gifted and talented students.

Research in the area of giftedness and bilingual education has been limited. Ernesto Bernal, one of the prominent early researchers on the subject, reported in 1994 that since the first gifted and talented programs began in the 1930s, new understandings about giftedness have led to a more inclusionary view of gifted education. According to Bernal, the field now emphasizes selection over identification and places more value on cultural diversity. In spite of the changing view, bilingual gifted education has proven to be isolated and problematic. Barkan and Bernal (1991) illustrate the shortcomings of bilingual gifted education in the early 1990s: "These children, if they are: 'identified' at all, are typically admitted only after they have mastered English and can receive instruction in an all-English classroom" (p. 144).

School systems on both coasts of the United States and in the Southwest have designed programs targeting bilingual gifted students, with some successful programs organizing as early as the late 1970s. Tucson, Arizona, was the site of one of the programs that was reported in the professional literature. The Tucson Unified School District in 1987 reorganized services for gifted students. The district at that time also used a Title VII bilingual gifted grant to research selection procedures, develop Spanish curriculum materials, and prepare bilingual certified teachers to earn certification in gifted education. Two points focused toward bilingual and gifted education integration were the inclusion of case study approaches and the involvement of language minority communities in identification (Barkan & Bernal, 1991). Additionally, the authors reported that during the 1989–1990 school year, the Tucson school district used a case study procedure that included these elements in the identification of bilingual first-grade gifted students in select schools:

Raven's Coloured Matrices
Teacher checklist of student behaviors
Parent questionnaire
Abbreviated version of the Wechsler Intelligence Scale for Children (WISC)

Rating of self-esteem
Samples of student work

Barkan and Bernal concluded that bilingually competent teachers of the gifted were the key to the education of gifted children who were limited English proficient (LEP). With the shortage of bilingual teachers across the United States, this critical key may prove elusive but should not be forgotten.

Characteristics of Potentially Gifted Bilingual Students

Gifted and *potentially gifted* are terms that often lack definitive parameters within the context of their use. This remains true when applying either term to bilingual students. Educators must also consider whether gifted programs for bilingual students are reflective of a bilingual emphasis or a gifted emphasis. I distinguish the bilingual gifted student as one who primarily demonstrates giftedness linguistically, whereas the gifted bilingual student may be gifted in a variety of areas and is also bilingual. Characteristics, identification, and programming must be consistent with the construct if the needs of the gifted student are to be consistently met.

"Both bilingualism and talent development are multidimensional phenomena involving cognitive, affective, cultural, environmental, and situational factors" reports Kloosterman (1997, p. 3). Although this is true, certain distinctions can be made between a student who demonstrates a linguistic giftedness and a student who is gifted in another area but is also bilingual. The bilingual gifted student will be more likely to demonstrate a rapid acquisition of a second language while demonstrating a high degree of manipulation and sophistication in the use of the primary language. This student might be nominated for a gifted program at two different points. He or she may draw attention based on the rapidity in which he or she exits from bilingual or English as a second language (ESL) services, and if criteria are in place to identify verbal giftedness in both languages, the student may qualify early for services. If the student is not identified early, linguistic talents may transfer rapidly to the second language, and the student may demonstrate gifted traits similar to non–second-language peers within a relatively short time, given the fact that traditional gifted students are often verbally gifted and flourish in the highly verbal classrooms of the U.S. educational system. In a 1998 report from the Office of Educational Research and Improvement of the U.S. Department of Education, reference is made to the argument of some educators that being bilingual is a special ability involving the constant negotiation between two linguistic worlds as well as the problem solving and sophisticated code switching required in such linguistic intelligence. The bilingual gifted student demonstrates this ability much earlier and at a much higher degree than bilingual peers.

The gifted bilingual student, however, may mirror more traditional gifted students, particularly those identified in systems in which multiple areas of giftedness are recognized and served. Giftedness in leadership, the visual and performing arts, and creativity can readily be demonstrated by bilingual students, provided the learning environment in which they are educated allows for experiences to demonstrate these talents as well as nurturing confidence, the lack of which may factor in to the demonstration of high ability. School settings may not always provide the context in which these areas of giftedness are most visible; it may be necessary to move beyond the boundaries of the campus to observe the manifestation of nonacademic gifted behaviors.

More elusive is the bilingual student who is academically gifted. A language-as-resource bilingual education program may be more ideal to recognize the bilingual student who is gifted in math, science, social studies, language arts, technology, or any other content area in which gifted services are provided. Bilingual and ESL programs that provide academic rigor and enrichment in all core areas, rather than focusing predominantly on second-language acquisition, better allow for the demonstration of potential giftedness in content areas. Gifted bilingual students given limited opportunities to demonstrate high levels of content performance in their dominant language may eventually be immersed in English-only classrooms in which the long-term acquisition of a second language may mask the academic talent of the student.

Both bilingual gifted and gifted bilingual students may not demonstrate gifted characteristics found on the many lists that have been designed by gifted education leaders over many years. Cultural traditions and beliefs, heritage, acculturation, and in some cases, poverty, may be critical variables impacting how gifted behaviors are demonstrated. Checklists of characteristics that have proven effective in searching for students for traditional gifted programs may not provide accurate profiles for bilingual students who are also gifted. Alternative characteristics need to be examined if increasing LEP student representation in gifted programs is a priority.

McLean (1995) comments on the first critical variable: culture. "Culture provides the substance and content for attitudes, thought, and action; it allows for a culture-specific idiosyncratic representation of knowledge among its peoples; it determines the kinds of cognitive strategies and learning modes that individuals use for solving complex problems within their society" (p. 8). The traditions that the family and cultural community of a bilingual student follow may provide several indicators of giftedness that are not visible in the culture of the school. These include, among many, storytelling and the oral tradition, depth and breadth of understanding of specific traditions, level of involvement in religious affiliations and community service, and the roles and responsibilities accepted within the family. Also, involvement in artistic endeavors reflecting what is valued in the culture may provide additional evidence of talent.

Educators responsible for gifted programs should also be knowledgeable of how giftedness is defined within a family and culture. Traditional gifted programs are highly representative of middle-class U.S. culture, and programs are often defined based on what is valued as gifted in mainstream society. If a family does not share these mainstream values, then giftedness may be defined in a very different manner. Cultural conflicts can also impact the demonstration of giftedness. For some families, competition and focus on self are not encouraged. Competitive children and those who draw attention to their talents may be more readily identified as potentially gifted in U.S. classrooms than those who have not been raised as such.

Rate of acculturation of a bicultural student may also be considered a possible atypical indicator of giftedness. A student who quickly adapts to the norms of peers in a school setting, which could include mannerisms, fashion, music, and various trends, may be demonstrating both reflective and conceptual thinking, as well as keen observation and analysis of the environment. How well the student adapts among the cultural contexts of the home, the neighborhood, and the school may also indicate a complex level of adaptability few have experienced. Acculturation is not likely to be found in a list of gifted characteristics used to identify gifted students.

Finally, poverty may be a variable impacting some bilingual students, depending on the circumstances surrounding their arrival in the school community. The potentially gifted student who is also living in a poverty situation becomes one of the most difficult students to identify for gifted services. Poverty can impact the demonstration of giftedness dramatically but not always in a negative way. Children of poverty who are creatively gifted may fill their lives with creative, rather than commercial, forms of self-entertainment and may use problem-solving skills to a much higher degree than their peers. Academically gifted children in poverty situations may seek unusual ways to quench an insatiable thirst for knowledge. Intellectually gifted children in poverty settings may apply their intellectual talents to survival or, in a negative sense, may become intellectually manipulative. Impoverished gifted young leaders may focus leadership skills into higher levels of familial responsibility or into neighborhood peer leadership roles. And the artistically gifted child of poverty may channel giftedness into projects of practical construction and design, entertainment, community beautification, or personal writings. A nurturing school environment facilitates some of these manifestations of giftedness becoming obvious, but it is more likely that the outside-of-school setting will provide more opportunities to observe these aspects of giftedness.

Identification Recommendations for Potentially Gifted Bilingual Students

Prior to embarking on a quest to identify gifted students from a bilingual population, certain questions must be addressed that can then serve as underlying assumptions for program development; identification methods; and curriculum, instruction, and assessment of this target population. These questions are illustrated in Table 1.1.

TABLE 1.1   **Fundamental Considerations for Identification of Potentially Gifted Bilingual Students**

Questions to Consider	Implications for Identification	Implications for Services
Will emphasis be placed on identification of students who are gifted linguistically or students who are gifted in multiple areas?	Specific instruments and criteria for selection will differ depending on the area or areas of emphasis. Moving beyond verbal measures requires broader investigation of types of giftedness and methods of identification.	Services for gifted students need to reflect how they were identified for a program. If students are identified using nonverbal or creative ability instruments, they will need services that emphasize what these instruments measure.
What measures are currently in use in either the bilingual or gifted programs that can provide data for selection consideration?	Many instruments used in bilingual programs can provide information on cognitive abilities and achievement, including measurement of gains on certain instruments. Some identification measures used in gifted education do not depend on a student's command of English.	Collaborative efforts can be made between educators of both gifted and bilingual programs to analyze data and recommend not only selection of bilingual gifted students but also to identify intersecting or parallel practices that can be integrated into gifted services for bilingual students.
What variables must be considered in order to change current identification procedures for gifted students to align with best practices outlined in research, including the use of multiple criteria?	Changes in identification methods require extensive information dissemination, involving those families both currently receiving services and those targeted. A comprehensive understanding of the literature on educational change is helpful.	Timelines for changes and implementation will be impacted by these variables. Parallel timelines need to be established in relation to changes in delivery of gifted services, curriculum, and resources used in the program.
What laws or guidelines have been established at the national, state, and district levels that will impact identification decisions?	Certain non-negotiables may need to be established prior to designing or redesigning an identification process.	Gifted programs must remain in compliance with all levels of governance. Adaptations may be required in both programs.
What are the community perspectives regarding gifted and bilingual programs, and how do these perspectives impact services in each?	Level of support for either program can have either positive or negative impacts on changes that impact both programs, including methods of identification and how instruments are used.	Strong support for both programs will not only facilitate full development of new or expanded services but also can decrease levels of criticism during preliminary stages of implementation.

TABLE 1.1   Continued

Questions to Consider	Implications for Identification	Implications for Services
What leadership roles in the district and on campuses will be impacted by the identification of gifted bilingual students?	An implementation of identification changes is only viable if leadership is in place to serve as a catalyst for changes and to orchestrate implementation and evaluation.	Strong leadership is needed in order to bridge concerns of stakeholders in both programs and develop strong networks of communication to ensure success.
What resources are available that reflect the talents that will be discovered through identification of gifted bilingual students?	Identification of students must reflect the curriculum, instruction, and assessment that are provided programmatically.	Teachers may be required to develop new materials, or resources may need to be expanded.

Research in the area of identification of bilingual gifted students has evolved from broader categorical topics (disadvantaged gifted, minority gifted, Hispanic gifted) to more focused areas of study. The early works of bilingual gifted advocates, such as Ernesto Bernal (1980, 1981), have provided more recent researchers with more discrete variables for the identification of these students. According to Cohen (1990), many school districts now include behavioral checklists, interviews, self-reports, autobiographies, and case histories to assist in the identification of gifted language minority students. The use of multiple criteria continues to be a focus after nearly 20 years of research on the topic of identification.

In a comprehensive look at identification instruments and criteria used to identify Mexican American gifted students, Garcia (1994) cites research showing that intelligence tests and achievement measures are biased against students who are limited English proficient. Expanding beyond the use of these standardized measures with the use of multiple criteria, those involved in identification decisions need to make thoughtful selections.

Garcia cautions that "even when multiple criteria are used, there is often a tendency to ignore qualitative or anecdotal data in favor of test scores such as group-administered intelligence tests and achievement tests" (p. 47). He proposes the use of qualitative instruments, such as portfolios, generic products, culture-specific or culture-sensitive checklists, parent interviews, and jot downs (gifted indicator matrices). In addition, when a student is bilingual, Garcia recommends that proficiency levels of both languages be considered, especially if any English-based measures are used, such as writing samples and verbally loaded standardized instruments.

Qualitative measures, currently popular for use in identification of under-represented gifted populations such as bilingual students, are not the panacea they may initially appear to be. Issues of validity and reliability may cloud the purpose of instruments, such as portfolios, resulting in valuable information being discarded when the issues become a focus (Paulson & Paulson, 1991). Nelson (1982) found behavioral checklists, a popular category of instrument used to identify gifted students, to be inaccurate and ineffective in the identification of gifted students when completed by teachers, unless the teachers received prior training in the use of the checklists. Clarification in the use of qualitative measures is critical if such measures are to maintain credibility in the identification process, and issues such as reliability, validity, and training should be examined when designing systems of identification for all gifted students. Addressing the issues proactively helps prevent the loss of the rich data these measures tend to generate.

Culture must also be considered when developing identification methods targeting potentially gifted bilingual students. Garcia (1994) points out that cognitive style, which he considers to be a culture-bound attribute, should be considered when screening bilingual students for gifted identification. Scores on instruments may be skewed if there is dissonance between the cognitive style of the student and the style required of the instrument.

Researchers have also focused in the past decade on specific characteristics of bilingual students that could help in gifted identification. Irby and Lara-Alecio (1996), in a study to report gifted attributes of bilingual students as reported by bilingual teachers, developed a list of characteristics organized into 11 clusters: motivation for learning, social and academic languages, cultural sensitivity, familial, collaboration, imagery, achievement, creative performance, support, problem solving, and locus of control. Few of these characteristic clusters would be found in traditional methods of identification.

Reyes, Fletcher, and Paez (1996) conducted a study of a project involving two rural elementary schools on the New Mexico–Texas–Mexico border with an ethnic composition of 97 percent Hispanic and 91 percent at or below the poverty level. The objectives of the project included the establishment of local identification committees to focus on community-valued characteristics; collaboration and involvement of parents, community, and staff; and development of multidimensional identification procedures that reflect a culturally relevant definition of giftedness. Lists of characteristics were identified by parents and community members from which inventories were developed to be completed by teachers, parents, and community contacts. Student self-identification forms, student portfolios, and tests of creative thinking and analogies were also included as part of the identification process. The researchers found that the major challenge to the project was the identification and implementation of nontraditional measures.

Clark and Gonzalez (1998) used a case study approach to examine the interaction of cognition, language, and culture as it relates to the identification of bilingual gifted students. Recommendations based on their findings included the cooperation of parents and teachers in the assessment process and the use of the following instruments: home language survey; parent and teacher ratings of cognitive, linguistic, and social abilities; qualitative use of English and Spanish tasks; cartoon conservation scales; language assessment scales; and the Test of Nonverbal Intelligence–2 (TONI–2). The researchers concluded that the cultural stimuli and perspectives used to interpret student performance were as important as the language used in testing.

One final study to be addressed in this identification overview was completed in 1999. Irby, Lara-Alecio, and Milke conducted a study of 175 Hispanic bilingual students in Texas to determine the degree of correlation between the Hispanic Bilingual Gifted Screening Instrument (HBGSI; Irby & Lara-Alecio, 1996) and the Naglieri Nonverbal Ability Test (NNAT; Naglieri, 1996). The HBGSI is a 78-item observational checklist stemming from an extensive review of the literature related to Hispanic gifted students. The checklist is completed by a student's classroom teacher. The HBGSI was found to significantly correlate with the NNAT. The researchers concluded that the HBGSI, presenting attributes relevant to Hispanic bilingual students, had promise as a referral instrument that would move students to an assessment phase of the identification process. "It is the intent of the HBGSI," state the researchers, "to provide bilingual teachers with a structure to make better referrals for assessment" (p. 20).

The Austin Independent School District in Austin, Texas, developed a system of identification that may prove to be a useful example for school districts addressing the unique demands of creating a system of identification of potentially gifted bilingual students. Directors of the gifted education and bilingual education programs collaborated in the development of a multiple-criteria screening profile that uses a combination of instruments recommended in the literature on bilingual gifted students. The bilingual identification profile parallels the system in place for other students, which helps ensure consistency in both identification and provision of gifted services. Measures include checklists of observed behaviors (academic and gifted characteristics), portfolios (academic traits), and standardized tests (verbal and nonverbal). Texas requires the use of multiple criteria, including data that are both quantitative and qualitative. The Austin district follows this requirement and has also carefully aligned the combination of instruments with the academic focus of its gifted program for students in kindergarten through twelfth grade. This includes the use of the Bilingual Verbal Abilities Test (1998), an instrument included in the identification process to better align bilingual gifted identification with the verbal focus of many services provided in a gifted program with an academic emphasis. The screening profile outlined in Table 1.2 is used by campus selection committees to select students for the gifted program.

The identification process using this profile is time consuming but allows for highly reflective selection and placement decisions requiring analysis of data collected from both listed instruments and those used in the bilingual program. Fully initiated during the 2001–2002 school year, the system holds promise in the urban district with a growing Hispanic population.

TABLE 1.2   **Screening Profile**

Criteria	Maximum Score	Target Score	Student Score	Comments
NOMINATION INFORMATION				
Teacher Nomination (required—complete all):				
Adapted/Purdue Academic Scales (language arts)	60	NA		
Adapted/Purdue Academic Scales (math)	60	NA		
Adapted/Purdue Academic Scales (science)	60	NA		
Adapted/Purdue Academic Scales (social studies)	60	NA		
Parent Nomination (required)	45	NA		
Peer/Self-Nomination (circle one—optional)	60	NA		
SCREENING INFORMATION				
Raven's Progressive Matrices	100th percentile	90th percentile		

Traits, Aptitudes, Behaviors
Record score for each characteristic: range is from 2 (weak) to 10 (strong)

Motivation ___   Interests ___   Communication Skills ___

Problem-Solving Ability ___   Memory ___   Inquiry ___

Insight ___   Reasoning ___   Imagination/Creativity ___

Humor ___

Narrative comments:

TABS OBSERVATION PERIOD (MINIMUM OF 6 WEEKS):

Bilingual Verbal Abilities Test	Percentile	Age Equivalent	CALP* Level	Comments
Student Scores				
BVAT Narrative Notes:				

Portfolio: Collect exemplary work in all areas	Average	Above Average	High	Comments
Portfolio (language arts)				
Portfolio (math)				

TABLE 1.2   Continued

Portfolio: *Collect exemplary work in all areas*	*Average*	*Above Average*	*High*	*Comments*
Portfolio (science)				
Portfolio (social studies)				
Portfolio Collection Period (minimum of 6 weeks):				

Additional Documented Evidence of Giftedness (Include any additional bilingual measures/documentation)

Criteria/Product/Performance	Comments/Score

*Cognitive academic language proficiency

Curriculum, Instruction, Assessment, and the Gifted Bilingual Student

Once gifted bilingual students have been identified, a new challenge arises: selecting or designing appropriate curriculum, instruction, and assessment resources to meet the complex needs these students bring to the gifted program. Much of the early literature on bilingual gifted education focused on methods of identification. A few researchers have expanded the focus into the areas of program models, curriculum, and instruction. Some early forays into the establishment of bilingual gifted programs explored not only identification methods but also dual language approaches to giftedness with bilingual content enrichment and flexible grouping (Brumberg & Toledo, 1980; Ferguson, 1986; Roby, 1982). These programs recognized the limited availability of curriculum for bilingual gifted learners as well as the need for staff development focusing on curriculum development and instructional strategies.

Emerging research begins to reflect an intersection among best practices in general education, gifted education, and bilingual education. Granada (2002) proposes a comprehensive approach to curriculum development, instructional design, and assessment development that is based on theory and practice in gifted education, bilingual education, and multicultural education. Curriculum in bilingual gifted education should be based in sound theory, developed within a structured framework, and reflective of state and national standards. Infused in the curriculum design are multicultural and linguistic components reflective of the cultures and languages of students being served in the bilingual gifted program.

This curriculum also must align with the model or models in place for the delivery of gifted services.

Instruction for the bilingual gifted student must be well designed and purposeful. Teachers of these students must avoid instruction that consists of loosely connected "gifted" activities gleaned from commercial resources or staff development workshops. Cumulative learning experiences are a necessity, particularly those that are child centered and that integrate depth and complexity in content learning and language development. The most exemplary curriculum will be rendered ineffective when paired with poor instruction, and the complex needs of bilingual gifted students do not allow for inefficient use of learning time. Learning experiences that allow bilingual/bicultural gifted students the opportunity to grow linguistically, that celebrate diversity, and that establish an atmosphere conducive to risk taking should be the prioritized instructional goal.

Granada (2002) also recommends that teachers of bilingual gifted students be proficient in multiple methods of assessment, including the use of preassessment tools. Assessment based on clear expectations becomes a cornerstone in the support of student development of advanced products and performances. Assessments should be an integral part of the instructional process, and methods to determine prior content knowledge or skill mastery prior to instruction must be used to avoid unwittingly basing instructional decisions on second-language abilities. When assessments inadvertently focus on a command of the English language, opportunities are lost to develop areas of talent.

The Bilingual Gifted Student and Creativity

Gifted students come in all shapes, sizes, and colors, and each is unique. Some gifted students are highly creative, whereas others may have to exert special efforts to generate original ideas or products. The same is true for the bilingual gifted student. A significant difference between this student and his or her monolingual English-speaking peers lies in the multiple perspectives associated with being bicultural and the unique mental processes associated with dual language capabilities. According to Lasagabaster (2000), "Concerning the relationship between bilingualism and creativity, most studies coincide in concluding that bilingualism fosters creativity" (p. 2). Creative people are those typically described as having the ability to generate ideas with fluency, think flexibly, produce ideas and products that are original, and elaborate in a variety of ways. Cataldi (1994) indicates that dual language learning "gives rise to mental flexibility, a superiority in concept formation, and a more diversified set of mental abilities" (p. 63).

Creative and intellectual processes may merge through problem solving and allow for metacognitive refinement, which is the ability to understand and verbalize how one thinks in gifted students. Diaz (1985) proposes that knowledge of two languages enhances metalinguistic awareness, serving as a critical component in the development of intelligence. The bilingual gifted student not only can be provided the opportunity to enhance metacognitive abilities but also has the added dimensions of this metalinguistic awareness and multiple cultural perspectives. This combination facilitates rich opportunities to enhance creative thinking, provided the contexts for learning, at school and in the home, encourage creative stimulation of the imagination.

Social and Emotional Needs of the Bilingual Gifted Student

The best gifted identification system aligned with a well-designed program model that delivers a rich and comprehensive bilingual/multicultural instructional program may still have a void to fill if the social and emotional needs of the students in the program are not addressed and supported. Many gifted students feel disengaged with their peers and recognize that they are different as a result of their giftedness. Asynchronous development may add to frustrations these students may experience, from the young child who reads at a very advanced level but whose hands cannot yet manipulate a pencil with ease to the gifted adolescent who may be a mature thinker but is socially immature and is dealing with the confusion of impending adulthood. Gifted students bring to the classroom very unique social and emotional needs, many of which have been documented in texts for students who are gifted. But what of the gifted student who, in addition to these complex attributes, has to deal with living in a world of two languages and two, if not more, cultures?

The bilingual gifted student faces issues that are difficult for them to understand and accept. The world in which they live in is defined by two languages, two cultures, and a continuum of multiple variables such as talents, norms, and rules. Whereas the mainstream gifted student wrestles with bringing meaning to concepts such as success, individuality, and achievement, the bilingual gifted student must view these same concepts from multiple cultural perspectives, and may struggle with the means to communicate what he or she is experiencing or needing help in understanding.

Bilingual gifted students may, at times, focus their talents on acculturation. Those that quickly adapt to the national culture and the ways of life of their peers may face conflicts with beliefs and traditions of the family and community. Competition, gender roles, and focus on the individual versus the group may increase in importance when examined through a student's multicultural lens.

Formal and informal counseling support for the bilingual gifted student may be the most effective means to address the combination of social and emotional needs of students in a gifted program. Vanderslice (1998) points out the need to provide support to students torn between competing cultures. These students may be caught between the need to demonstrate giftedness and adherence to family patterns and values. Vanderslice recommends that counselors become familiar with cultural backgrounds and values of minority groups to aid in this support. This recommendation should extend to teachers working with the students as well, and a concerted effort should be made to include a strong parental educational component as part of the bilingual gifted program.

Summary and Conclusion

The student who is bilingual, bicultural, and gifted presents a unique and considerable challenge, and research on this population is far from expansive. Researchers and practitioners in gifted education are focusing more and more on issues relative to these students, perhaps as an outgrowth of the projected future demographics of the United States. Reviewing the literature provides some promising recommendations for the successful development of programs to identify and serve the bilingual gifted student population.

Barkan and Bernal (1991) offer the following recommendation: "Programming for bright language minority students must be linguistically and culturally inclusive, building on the assets a child brings to school rather than denigrating the LEP child's first language or implicitly attempting to replace one language and culture with another" (p. 146).

Cohen (1990) makes the following recommendations for improvement of identification and programming for gifted language minority students:

- Broaden the concept of giftedness.
- Expand research on giftedness and minority language students.
- Employ more well-rounded assessment techniques, including the use of multiple criteria.
- Increase staff awareness of their potential for developing a gifted and talented program.
- Explore various program models.
- Increase awareness of different ways giftedness may be manifested in different populations.

A report on talent and diversity (Office of Educational Research and Improvement, 1998) suggests addressing bilingual gifted issues through a learning process.

> School staff needs progressive, substantive staff development to supplement and expand their knowledge of other cultural and linguistic groups. They also need support in learning how giftedness manifests itself within cultural norms. This knowledge, when supported with opportunities to pilot new programs geared toward introducing LEP students to high-status knowledge, will aid both in the development of new identification procedures that, while perhaps imperfect, will

result in expanding the numbers of LEP students participating in gifted and talented programs. (pp. 14–15)

In addition, the following basic starting points are recommended:

- Establishing a cognitive and philosophical shift that views youth—including youth not yet proficient in English—as high-ability students with outstanding talents that need multipronged identification procedures to identify and nurture them.
- Forging a commitment to the long-term social benefit of redesigning gifted education to include and meet the needs of students who are LEP.
- Collaborating across programs; there must be a willingness to negotiate and entertain different points of view.
- Building on strengths and program maturity.
- Establishing a clear and coherent vision of inclusive gifted education.
- Bringing the issue of students who are LEP and gifted education to a heightened level of public awareness.
- Creating an action plan with realistic timelines.
- Securing adequate teacher training and inservice programs, including training in identification procedures for bilingual education teachers. (p. 16)

The identification and program planning for gifted bilingual students is not easy. There is much to learn and researchers and educators have only begun to scratch the surface as they attempt to understand and support these unique individuals. If politics, biases, and lack of knowledge are the guide, failure is destined. However, if solutions are approached with compassion, understanding, and integrity, the path to success will yield endless benefits along the way.

REFERENCES

Barkan, J. H., & Bernal, E. M. (1991). Gifted education for bilingual and limited English proficient students. *Gifted Child Quarterly, 35*(3), 144–147.

Bernal, E. M. (1980). *Methods of identifying gifted minority students.* (ERIC Document Reproduction Service No. ED 204 418)

Bernal, E. M. (1981). *Special problems and procedures for identifying minority gifted students.* Paper presented at the Council for Exceptional Children Conference on The Exceptional Bilingual Child, New Orleans, LA. (ERIC Document Reproduction Service No. ED 203 652)

Brumberg, S. F., & Toledo, V. (1980). *Final evaluation report for the C. S. 211 bilingual gifted and talented program, 1978–1979.* (ERIC Document Reproduction Service No. ED 200 694)

Cataldi, R. J. (1994). Bilingualism and early language acquisition—great assets. *NASSP Bulletin, 78*(564), 62–64.

Clark, E. R., & Gonzalez, V. (1998). Voices and voces: Cultural and linguistic dimensions of giftedness. *Educational Horizons, 77*(1), 41–47.

Cohen, L. M. (1990). *Meeting the needs of gifted and talented minority language students.* ERIC Digest #E480. (ERIC Document Reproduction Service No. ED 321 485)

Crawford, J. (1998). Language politics in the U.S.A.: The paradox of bilingual education. *Social Justice, 25*(3), 50–69.

Diaz, R. M. (1985). *The intellectual power of bilingualism.* Paper presented at a Conference on Early Childhood First and Second Language Acquisition, Fresno, CA. (ERIC Document Reproduction Service No. ED 203 368)

Ferguson, L. (1986). A fair share: Opening doors for the gifted bilingual student. *Equity and Choice, 2*(3), 5–13.

Garcia, J. (1994). Nonstandardized instruments for the assessment of Mexican-American children in gifted/talented programs. In S. B. Garcia (Ed.), *Addressing cultural and linguistic diversity in special education: Issues and trends* (pp. 46–57). Reston, VA: The Council for Exceptional Children.

Granada, A. J. (2002). Addressing the curriculum, instruction, and assessment needs of the gifted bilingual/bicultural student. In J. A. Castellano & E. Diaz (Eds.), *Reaching new horizons: Gifted and talented education for culturally and linguistically diverse students* (pp. 133–153). Boston: Allyn & Bacon/Longman.

Irby, B. L., & Lara-Alecio, R. (1996). Attributes of Hispanic gifted bilingual students as perceived by bilingual educators in Texas. *SABE Journal, 11,* 120–142.

Irby, B. L., Lara-Alecio, R., & Milke, B. (1999). *Assessment from multiple perspectives for second language learners: An analysis of the Hispanic Bilingual Gifted Screening Instrument.* Paper presented at the Annual Meeting of the National Association for Bilingual Education, Denver, CO. (ERIC Document Reproduction Service No. ED 430 404)

Kloosterman, V. I. (1997, Spring). Building a bridge: A combined effort between gifted and bilingual education. *The National Research Center on the Gifted and Talented Newsletter,* 3–6.

Lasagabaster, D. (2000). The effects of three bilingual education models on linguistic creativity. *International Review of Applied Linguistics in Language Teaching, 38*(3/4), 213–228.

Marland, S. P. (1972). *Education of the gifted and talented.* Report to the Congress of the United States by the U.S. Commissioner of Education, Washington, DC: U.S. Government Printing Office. (ERIC Document Reproduction Service No. ED 056 243)

McLean, Z. Y. (1995). History of bilingual assessment and its impact on best practices used today. *New York State Association for Bilingual Education Journal, 10,* 6–12.

Naglieri, J. A. (1996). *Naglieri nonverbal ability test.* San Antonio, TX: Harcourt Brace.

Nelson, H. (1982). The identification of black and Hispanic talented and gifted students—grades K through 6: In search of an educational standard. In *Identifying and educating the disadvantaged gifted/talented: Proceedings from the Fifth National Conference on Disadvantaged Gifted/Talented* (pp. 63–90). Ventura, CA: Ventura County Superintendent of Schools.

Office of Educational Research and Improvement. (1998). *Talent and diversity: The emerging world of limited English proficient students in gifted education.* (MIS Publication No. ORAD-98-1100). Washington, DC: U.S. Department of Education.

Paulson, F. L., & Paulson, P. R. (1991). *The ins and outs of using portfolios to assess performance (rev. ed.).* Paper presented at the Joint Annual Meeting of the National Council of Measurement in Education and the National Association of Test Directors, Chicago, IL. (ERIC Document Reproduction Service No. ED 334 250)

Reyes, E. I., Fletcher, R., & Paez, D. (1996). Developing local multidimensional screening procedures for identifying giftedness among Mexican American border population. *Roeper Review, 18*(3), 208–211.

Roby, W. (1982). *1981–82 project evaluation for Encendiendo Una Llama: A program for bilingual gifted and talented students.* (ERIC Document Reproduction Service No. ED 227 688)

Vanderslice, R. (1998). Hispanic children and giftedness: Why the difficulty in identification? *The Delta Kappa Gamma Bulletin, 64*(3), 18–23.

CHAPTER

2 ESL Students in Gifted Education

NILDA AGUIRRE

It is the supreme art of the teacher to awaken joy in creative expression and knowledge

—Albert Einstein

It is paradoxical that many educators continue to believe that English language proficiency is essential prior to placement in gifted programs. Giftedness is not a trait inherent to native English speakers. Gifted programs must mirror the population of any given community. Therefore, if there has been an increase of minorities in a particular community, there should be a proportionate increase in representation of this same group in gifted education. National studies have repeatedly documented that students who are limited English proficient (LEP) are grossly underrepresented in gifted education.

Population forecasts indicate that the number of language minority student enrollments exceeds projections. The number of students who are LEP has increased dramatically in recent years, by 967,670 in 6 years according to the nation's state education agencies (SEA). In addition, Spanish language students who are LEP represent almost three quarters of the overall population (Fleischman & Hopstock, 1993). According to a report published by the U.S. Department of Education (1988), *Talent and Diversity: The Emerging World of Limited English Proficient Students in Gifted Education,* Hispanic students who are LEP are hindered by current gifted and talented criteria most likely because they come from conditions of poverty. The challenge for the educational system is to establish a cognitive and philosophical shift that will help overcome these barriers without reducing expectations.

Early intervention is crucial if the number of students who are gifted LEP is to increase. A multifaceted identification procedure should be added to the language assessment test that determines language proficiency. Providing adequate assessment of student abilities, strengths and passions will direct the educational plan and ensure that needs are met early.

Dispelling the Myths

Many myths surround students who are gifted LEP. According to one of the common myths, students who are LEP must exit English for speakers of other language (ESOL) classes before they are tested and placed in the gifted program. Educators, researchers, and policymakers need to design a program for students who are gifted LEP to be placed and served as they acquire English proficiency. This is not a novel idea. Many are implementing this concept and have created "pregifted" classes where potential students who are gifted LEP are nurtured and challenged. The learning environment is demanding and the expectations are high. Students are not held back; they are propelled forward. English language proficiency becomes the byproduct of this innovative approach. Children are exposed to a language rich environment that integrates critical and high-order thinking, as well as the use of multiple intelligences. This concept is explored later in this chapter. There are additional myths that have been associated with students who are gifted LEP, including the following:

- Students who are LEP are less capable and not able to keep up with the other students who are gifted.
- Students who are LEP are different and will have to acculturate before they can understand aspects of giftedness valued by the dominant culture.
- Parents of students who are LEP are not as involved as parents of other children who are gifted.
- Students who are LEP are accustomed to working in groups and will not do well when they have projects that require independent research and work.
- Students who are LEP have accents and limited vocabularies; therefore, they are unable to verbalize or articulate like other children who are gifted.

Bridging the ESL and gifted divide will contribute to dispelling the myths surrounding students who are gifted LEP. Awareness is crucial in order to accomplish this. Current educational reform aims to improve the academic achievement of all students. Access to challenging curriculum and high-quality academic programs are part of the plan. The groundwork has been initiated for educators who have considered certification in both ESOL and gifted education. These teachers now have an opportunity to bridge the divide. The reform must develop from within the fields of ESL and gifted education. Conceptualizing a program to serve students who are both LEP and gifted should be the rule, not the exception.

For some time, educators have expressed frustration at not being able to identify students who are LEP and who demonstrate gifted ability in class. They argue that using standardized intelligence quotient (IQ) tests as primary measures of giftedness does not take into consideration the linguistic and cultural differences of students who are LEP. Renzulli (1978) indicated that "more creative persons come from below the 95th percentile than above it, and if such cut-off scores are needed to determine entrance into special programs, we may be guilty of actually discriminating against persons who have the highest potential for high levels of accomplishment" (p. 1782). Three percent is a conservative estimate of the population that is considered gifted. However, studies indicate that LEP and other minority groups fall below 50 percent of the expected numbers (Chan & Kitano, 1986). Differences in learning styles largely contribute to underrepresentation. Different cultures have different values. That is, they are not automatically aligned with the dominant culture. For example, Hispanic children differ from the dominant culture in that they are raised to value and respect their elders and to respect teachers and authority. This could hinder a student's performance if the teacher is playing devil's advocate and expects students to contradict or challenge him or her. These children are perceived as uncooperative or not participating in the activity, which may result in lower grades. The dominant culture values competition, independence, and initiative. Many minority students possess special talents that are valued within their own culture; however, these special talents are not recognized by the dominant culture as signs of giftedness.

Most of this author's experience with students who are gifted LEP is a result of working with project GOTCHA (Galaxies of Thinking and Creative Heights of Achievement), a former Title VII academic excellence program funded by the Office of Bilingual Education and Minority Language Affairs (OBEMLA) under

TABLE 2.1   Characteristics of Students Who Are Linguistically and Culturally Diverse

- Eagerly shares his/her native culture.
- Shows strong desire to teach peers words from his/her native language.
- Has a strong sense of pride in his/her cultural heritage and ethnic background.
- Eagerly translates for peers and adults.
- Balances appropriate behaviors expected of the native culture and the new culture.
- Possesses advanced knowledge of idioms and native dialects with ability to translate and explain meanings in English.
- Understands jokes and puns related to cultural differences.
- Reads in native language two grades above his/her grade level.
- Functions at language proficiency levels above that of nongifted peers who are LEP.
- Able to code switch.
- Possesses cross-cultural flexibility.
- Has a sense of global community and an awareness of other cultures and languages.
- Learns a second or third language at an accelerated pace (formal or informal).
- Excels in math achievement tests.
- Demonstrates strengths in the creative areas of fluency, elaboration, originality, and flexibility.
- Demonstrates leadership abilities in nontraditional settings: playground, home, church, clubs, and so on.

From *Characteristics of Students Who Are Linguistically and Culturally Diverse*, by N. Aguirre and N. Hernandez, 1999, Baton Rouge, LA: Modern Language Services.

the U.S. Department of Education. Project GOTCHA was developed to meet the needs of high-ability learners who were not proficient in English. For nine years (1987–1996), project GOTCHA was disseminated in more than 15 states. Project GOTCHA's identification component consisted of a multifaceted approach that took into account parent or community nominations, teacher nominations, analysis of creative ability, Renzulli's Behavioral Checklist (adapted), Torrance Test of Creative Thinking Skills, and leadership ability. The results are recorded on a matrix and the ESL/gifted committee would meet and determine eligibility for placement based on the points obtained. As project disseminator, this author collected the data and interviewed the teachers implementing the program. As a result, a list of characteristics representative of students who are gifted LEP was generated. Table 2.1 presents the list of these characteristics.

Issues of Testing, Evaluation, and Assessment

Schools systems must examine their current criteria when identifying students who are LEP. Federal law requires screening students who are LEP for English language proficiency when they enter school. Screening is typically done by having parents complete a home language survey during the registration process. At the same time, further assessments should be conducted to determine any other special needs a child might have.

> Where inability to speak and understand the English language excludes national origin minority group children from effective participation in the educational program offered by a school district, the district must take affirmative steps to rectify the language deficiency in order to open its instructional program to these students. Any ability grouping or tracking system employed by the school system to deal with the special language skill needs of national origin minority group children must be designed to meet such language skill needs as soon as possible, and must not operate as an educational dead-end or permanent track. (*Lau v. Nichols*, 414 US 563)

This citation is from the landmark decision by the Supreme Court in the case of *Lau v. Nichols*. It is important to acknowledge that school systems must avoid practices that exclude "national origin minority group children from effective participation in the educational program offered by a school district." *Effective participation* can be interpreted as providing students who are LEP with access to gifted educational programs. Legal history calls for students who are LEP to be served. One question to be asked is, Are teachers only referring bilingual or ESL students to ESL/bilingual or two-way immersion programs? Or, can one interpret that to mean, *all* educational programs available to *all* children. Many have interpreted this ruling to mean special programs that teach English. Think outside the box for a moment. What precludes a school system from developing a program within a program to address the needs of children who are gifted LEP? A deeper under-standing is needed of all educational programs to ensure that all the needs of students who are LEP are met. This can be easily accomplished if, as part of the ESL certification requirements imposed by most states, a course is developed that provides in-depth information regarding special services for students who are learning disabled, as well as those who are gifted and talented. ESL certification courses lack information about other needs of children who are LEP. All ESL/bilingual programs should consider a gifted and talented component.

In the quest to find the most appropriate evaluation process to use with students who are LEP and are referred for gifted education, many overlook the obvious: the examiner. The person administering the test is critical in determining whether a student performs at a maximum level, which affects eligibility. Simple nonverbal communication by the test administrator can cause interference, which suggests to the child, "This is too difficult for you; you can't speak English; remember, you only have this one chance." The Kaufman Brief Intelligence Test (K-BIT) is widely used by some systems as a prescreening measure; the instructions clearly state that if a child is not proficient in English he or she should be allowed to answer those items in his or her heritage language. Most examiners will not take the time to provide the opportunity for fair testing. It takes longer and requires a translator. Those who have worked with children who are LEP and have tested them successfully routinely conclude that different methods of assessment are crucial if one is to get a true picture of a child's abilities. The federal government does not mandate criteria for assessing giftedness. This occurs at the state or local level. Those policies need to be reviewed to determine if they are the *best* policies. If a local school system has experienced a growth in the language minority population, it may be time to revise the criteria so they are more inclusive and to cast a wider, deeper net. The results of ignoring these evaluations is potentially devastating to the child and to society. Talents will not be nurtured. Motivation and enthusiasm will be squelched. Creativity will be ignored. And, potentially, children may become discipline problems and possibly drop out of school. We will then conclude that the system has failed them. They have not been challenged or engaged in the educational process. They may gravitate to outside influences, such as gangs, where they can demonstrate gifted behaviors, such as leadership. This is not meant to alarm, but to alert, all that the educational system must tailor programs to meet the needs of the fast-growing minority student population who are also gifted. There is a universal myth that "gifted kids will get it on their own," but nothing is further from the truth!

The Benefits of Pregifted Programs

The importance of adopting a "pregifted program" for students who are potentially gifted LEP must be recognized. Findings from sites implementing "pregifted programs" affirm the need for these programs and reveal the success of students

TABLE 2.2

States	Schools Implementing GOTCHA	Teachers Trained	Year	Total Students Served	Year	Parents Trained	Year	Evaluated for District's Gifted Program	Students with LEP Meeting Eligibility
Florida	12	28	87–96	2,520	90–96	1,800	94–96	126	48
California	4	5	90–96	360	90–96	150	95–96	30	6
Iowa	1	2	92–96	28	92–96	10	95–96	0	0
Louisiana	3	6	93–96	54	93–96	38	95–96	4	3
Michigan	2	3	93–96	32	93–96	18	95–96	4	3
New York	18	24	92–94	186	92–94	95	93–94	18	15
Georgia	2	2	92–96	18	N/A	0	—	0	0
Nevada	1	1	87–90	8	N/A	0	—	0	0
Texas	5	5	90–92	68	N/A	0	—	9	2
N. Dakota	1	1	95–97	5	N/A	0	—	0	0
Washington	2	2	95–97	5	N/A	0	—	0	0
Illinois	2	2	90–93	43	90–93	35	92–93	5	4
Total Impact	53	81	87–96	3,340	87–96	2,146		196	81

Note: The numbers in column 5 are the total numbers of students who were served during the life of the project.

The number of students referred for evaluation passed the rigorous screening criteria set by their state or local system. Many parents did not give permission for their children to be screened. In some cases the teachers did not refer students until they exited ESOL. Some schools chose not to refer students for gifted and kept the students in the pregifted program.

who were fortunate enough to participate in them. School system leaders who believe in gifted education for children who are LEP have shared some of the ideas that made their programs successful. They suggest the following criteria in order for the program to succeed: (1) ESL teachers who are also certified or knowledgeable about gifted characteristics and strategies, (2) ensuring that all administrators and staff assist students in reaching their maximum potential, (3) a learning climate conducive for academic success, and (4) a collective belief that the myths surrounding students who are gifted LEP are false.

Project GOTCHA advocates pregifted programs as viable solutions for gifted students who are LEP to achieve and have their needs met. Project IGNITE (Identifying Gifted Students in and through ESOL), a Title VII program enhancement grant, has been very successful in placing gifted children who are LEP in gifted classes after 2 years in the pregifted program. More than 34 percent of the students who participated in project IGNITE in the East Baton Rouge Parish School System were eligible for the district's gifted and talented program. School systems that have adopted this concept find that the passage rate of minority students exposed to gifted curriculum and strategies, integrated with ESL methods, far exceeds the traditional approach of waiting for students to exit ESOL prior to referring them for gifted programming. Table 2.2 contains a report of schools that submitted data as a result of having implemented project GOTCHA. It includes cumulative totals of students impacted per state during the years of implementation. The data reflect that 41 percent of the students referred for evaluation met the eligibility criteria set forth by the state. In the early 1990s, the mindset of many in education was to only refer students for gifted programs once they exited the ESOL program. This practice resulted in students who are LEP not being reported as such. Rather, they were reported by ethnicity only.

Curriculum and Instruction for Gifted LEP Students

Curriculum and instruction are crucial to the success and achievement of gifted students who are LEP. It is not easy to teach gifted children. They question, challenge, investigate, explore, take risks, and expect more. Gifted children who are LEP have the same desires as other children but with an added dimension: learning English, and learning it well. Unlike most white middle-class gifted children, many gifted students who are LEP are not perfectionists. This may explain why a gifted child who is LEP does not speak in front of peers but can still achieve straight A's every time he or she takes a test.

Gifted students who are LEP require a curriculum that integrates gifted strategies and provides for accelerated English learning practices. Most gifted programs are accelerated and the curriculum is often compacted to provide opportunities for extensions and enrichment. The same concept holds true for gifted children who are LEP. That is, they acquire English language proficiency twice as fast as their nongifted LEP peers. Findings from project GOTCHA and project IGNITE concur that gifted children who are LEP are capable of completing ESL programs in less time if they are taught using accelerated English instruction combined with gifted strategies. This is substantiated by the results obtained from project IGNITE, where 565 students were screened over a period of 2 years. Ninety-two students were eligible to participate in the program. During the school year, these students were instructed in small groups. Each student served as a catalyst for the other. Project IGNITE provided a forum for acquiring English proficiency in an accelerated academic program that also emphasized creative problem solving, higher-order thinking skills, and academics integrated with the arts. This unique combination not only kept these students engaged but also empowered them to create, inquire, and research on their own. When the program ended 32 students were eligible for participation in the district's gifted and talented programs. The process is not easy. All involved need to support the mission of identifying and instructing gifted students who are LEP.

The Role of Language

Pride in one's cultural heritage and native language is one of the characteristics often found in gifted students who are LEP. In working with gifted children who are LEP, this author found that they sought opportunities to talk about their country, to teach their friends words from their language, and demonstrated interest in learning more about their country through projects. Acceptance of children's culture and language sends a powerful message. Not only does it validate feelings of self-worth but it also teaches them to respect and accept other cultures and languages as well. When children are learning English, there is a period of transition in which they feel empowered by being able to speak a language their parent(s) might not speak or understand. If teachers and peers fail to respect a child's language, the situation could backfire at home where the child chooses only to speak English and not to communicate with parents or other family members. Parents may feel embarrassed that their child negates the culture and language and may try to speak in English, however limited, to the child. This creates two problems: (1) The English spoken by the parent at home may not be standard English and (2) the child will miss out on continued proficiency in his or her native language. The ramifications are damaging to the child, parents, family, and society. The child might have eventually been fluent in two or more languages, thereby having been afforded additional opportunities in the job market as an adult. Parents have expressed their disappointment in teachers and administrators not capitalizing on the strength of the diversity that exists at the school their child attends. Diversity is the strength of the United States. The United States is a tapestry of cultures and languages that form patterns of peace and beauty. Gifted students who are LEP who are taught to value and respect their culture and language contribute to the tapestry.

Ensuring the successful retention of students with English as a second language (ESL) in gifted education depends largely on the support that students receive while they are in the program. Some ESL students lead very unstable lives because parents move to available work locations thereby causing children to change schools. In many instances, the inability to retain gifted ESL students is beyond the parameters of the school. Parental participation is crucial, but so is the involvement of the school in the community. The school and the community must unite to function as an entity. Issues that are important to parents should be brought forth at PTA meetings. The administration needs to work hard at knowing each family and recognizing when a family has problems and might need help. There needs to be a bond between parents, the school, the child, the teacher, and the administration. As the Chinese proverb says, it takes a whole village to educate one child.

The family needs to believe that they are an integral part of the educational system, and they need to understand the benefits that their child will receive in a gifted program. Parent training sessions and conference meetings are essential in keeping parents informed of their child's progress and potential. A caring environment plays an important part in retaining students in programs. Gifted programs are no different. Gifted ESL students must believe that they are accomplishing their goals and fulfilling their needs.

Gifted LEP Students: Having Their Say

Following are some of the thoughts, comments, suggestions, and warnings offered by students interviewed over the years.

I love my gifted class. I feel important when I know the answers. I like my teacher. She makes school fun. (Alicia, second grade, Miami-Dade County, Florida)

I wish my parents would understand what I do in school. They think we play all day. Being gifted means that your teacher thinks up all different ways of doing stuff so we don't get bored. (Thomas, second grade, Dade County, Florida)

If I could just be in a gifted class that lasts all day. I get so bored in my regular class. The teacher repeats things over and over again. I lose interest many times. I love my gifted class. That's where I belong. (Maria Elena, seventh grade, Lee County, Florida)

I would like for all teachers to interview us and figure out how we like to learn and what we want to learn. School would be much more interesting. Isn't that what they do in college? (Chamele, fifth grade, Broward County, Florida)

I love to make puppets, write my own scripts, choose the music, design the stage, create the program, to sum it all up...I like to do my own thing, and the best thing is that my teacher lets me. (Kemery, third grade, Broward County, Florida)

Everyone thinks that being gifted means you get straight A's. It's not about grades, it's about what I like to learn. I like my friends in gifted. They don't make fun of how I speak. I have been in America for 2 years and speaking English is very hard for me. That's why I love to write. No one hears me mispronounce words. (Abel, eighth grade, De Anza, California)

I don't like being in gifted. My teacher goes too fast. I can't understand. My parents say to me that I am smart and will do well, but I am scared of failing. I will try very hard to learn quickly. I just need a little more time. (Mathis, sixth grade, Broward County, Florida)

When I go to college I want to teach gifted kids like myself. I will know how to understand children who come from Mexico and are gifted. I can make a change for the better. (Melissa, fourth grade, Fabens Independent School District, Texas)

If I could change one thing in life it would be the following: I would want my parents to have had the opportunity to study so they can get a good job and not have to move all the time. I like being in gifted at this school. I hope papa keeps his job for a long time. (Jaime, sixth grade, Yakima, Washington)

These are testimonials from students who were once served in gifted classes or in pregifted programs. These students are concerned about the future of their families. They crave stability and profess a desire to continue their education. I was inspired by these children to continue disseminating information about gifted education for ESL students. Many educators are concerned with teaching children who are LEP English. I would like to encourage educators to search deeper and allow students' passions to flourish. Learning English should not be the focus of any child's education.

Summary and Conclusion

Identifying gifted students who are LEP is only the tip of the iceberg. Gifted students who are LEP should be provided with an individualized education plan to meet their academic needs. The educational progress of these students depends on educators making the children's educational experiences relevant and meaningful. Gifted and talented individuals have shaped the world: Albert Einstein, Wolfgang Amadeus Mozart, Pablo Picasso, Henry Ford, Simon Bolivar, and Mohandas Gandhi are only a few. Gifted and talented students of today will shape the world of tomorrow. The time has come to combine gifted and ESL programs. Education has seen many changes in the past decade. The "educational revolution," as I like to call it, has intensified the teaching profession, making all reach and teach like never before. Educators and all stakeholders must embrace these challenges and strive to create a community of learners where each child can reach his or her potential.

REFERENCES

Chan, K. S., & Kitano, M. K. (1986). Demographic characteristics of exceptional Asian students. In M. K. Kitano & P. C. Chinn (Eds.), *Exceptional Asian children and youth* (pp. 1–11). Reston, VA: The Council for Exceptional Children.

Fleischman, H., & Hopstock, P. (1993). *Descriptive study of services to limited English proficient students Volume 1: Summary of findings and conclusions.* Arlington, VA: Development Associates.

Lau v. Nichols, 414 U.S. 563 (1974).

Project Ignite. (1999). *Identifying gifted LEP students in and through ESOL.* Title VII Enhancement Grant awarded to East Baton Rouge Parish School System. U.S. Department of Education: Office of Bilingual Education and Language Minority Affairs.

Renzulli, J. S. (1978). What makes giftedness? Re-examining a definition. *Phi Delta Kappan, 60*(3), 180–184, 1782.

U.S. Department of Education. (1998). *Talent and diversity: The emerging world of limited English proficient students in gifted education.* Washington, DC: U.S. Government Printing Office.

Zappia, I. A. (1989). Identification of gifted Hispanic students: A multidimensional view. In C. J. Maker & S. W. Schiever (Eds.), *Defensible programs for gifted students from underserved populations: Cultural and ethnic minorities* (pp. 10–26). Austin: PRO-ED.

3 The "Browning" of American Schools

Identifying and Educating Gifted Hispanic Students

JAIME A. CASTELLANO

They represent all 22 Spanish-speaking countries and territories of the world. They are Mexican, Puerto Rican, Cuban, and Spaniard. They also come from Argentina, Belize, Bolivia, Chile, Colombia, Costa Rica, the Dominican Republic, Ecuador, El Salvador, Equatorial Guinea, Guatemala, Honduras, Nicaragua, Panama, Paraguay, Peru, Uruguay, and Venezuela. School-age children from each of these countries are most likely represented in gifted educational programs throughout the United States.

The census 2000 data suggest that the "browning" of U.S. schools will continue. Deduction leads me to believe that over the next few years the number of Hispanic students eligible for gifted education will steadily increase. This chapter provides readers with a comprehensive overview of identification and education of gifted Hispanic students. From an educational perspective, Hispanics are the majority student groups in school districts in California, Florida, Illinois, New York, and Texas, among other states. They impact virtually every school-based program that exists, including gifted education.

However, Hispanics are still considered an underrepresented group in gifted education and will continue to be so if tradition prevails in how we look at the best and brightest students in the United States. The time for a paradigm shift is now. This chapter offers some alternatives for consideration in this regard. There should be no gatekeepers in gifted education. Rather, we should acknowledge that there is no other program best suited to represent diversity in terms of intelligence, language, and ethnicity than gifted educational programs.

What the Research Says

Data released by the U.S. Census Bureau about the nation's Hispanic population underscore the need for President George W. Bush and Congress to make appropriate decisions about the nation's budget, especially with respect to children and education. According to the report, more than one third (35.7 percent) of Latinos are less than 18 years of age. Other data show that they represent the second-largest group of students in the nation's schools. However, Latino children are underrepresented in Head Start, early childhood developmental programs, after-school programs, and rigorous academic courses, including gifted education. If we equip Latino children, and all children, with high-quality education and ensure their well-being, we will have a tremendous pool of talent ready to lead the nation forward, and every U.S. citizen will benefit (Yzaguirre, 2001).

Educational investments are especially important because census data show that educational disparities between Latinos and other U.S. citizens is striking. In 2000, 57 percent of Hispanics 25 years old and over had graduated from high school, compared to 88 percent of non-Hispanic whites in the same age category. More than one fourth (27.3 percent) of Hispanics have less than a ninth-grade education level; in contrast only 4.2 percent of non-Hispanic whites were at this education level. Only 1 in 10 Hispanics (10.6 percent), compared to almost 3 in 10 non-Hispanic whites (28.1 percent), had a college degree. Data also show that the poverty rate for Hispanic children is more than three times that of non-Hispanic white children.

According to Cantu (1998), gifted and talented students represent one of the greatest resources in the United States. They may become the leaders, inventors, artists, scientists, and problem solvers of tomorrow. But trends in gifted and talented education throughout the United States indicate that a significant number of students with exceptional abilities are not receiving high-quality services either because they have not been identified as gifted or because programs in which they are enrolled do not address their unique strengths and needs. The National Educational Longitudinal Study (NELS) found that the representation of racial and ethnic groups in gifted and talented programs favors some groups more than others. The study found that gifted and talented programs are comprised of the following:

- 17.6 percent of all Asian students.
- 9 percent of all white students.
- 7.9 percent of all African American students,
- 6.7 percent of all Hispanic students.
- 2.1 percent of all Native American students (Resnick & Goodman, 1997).

Hispanics are united by customs, language, religion, and values. There is, however, an extensive diversity of traits among Hispanics. One characteristic that is of paramount importance in most Hispanic cultures is family commitment, which involves loyalty, a strong support system, a belief that a child's behavior reflects on the honor of the family, a hierarchical order among siblings, and a duty to care for family members (Griggs & Dunn, 1996). This strong sense of other-directedness conflicts with the U.S. mainstream emphasis on individualism (Vasquez, 1990, in Griggs & Dunn, 1996). Indeed, Hispanic culture's emphasis on cooperation in the attainment of goals can result in Hispanic students' discomfort with conventional classroom competition in the United States. This mismatch often means these students are misidentified, or underidentified, for gifted education programs.

Hispanic Student Testing in the United States

In September 1999, the President's Advisory Commission on Educational Excellence for Hispanic Americans outlined an action agenda for the testing of Hispanic students in the United States. Its first guiding principle suggested that all Hispanic students must be tested with assessment instruments that are fair and accurate (Hernandez, 1999, p. 7). Furthermore, it is important to distinguish among testing needs of Hispanic students who are (1) fluent English speakers, (2) English language learners, and (3) fully bilingual and biliterate. These multiple levels of proficiency are further confounded by the limitations placed on teachers (and psychologists) by virtue of state laws and regulations as well as local board policies. Few are based on reliable and replicable research (p. 9).

Recognizing this mural of complexities, it is incumbent on states (and local school districts) to frame their testing policies to assure that Hispanic students (and other culturally and linguistically diverse student groups) are tested with assessments specifically designed to measure their levels of English language proficiency for diagnostic and instructional purposes. Their achievement levels in core content areas of the curriculum (as well as cognitive ability, i.e., on IQ tests) must also be measured with assessment instruments in the language with which they are most proficient (p. 9).

In school districts across the United States that serve large numbers of culturally and linguistically diverse students, these recommendations should be considered for all student groups. When testing for possible placement into gifted education programs, professional organizations, such as the National Association for Bilingual Education's Special Interest Group on Gifted Education and the Special Populations Division of the National Association for Gifted Children, advocate that the evaluation process must reflect a best practices approach. Both of these organizations' national conferences regularly include concurrent sessions on the identification and assessment of Hispanic and other culturally and linguistically diverse students for gifted education.

Identification and Education of Gifted Hispanic Students

Historically speaking, Hispanic students have been disproportionately underrepresented in educational programs serving the gifted. To reverse this trend, the actualization of a paradigm shift includes a change in how to look at our best and brightest Hispanic students, with a shift in philosophy, cognition, commitment, and collaboration being of equal importance. In order to overcome the barriers to identifying this population of students for gifted education programming, the following considerations should be taken into account: characteristics and cultural considerations, assessment and evaluation, and alternative assessments and demonstration of need.

Characteristics Checklists and Cultural Considerations

Attempting to describe and discuss the wide range of concerns regarding gifted Hispanic students is both challenging and far-reaching. The combination of relevant cultural, linguistic, socioeconomic, political, personal, and other variables unique to each individual exacerbates any discussion of the issue (Diaz, 1999). Furthermore, although Hispanics share a common origin and linguistic base, the groups that make up the Hispanic population are not monolithic; they differ significantly in many important ways. According to Bean and Tienda (1987), Hispanics living in the United States come from 22 different countries or territories. Their unique experiences have influenced them in different ways, both before and after immigration to the United States. These differences are crucial when considering the identification and development of giftedness among Hispanic students.

Any multicriteria identification procedure typically includes a checklist of gifted behaviors that is most often completed by the child's teacher. With regard to Hispanic students, the work by Bernal and Reyna (1974) continues to be one of the standards used today. Table 3.1 represents universal characteristics of giftedness, cultural values often characteristic of Hispanics, and the behaviors resulting from their interactive influence. Bernal's work reveals the importance of going beyond what is commonly held to be true about gifted behaviors and considers the influences of culture and other factors.

As our collective knowledge level increases about giftedness in historically underrepresented student groups, so has our ability to identify and assess them. A multiple-criteria approach should make allowances for the cultural or linguistic idiosyncrasies that define individual children. However, the importance of identifying gifted characteristics that are cornerstones for academic achievement and increased cognitive attainment cannot be underscored. Table 3.2 is a checklist, modified from the work conducted at Kent State University in 1992 that identifies characteristics of young children who are gifted. The work was funded by the U.S. Department of Education's Jacob K. Javits Gifted and Talented Students Education Act; Office of Educational Research and Improvement (OERI). The gifted characteristics are clustered around four primary identifiers: (1) exceptional learner (acquisition and retention of knowledge), (2) exceptional user (application and comprehension of knowledge), (3) exceptional generator (creator of knowledge), and (4) exceptional motivator (pursuer of knowledge). In conducting research on characteristics of other historically underrepresented student groups, this author concluded that the characteristics generated by the work at Kent State University transcend culture, ethnicity, and linguistic differences. In other words,

TABLE 3.1   Characteristics of Giftedness, Cultural Values, and the Behaviors Resulting from Their Interactive Influence

Absolute Aspects of Giftedness	Cultural Values Often Characteristic of Hispanics	Behavioral Differences
High level of verbal ability	Traditional language of the family	Fluent communication with peers and within community, even if using nonstandard English
Emotional depth and intensity	*Abrazo*, a physical or spiritual index of personal support	Touching, eye contact, feelings of support to achieve maximum academic productivity required
Unusual sensitivity to feelings and expectations of others	Family structure and dynamic-male dominance	Personal initiative, independent thought, and verbal aggressiveness often inhibited in females
Conceptualization of solutions to social and emotional problems	Nuclear and extended family closeness	Often assumes responsibility for family or younger siblings
Unusual retentiveness; unusual capacity for processing information	Traditional culture	Successfully adapts and functions in two cultures
Leadership	Collaborative, rather than competitive, dynamic	Accomplishes more, works better in small groups than individually

these characteristics speak to universal traits. For example, when asked how giftedness is perceived in their own children, Hispanic, Haitian, and Haitian American adults identified many of the same characteristics.

Assessment and Evaluation

The assessment and evaluation of Hispanic students for gifted education should include a combination of qualitative and quantitative data that embraces a multiple-criteria philosophy. If an evaluation of a student's cognitive ability is required for eligibility, careful consideration should be given to the type of "IQ" test to be administered. Should a verbally stacked, English intensive, culturally biased instrument be used, or should the playing field be balanced by administering performance-based "IQ" tests that still measure a student's cognitive ability. Tests such as the Naglieri Nonverbal Ability Test and the Universal Nonverbal Intelligence Test are

TABLE 3.2 Cross-Cultural Validation for the Identification of Exceptional Potential or Gifted Behavior

Characteristic	Hispanic	Haitian	African American	Bilingual/ ESOL	Low Socioeconomic Status
Exceptional learner (acquisition and retention of knowledge)					
1. Exceptional memory					
2. Learns quickly and easily					
3. Advanced understanding					
Exceptional user (application and comprehension of knowledge)					
4. Exceptional use of knowledge					
5. Advanced use of symbols					
6. Demands a reason					
7. Reasons well					
Exceptional generator (creator of knowledge)					
8. Highly creative					
9. Atypical thinking					
10. Self-expressive					
11. Keen sense of humor					
12. Curiosity					
Exceptional motivator (pursuer of knowledge)					
13. Perfectionism					
14. Initiation					
15. Reflective					
16. Long attention span					
17. Leadership					
18. Intensity					

Adapted from Jacob K. Javits Gifted and Talented Students Education Act. Early Assessment for Exceptional Potential—United States Department of Education Grant #R206A00160, Kent State University, 1992.

being used with success by school districts across the country in identifying Hispanic and other underrepresented groups for gifted education.

In the school district of Palm Beach County, Florida, gifted education program administrators revised the plan that targets historically underrepresented students. One of the new eligibility criteria is the formation of a student portfolio that must contain at least three different forms of quantitative data and three different forms of qualitative data. Based on the portfolio contents, the student receives a rating of adequate, commendable, or exemplary. A rating of adequate represents work samples indicating the student is experiencing success meeting grade-level goals, objectives, and benchmarks. A rating of commendable is given if the portfolio contents show that the student is working 1 year above grade level. Finally, an exemplary rating demonstrates that the student is working 2 or more years above grade-level expectations. The student portfolio is reviewed by the school's child study team who must agree on the rating. Following are examples of accepted quantitative and qualitative data:

Quantitative Information	*Qualitative Information*
Reading running record (if available)	Nomination form/checklist
Past school performance (if available)	Teacher anecdotes
Language proficiency test results	Parent interview comments
IQ test scores (if available)	Student interview comments
Achievement test scores (if available)	Writing samples
State-level testing results (if available)	Performance-based products
Awards, accomplishments, achievements	Other
Other	

Finally, Burnette (2000) promotes a best practices approach to the assessment and evaluation of culturally and linguistically diverse students. In general, these practices can be organized according to four principles:

1. Convening a full, multidisciplinary assessment team—parents, educators, and assessors are part of any assessment team. Other integral members of the team include interpreters and a person who is familiar with the student's culture and language.
2. Using strategies that promote the individual's areas of strengths.
3. Determining the language to be used in testing—assessment of language dominance and proficiency should be completed before further testing is conducted for students whose home language is other than English.
4. Conducting a tailored, appropriate assessment of the child and environment. Ideally, nonbiased, appropriate instruments should be combined with other sources of information (observations, interviews) from a variety of environments (home, school, community) to produce a multidimensional assessment.

Alternative Assessments and Demonstration of Need

Frequently, a student demonstrates a need for gifted education programming by the results generated from the administration of a norm-referenced standardized test of academic achievement. Such protocols are available in English and Spanish. To further support the need for gifted education, informal methods of assessment should be employed. *Informal* is used here synonymously with alternative assessment and implies that these assessments can be incorporated easily into classroom routines and learning activities. The results are indicative of the student's performance on the skill or subject of interest. Alternative assessments can be divided into structured and unstructured techniques. Structured assessments are most often planned by the teacher and reflect purpose and specificity. Examples include checklists, cloze tests, criterion-referenced tests, rating scales, questionnaires, and structured interviews. Notice that some of these tests have relatively easy scoring.

Unstructured assessment techniques as a form of alternative assessments range from writing stories to playing games. And even though they are somewhat more difficult to score, they do provide valuable information about the skill level of students. Types of unstructured assessments include writing samples, homework, logs or journals, games, debates, brainstorming, story retelling, anecdotal accounts, and naturalistic observations. When combined with more formalized assessment techniques, alternative assessments help provide a comprehensive profile of a student.

Psychologists and the Assessment of Hispanic Students for Gifted Education

What the psychologist brings, or doesn't bring, to the assessment process in terms of attitudes and experiences, among other behaviors, often determines the eligibility of historically underrepresented students (Hispanic) for gifted education. In order to maximize the possibility for such students this author has developed a list of recommendations, or best practices, that psychologists and others who assess these students should consider. As a nationally recognized advocate for the inclusion of more historically underrepresented students in gifted education, this author has been called repeatedly to advise, consult, and provide testimony on how to best assess these students. And recently, on a more regular basis, questions have been raised regarding the psychologist–student relationship and what can be done to maximize testing conditions and results.

Many school districts can easily document their attempts to recruit school psychologists who represent the diversity of the local school district. Hispanic, particularly those that are bilingual, and African American psychologists are simply difficult to find, let alone hire. There simply are not enough available. As a result, many school districts continue to use Anglo psychologists to evaluate poor, minority, immigrant, limited English proficient, and culturally diverse students.

The best practices recommendations, which others may interpret as guiding principles, suggest that there are certain dynamics that must be considered when evaluating and assessing Hispanic students, and other underrepresented students, for gifted education programming. Many of them center around the specific culture of the student being tested. However, it is this author's contention that many of the cultural aspects taken into account are very similar for Hispanic, African American, and Haitian students who are poor, immigrant, and have problems with English proficiency. Sure, surface culture elements define each group as unique, but deep cultural elements that define who they are are more similar than different.

Recommendations/Best Practices/Guiding Principles

Inclusionary methodology dictates that any process implemented to evaluate the academic and cognitive ability of underrepresented students for gifted education must be flexible enough to accommodate the needs of the student being tested. Not vice versa. As adults, psychologists have the education, ability, and flexibility to set the stage for optimal student performance. The following recommendations/best practices/guiding principles will assist them in this endeavor.

Setting the Stage.   Psychologists should consider making a minimum of two visits to the student's classroom prior to the actual assessment.

1. The first visit could last as long as 30 minutes and is preplanned with the classroom teacher. Usually, 15 to 20 minutes will suffice. The purpose is to match a name with a face and to simply observe the student in the context of the classroom. Anecdotal observations are recorded in writing.
2. The second visit could last as long as 45 minutes. It is also planned with the teacher ahead of time, and it is understood that there will be deliberate contact with the student. Engaging the student through a small group activity with at least two or three of his or her classmates chosen by the teacher is suggested. The activity can be as simple as challenging the group to use their critical-thinking and problem-solving skills to answer a brain teaser as quickly and efficiently as possible. Anecdotal observations of the targeted student are recorded in writing.

Taking the time to establish a rapport with a student who may be culturally or linguistically different has the potential of paying big dividends later. And besides, it makes sense.

The Testing Situation.   Psychologists should consider "chunking" the time it takes to evaluate a student if the process is to be completed before the end of the school day. Chunking implies that there will be opportunities for the student to rest between subtests or given periods of time. Allowing the student to "refuel" may enhance the overall testing experience, including the results.

An informal interview lasting 5 to 10 minutes should be held with the student just prior to testing. This is an ideal opportunity to capitalize on the former visits to the classroom and increases the comfort level of the student. It is at this time that the psychologist genuinely dialogues with the student about what will occur and affords the student an opportunity to ask questions. Appropriate physical and environmental conditions are also arranged accordingly to optimize the testing process.

Testing in the Heritage Language of the Student (If Needed). It goes without saying that testing must occur in the heritage language of the student if the child study team deems it appropriate. Heritage language assessment is supported by federal legislation, the Individuals with Disabilities Education Act (IDEA), and makes good sense. However, because a psychologist may speak the language of the student being tested does not necessarily equate to knowledge about literacy and bilingualism, and principles of second-language acquisition, and these factors do impact the testing process.

This author's experience as an elementary school principal and district administrator has been that bilingual psychologists often fall into the same trap as Anglo psychologists who test culturally and linguistically diverse students. It would behoove them to also follow the recommendations spelled out in this writing. In addition, when testing does occur in a language other than English, it is incumbent that they have at least a basic knowledge in the following areas:

1. A basic foundation of the second-language acquisition process.
2. A basic foundation of bilingualism and how it is captured in the school context.
3. A basic familiarity with the current research on literacy development.
4. A basic familiarity with the current research on English as a second language.

This background knowledge further empowers the bilingual psychologist, providing additional tools to heighten effectiveness while also serving as an advocate for culturally and linguistically diverse students.

If there is no psychologist available who speaks the heritage language of the student, the following guidelines surrounding the use of translators or interpreters should be used as benchmarks to make the best of the situation.

1. Obtain the services of an experienced translator who is articulate, and can read and write the heritage language of the student.
2. Translators should be provided the necessary training in the following areas to increase the reliability and validity of the testing process.

a. In the terminology specific to each area of exceptionality. More importantly, they must possess the ability to substitute technical language for more culturally appropriate and sensitive language without changing the content of the message.

b. In the rules and regulations that govern the psychological assessments of culturally and linguistically diverse students spelled out in federal, state, and local policies.

c. In how they interact with parents in what at times may be very passionate, emotionally charged meetings.

d. In the rights of parents as outlined in the IDEA and their procedural safeguards presented by the local school district.

When Testing Is Over.   Once the "official" testing is over, it is recommended that the psychologist summarize what was done and what will happen next. It is important for students to know that there will be closure and that their parents will be provided with an explanation of the results. To further cement their rapport the psychologist should personally escort students back to the classroom generating informal conversation that is genuine and direct. Validating the student by personalizing comments leaves both parties with a "feel good" attitude after everything is said and done.

Issues of Curriculum and Instruction

To meet the needs of gifted and talented Hispanic students, qualitatively different instruction should be planned. Qualitatively different instruction refers to those learning experiences that reflect the development of critical and creative thinking skills, content acceleration, and effective education. Mere quantity of work is not desired. Any program targeting these students must emphasize the following four major variables:

1. Basic emphasis: A gifted student's ability to master course content with ease is one consideration in placing the student at an appropriate instructional level.

2. Cognitive emphasis: This component stresses the critical-thinking skills of analysis, synthesis, and evaluation.

3. Creative emphasis: Fluency, flexibility, originality, elaboration, and divergent thinking are components commonly associated with creativity.

4. Affective emphasis: Emotional growth, social growth, aesthetic awareness, and conceptual moral growth are all part of the affective emphasis.

These variables should be woven into the gifted Hispanic student's yearly program. There may be lessons in which one area is emphasized, but generally, the variables are correlated into a comprehensive program. And, of course, students should be allowed to participate speaking and writing in the language with which they feel most comfortable. This is certainly consistent with maintaining ethnic identity, accommodating learning style differences, and providing an accelerated and enriched curriculum. Furthermore, empowering this population of students is important to their success and to the success of the overall program. Providing support systems that focus on social, academic, and familial issues are equally important and should be a justifiable part of their program focus.

Effective Program Models

Large urban school districts may consider establishing a magnet center model, in which teachers trained in gifted education provide a full-time, differentiated curriculum to students drawn from a number of neighboring schools. The unique advantage of this model is that because they are grouped homogeneously, students encourage one another to achieve higher performance levels in core subjects. Another model to serve high-ability Hispanic students involves establishing a cadre of resource teachers specifically trained in curriculum differentiation. These resource teachers team with either regular or bilingual teachers to implement strategies such as designing instructional units around thematic or topical concepts that allow for interaction of disciplines and activities appropriate for different ability levels, learning styles, group size, or individual students. Curriculum differentiation for gifted and talented Hispanic students may include projects, presentations, and participation in activities that reflect the development of critical and creative thinking skills and content acceleration, and that affect education, such as service projects, developing and conducting research so as to add to a current body of knowledge, solving a community problem, and challenging or questioning as a way to stimulate change, among others.

The resource room model works as a send-out program from the regular classroom for a portion of the day. Students who are excelling at a level the classroom teacher cannot easily challenge may spend part of the day in the resource room. The resource room model provides an opportunity for students to work part time with their academic peers and may include multiage grouping. It provides enrichment to supplement what is being taught in the regular classroom, acceleration to challenge students at an advanced level, and independent study based on student interest and advancement level. The resource room model also provides the teacher the opportunity to act as a coach and facilitator to support and promote student performance at the highest level.

Program models to meet the needs of gifted Hispanic students can be as varied as a district's creativity allows them to be. There are both full-time and part-time models to consider, each with its own set of advantages. Important considerations for choosing the most appropriate model for students include funding, total number of participating students, space, personnel, and a commitment to meeting specialized needs, among others.

Professional Development and Training

Arguably, one of the most comprehensive professional development and training programs took place in the San Diego City school district through project EXCEL, a Title VII bilingual/gifted grant implemented from 1989 to 1994. The training component built on and extended the San Diego schools gifted and talented education (GATE) teacher certification process with a focus on the culturally and linguistically diverse gifted child. This certification process included seven categories: characteristics of gifted and talented students, identification of the gifted and talented, theoretical foundations of giftedness, curriculum for gifted and talented learners, instructional strategies, parenting the gifted, and professional growth through participation in local and statewide gifted organizations.

The goals of the teacher training component were to develop and enhance teacher characteristics conducive to the learning to be done by the gifted and to foster the understanding that preparedness, or skill level, is not necessarily synonymous with giftedness, especially as the culturally and linguistically diverse child is served (Perez, 1993, pp. 23–24). As a result of project EXCEL, the San Diego City school district has more than 100 bilingual teachers of the gifted who honor both the English language and heritage language of the children.

As with any teacher training program, two factors ensure the successful implementation of newly acquired skills and information: funding and the opportunity for follow-up collaboration and sharing. Professional development for teachers serving gifted Hispanic students is typically a long-term process requiring ongoing articulation that allows teachers to bring out their own intellectual and creative abilities. As with project EXCEL, training should embrace diversity because it is the very nature of giftedness in all groups of students (Perez, 1993).

Parental Involvement

The gifted education program in any school district has the responsibility of sharing information with parents, who are important to the overall development of their children. Information can be shared through written correspondence or by convening meetings, conferences, workshops, and so on. Whatever the form, it is imperative that the communication also be in the language most comfortable for parents. One of the primary objectives of a parental involvement program is to encourage opportunities for parents to actively participate. For example, for Spanish-speaking parents, bilingual gifted education staff and parents of participating students can cooperatively develop a handbook in Spanish to assist other parents in nurturing gifted potential at home.

Hine (1994), working with 10 Puerto Rican students and their parents, identified the following eight family factors that contribute to high achievement:

1. Parents should let their children know they value achievement in school.
2. Parents should help their children develop strong language skills.

3. Parents must make their children understand that they believe their children will be successful both in school and, later, in the workplace.
4. Parents must provide a strong family support system for their children.
5. Parents who nurture a strong family bond at home help their children develop a positive image of themselves and their culture, and gain the self-confidence necessary to meet the challenges they face at school and in the community.
6. Parents should help their children understand that their futures can be bright with preparation and hard work. Instant success stories don't usually happen in real life. The great majority of successful adults dealt with many challenges and obstacles along the way.
7. Parents should not let their children use cultural biases held by people at school or in the community as an excuse for failure.
8. Parents should become involved in their children's school and extracurricular activities. By encouraging a "social bond" with the school and community, they will help the children grow in confidence and self-esteem.

The school district's position should also reaffirm that parents are their children's first and best teachers. This being the case, gifted program personnel should encourage parents to attend informational presentations that foster the parent–gifted child relationship. Parents should also be encouraged to borrow and review materials available at the school, serve as volunteers in classrooms or resource centers, assist with field trips, and be involved in other after-school activities. Parents can also assist a specific student or group of students as a mentor or resource person.

The formation of support groups for parents is still another way for them to participate. This option allows them to share with one another in an informal collaborative environment, and to meet other friends and family members of gifted students. Finally, open channels of communication between parents and school personnel enhance opportunities for appropriate learning experiences and meaningful extensions of learning in the gifted program.

Summary and Conclusion

Programming for gifted Hispanic students includes many options. Components that should be given special consideration include (1) maintaining ethnic identity, (2) extracurricular cultural enrichment, (3) learning style differences, (4) counseling, (5) parent support groups, (6) development of significant program models, (7) accelerated and enriched curriculum, and (8) career development. Although it may not be possible to include all of these components at the outset, it is desirable to include all of them eventually if minority gifted children (Hispanic) are to have an optimal opportunity to develop and use their abilities (Davis & Rimm, 1998). Hispanic students who demonstrate skills and characteristics of the gifted and talented need, and deserve, an additive learning environment where, as a group, they are viewed as an asset to the district's overall gifted education program. They should be viewed as intelligent, and as such, challenged to fly to their greatest heights through the programs, services, and opportunities available to them.

REFERENCES

Bean, F. D., & Tienda, M. (1987). *The Hispanic population of the United States*. New York: Russell Sage Foundation.

Bernal, E. M., & Reyna, J. (1974). *Analysis of giftedness in Mexican American children and design of a prototype identification instrument*. Austin, TX: Southwest Educational Development Laboratory. (ERIC Document Reproduction Service No. ED 360 871)

Burnette, J. (2000, December). *Assessment of culturally and linguistically diverse students for special education eligibility*. ERIC Clearinghouse on Disabilities and Gifted Education. Reston, VA: The Council for Exceptional Children.

Cantu, L. (1998, June–July). Traditional methods of identifying gifted students overlooks many. *Intercultural Development Research Association Newsletter*.

Davis, G. A., & Rimm, S. B. (1998). *Education of the gifted and talented*. Boston: Allyn & Bacon.

Diaz, E. I. (1999). Hispanic Americans. In A. Y. Baldwin and W. Vialle (Eds.), *The many faces of giftedness: Lifting the mask* (pp. 23–44). Toronto, Canada: Wadsworth.

Griggs, S., & Dunn, R. (1996). *Hispanic-American students and learning style*. University of Illinois at Urbana-Champaign. Children's Research Center. Champaign, IL.

Hernandez, S. (1999, September). *Testing of Hispanic students in the United States: An action agenda*. President's Advisory Commission on Educational Excellence for Hispanic Americans. Washington, DC.

Hine, C. Y. (1994). *Helping your child find success at school: A guide for Hispanic parents*. National Research Center for the Gifted and Talented. Stoors, CT.

Perez, R. S. (1993). *Project EXCEL: A Title VII bilingual/gifted project*. San Diego City Schools: San Diego, CA.

Resnick, D., & Goodman, M. (1997, Fall). *Northwest Education*. Northwest Educational Laboratory Resources.

Yzaguirre, R. (2001, April). Census shows disparity in education of Latino children. *Hispanic Magazine*, 104.

4

Gifted Education and African American Learners

An Equity Perspective

KEN DICKSON

The rationale for this chapter is forthright. It examines underrepresentation of African American students in schools in their roles as social institutions. Educational institutions, like political and economic institutions, continue to be agents of social change in terms of improving quality of life. Social institutions enjoy certain rights and have certain responsibilities to the societies they serve. The responsibilities must be carried out fairly in terms of the needs of that society. While carrying them out, the institution must garner and maintain support from parts of society that do not particularly require its services. The spirit of the law guides some of the responsibilities. The letter of the law guides others. Both the spirit and letter of the law can be elusive, particularly when they have connections to major social transformations, such as school desegregation laws in the middle of the twentieth century. School desegregation law (*Brown v. Topeka Board of Education*, 1954) is a social transformation never witnessed. It is doubtful if there has ever been a greater social and ideological transformation in the United States. The whole idea was troubled from the onset because racial and ethnic minority groups, including African Americans, were not desegregated. They were eliminated. There were no options available to African Americans but to seek their rights and privileges, and to pursue improved quality of life, but they were ill prepared to deal with such a major social transformation. Vestiges of that ill preparedness still exist. Nowhere are they better evidenced than in the social institutions of education and educational services for the gifted. (Education services for the gifted herein will be expressed as "the field".)

African American learners continue to be underrepresented in the field. African American adults, including professional staff and parent or caregivers are underrepresented as well. Given the nature, persistence, and magnitude of under-representation among African Americans in the field, there are numerous proposals to be shared. This chapter is framed around five transformative proposals aimed at gifted education and African American caregivers and educators that together will move toward maximizing ideals of equity, diversity, and excellence.

1. Practice the belief statements that characterize the foundation, mission, and purpose for education and the field. The statements commonly support ideals of equity, democracy, egalitarian principles, civil rights, and social justice. These ideals must become the main ideology that informs the paradigms, which influence the theories and practices that characterize the field.
2. Engage in formal discussions specifically designed to lead to pragmatic initiatives to modify current paradigms, inclusive of eliminating underrepresentation.
3. Increase efforts to upgrade the fields' qualities including competencies regarding exceptional potential in African American learners.
4. Continue to challenge psychometric dependency and eventually eliminate it. Like drugs and alcohol, psychometrics easily can be and often is abused. It, therefore, can stand in the way of equity and to what is just and fair.
5. Commit to implementing the perspectives suggested in writings by African Americans and other ethnicities on race and education in general and African Americans and gifted programs in particular.

Moving toward Equity, Diversity, and Excellence

Purpose

This chapter has a three-part purpose. First it will increase awareness about African Americans and their relationships to gifted education. It focuses on African Americans participation in the field. This includes an examination of why participation is low and how to increase it among learners as well as African American adult stakeholders. The chapter does not necessarily focus on the few African American learners the system has identified and is serving. Rather, the chapter focuses on the system and ways that it can be improved to help the many African American learners it underidentifies and ultimately misses.

The second part of the purpose is to offer readers rationale, pragmatic ideas, and opportunities to reexamine perspectives on giftedness as they relate to social justice and to African Americans. The third and overarching purpose is to offer readers encouragement to do what they can with what they have, considering the following:

- Bringing harmony to where there is dissonance.
- Bringing definition to vagueness.
- Successfully challenging indifference.

- Stimulating thought.
- Rejuvenating spirits.
- Inspiring the unmotivated, and, most of all, celebrating the vitality, essence, and promise of African American learners everywhere.

Organization

Ongoing formative and summative investigation and assessment reflecting for more than 20 years of practices and activities influences the content and provides the background and data sources for this chapter. The focus of the 20-year investigation has been on activities and practices associated with educational equity, diversity, and achievement in exceptional-needs education. These practices and activities align with the principles of cyclical action research. Components of action research principles, therefore, are the templates for this chapter. They include design, general and specific activities, data sources, demographics, and focus areas.

Design. The action research design consists of the following activities:

- Identifying and engaging in an exploration area or problems to be solved.
- Intervention strategies.
- Implementation methods.
- Classroom, program, and project initiatives.
- Organizational observations, data collection, and interpretation.

The outcomes of these activities influence or recycle the original exploration for a newly stated exploration area, which continues the line of investigation. This includes engaging in various forms of informal, qualitative, formative, subjective, interpretive, and experiential inquiry. Strong emphasis is placed on observational and experiential aspects of inquiry.

General Activities. General activities involved in the action research included self-reflective inquiry based on adapted principles of cyclical action research. The action research design included identifying pragmatic requirements associated with administrator and teacher practitioner competencies regarding equity, diversity, and achievement.

Specific Activities. Specific activities involved in the action research and critical to this chapter are reflections of more than 20 years of administrative practices focused on gifted educational services, integrated curricula, and leadership in multicultural equity and diversity initiatives. Included in these reflections is the appreciation gained from activities and practices involving curriculum and instructional supervision; leadership in local, state, and national advocacy groups; professional development; exceptional-needs education; consulting; research into practice applications; and product development. Additional reflections involved gaining understanding from participation in and contributions to various national, state, and local organizations devoted to social justice.

The focuses of these activities was on equity and diversity as related to achievement among learners in exceptional educational environments. This included learners who were identified and not identified as gifted, as well as culturally and linguistically diverse learners and children of poverty.

Data Sources.　Primary data sources influencing the research design included four geographic regions of the United States, including six states and five primary sites. A primary site is defined as one in which at least 2 years of data collection occurred. The five sites included the south, the upper midwest, the southeast, the mountain west region, and the western plains region. Each site meets urban/suburban characterizations.

Secondary data sources included reflections, observations, and anecdotal comments from more than 20 years of participation and contributions to local, state, and national forums on equity, diversity, and achievement concerns. These forums were conducted at various sites and were facilitated by various advocates involved in cultural and academic diversity.

Demographics.　The primary data sources included five metropolitan areas with populations from 100,000 to 600,000 people. The total African American population from each site was approximately 71.1 percent. Each site included at least one public school system with K–12 enrollments ranging from 25,000 to 70,000 students.

Focus Areas.　A major focus of these activities and practices included reflections on access, support, and opportunity for learners with exceptional needs or learners who are members of a special population. The major emphasis focused on disproportionality concerns in exceptional-needs environments, including special and gifted education. In special education, it included overrepresentation of racial ethnic minorities. In gifted education, it included underrepresentation of racial ethnic minorities. Additional emphasis was placed on basic applied research in terms of cultural competencies in practitioners, including research, analysis, assessment, design, reporting, and conducting technical assistance related to practice with various audiences. The technical assistance focused on improving individual competencies and was commonly disseminated through presentations in national and state assemblies.

Underrepresentation: Can We Overcome It?
It's a Matter of the Heart and Head

Why are African American learners underrepresented in educational services for the gifted? How can this underrepresentation be overcome? These questions have been asked for years. For just as many years, formal and informal responses to the questions have been suggested. The answers have ranged from uninformed opinions to validated research. This response provided in this chapter expands on what has been previously learned and is intended to encourage greater efforts to transfer what has been learned into practice.

The response begins with two perspectives. One perspective focuses on opening our hearts. This perspective is influenced by a lyric ("open your heart to what I mean") from Nina Simone's *Young, Gifted and Black* (1969). Simone conveys a message to listeners that to be young, gifted, and black is a lovely precious dream—not a reality. Unfortunately, Simone's message echoes realities found in many educational environments for African American learners and those that provide services for the gifted. Their proportionate participation remains a dream. Despite broadened definitions of giftedness, and ample resources concerning positive attitudes as related to diversity, African American learners remain underrepresented in many services for the gifted.

The second perspective focuses on the now-legendary and frequently cited quote by the founder of the Effective Schools Movement, the late Ron Edmonds. Edmonds (1979) asserts

> We can, whenever and wherever we choose, successfully teach all children whose schooling is of interest to us. *We already know more than we need* in order to do this. Whether we do it must finally depend on how we feel about the fact that we haven't so far. (p. 29, emphasis added)

Edmonds's quote relates to our head, our cognitive sense of morality, ethics, justice, and fairness. Edmonds and Simone are not names we instantly associate with the field in terms of research, practice, or advocacy. Each, however, is a gifted individual who has made significant contributions in terms of vision and product. Simone's and Edmonds's visions and products are gifts to our hearts and heads and support the intents in this chapter.

Overcoming or transforming inequities are indeed matters of the heart and head. Historical accounts of endeavors of many kinds have shown that efforts to transform the status quo through the head only, absent the heart, are destined to reap little change. Consider the lyric and the quote in terms of their applicability to the field. Through such considerations, the Simone lyric suggests that we find ways to touch the hearts of those who have the will to transform educational inequities such as underrepresentation.

Reconsider Edmonds's quote in terms of its applicability to the field. It suggests that we find ways to touch heads as well as hearts. Focusing primarily on general educators, Edmonds asserted that they already knew more than they needed to successfully teach all children whose schooling is of interest to them. Consider his assertion in terms of the field. Part of the quote asserts that the field already has more than enough "know how" to be successful in overcoming underrepresentation of African American learners. In recent years, the field has been informed with a significant quantity and quality of documentation on how to eliminate the underrepresentation inequity. The documentation has dissected the concern from several angles. Many previously known concepts were revisited as still useful and many new concepts have been offered as possibilities. What, then, is the problem? Overcoming underrepresentation is an achievable reality. Unfortunately, it is difficult to do, as evidenced by its persistence.

What We Know About Underrepresentation and What We Can Do About It

Underrepresentation is a practice. Its pervasiveness and persistence qualifies it to be characterized as such because it meets the classic definition of the term. A practice, or to practice, requires that a course of actions be repeated to improve performance—but whose performance and at what price? Actions associated with underrepresentation have been intentionally put into place to serve specific needs or to achieve specific goals of the greater society.

How can underrepresentation be decreased and eventually eliminated? For decades the field has been fortunate to have several stakeholders committed to the underrepresentation issue. These stakeholders include researchers, theorists, practitioners, and advocates working independently and collaboratively with their peers in special education. They have examined the whole area of disproportionality, including overrepresentation of African American learners in special education and their underrepresentation in gifted education, to great depths.

They have produced significant data, including a 1992 report by the Office for Civil Rights Elementary and Secondary School Civil Rights Compliance (U.S. Department of Education, 1992), indicating that African American learners represent 21 percent of the general school population but only 12 percent of the gifted population—an underrepresentation rate of 41 percent. In related data, the stakeholders have identified many problems that cause underrepresentation and offered as many strategies to solve them. The stakeholders have learned that the problems causing underrepresentation are not accidents or regrettable misfortunes beyond human control. The factors are entirely in the realm of human control; they are conceived, developed, and perpetuated by humans. The factors have generally been reported as school concerns, but in reality these factors reflect larger specific concerns existing in the present and recent past of society. The concerns are sociocultural in nature. They are rooted in political issues associated with power, privilege, control, economic stratification, cultural attitudinal misalignment, confusion, conflict, and fear of differences.

Many people have spent many years identifying and examining the causes of underrepresentation. Consider Edmonds's assertion, "We can, whenever and wherever we choose, successfully teach all children whose schooling is of interest to us. We already know more than we need in order to do this." Following is an examination of some of the abundant knowledge about factors of underrepresentation among African American learners advanced by stakeholders writing on the subject over the years (e.g., Adderholdt-Elliot, Algozzine, Algozzine, & Haney, 1991; Baldwin, 1987, 1989, 1999; Ford, Grantham, & Harris, III, 1996; Ford & Harris, III, 1991; Frasier, 1979, 1989; Frasier, Garcia, & Passow, 1995; Fraiser, Martin et al., 1995; Hilliard, 1999; Kitano, 1991; Patton & Baytops, 1995; Richert, 1985, 1987; Shade, 1990; Shade & Edwards, 1987; Shade, Kelly, & Obeg, 1997):

- Beliefs of the culture that giftedness and African American represents an anomaly.
- Lack of clarity regarding a definition of giftedness, particularly regarding African American perspectives.
- Negative racial attitudes.
- Limited and limiting resources, including who maintains power over them and has access to them.
- Eurocentric perspectives and values, including what is taught and how it is measured.
- Overreliance on testing; not enough assessment and use of appropriate interventions.
- Failure to use African American culture as a link to precocity.
- Misalignments and disconnections between gifted programs and general education environments.
- Overreliance on untrained teachers' input for identification processes.
- Failure to involve African American parents in identification processes and to address their concerns regarding gifted programming and their children's participation.
- Lack of federal resources with guidelines and requirements for inclusiveness.

In recent years, efforts to understand why underrepresentation occurs have been reported in *Minority Students in Special and Gifted Education* (National Academy Press, 1999). The results of the report cites the following conclusions:

- Giftedness is not a fixed trait; context plays a critical role in achievement and behavior.
- There are biological, social, and contextual contributors to early development that differ by race or ethnicity.
- Schooling independently contributes to the incidence of giftedness among students in different racial or ethnic groups by the opportunities it provides.
- The data is inadequate to address concerns as to whether gifted programs are beneficial or risky.
- Early identification and intervention is more effective than later identification and intervention. Strategies focused on a developmental orientation designed to recognize gifted behaviors early should be the philosophy rather than operating on a "wait 'til they succeed" philosophy.

Given the pervasiveness and persistence of underrepresentation, eliminating it is a complex task. Its causes are clear, but its widespread elimination cannot yet be achieved.

What are some of the obstacles preventing the elimination of underrepresentation? Perhaps the investigations from the field of special education on disproportionality will provide some perspectives. Special education has had a long history of accomplishments with a large group of stakeholders examining disproportionality (e.g., Allen & Graden, 1995; Chalfant & Pysh, 1989; Elliott & Fuchs, 1997; Feuerstein, 1979; Fuchs, Fuchs, & Barr, 1990; Harry, 1994; Jacob-Timm & Hartshorne, 1998; Lee, 1996; Luft, 1995; Markowitz, 1995, 1996; Quinn & Jacob, 1999; Reschly, 1997; Reschly, Kicklighter, & McKee, 1988a, 1988b, 1988c; Reschly & Yssekdyke, 1995; Shapiro & Skinner, 1990; Shinn, 1995; Ysseldyke & Christenson, 1993; Ysseldyke et al., 1997).

Significant federal support, such as the Individuals with Disabilities Education Act (IDEA, 1997, P.L. 105-17), has helped many initiatives focus on the disproportionality. Some outcomes of the investigations have relevant correlations to issues concerning underrepresentation in gifted education. They include

- Attitudes, perceptions, laws, and policies are difficult to change.
- Time, space, and training is not always available.
- Social patterns are often effectively stronger than the legislation addressing change. As a consequence, many legislative acts fail to achieve their intended purposes and address only individual components of particular systems, resulting in piecemeal and scattered change.
- Territorial issues on the part of special and general educators result in an attitude that a student belongs to either special or general education.
- Reorganizing and reorienting schools to support students in different and diverse ways is difficult.
- There may be a lack of ethnic or cultural sensitivity on the part of school staff.
- Communities are often not ready to support the major changes necessary to implement strategies that address disproportionality, particularly if the changes necessitate increased funds or shifting funds from popular school activities.
- Involving parents, guardians, and families from diverse ethnic and racial backgrounds is sometimes difficult.
- Misconceptions exist about how procedural safeguards operate concerning students who are in need of different educational strategies or different types of support.
- Traditionally, special education has been a "place" rather than a set of services or educational strategies.
- Classroom teachers are overloaded and grappling with many responsibilities, but without needed support.
- Class sizes are large. There is limited time for staff planning, meeting, and consultation, particularly with related services; development and training is rarely schoolwide and typically not ongoing.

- Funds for staff training are limited.
- Classroom teachers lack skills to strategize and problem solve with their colleagues using a consultative model.
- There is limited support and guidance for the novice teacher.

These are some of the reasons for underrepresentation of African American learners in gifted programs. They are obstacles that help perpetuate underrepresentation. Suggestions to reduce, and eventually eliminate, the problem are offered next.

- Examine underrepresentation causes and obstacles. Prioritize those that are most troubling; have been the most difficult to implement; or have been least effective in terms of fairness, achieving access, support, and opportunity to learn.
- Assess or reassess the capacity of existing personal, peer, and institutional resources that you want to use or have been using. Carefully direct them toward the priorities you have established.
- Intensify collaborative efforts initially within peer groups, then across wider audiences—particularly those audiences not previously considered as possible collaborators (some suggestions are mentioned later in the chapter).

Underrepresentation: A Desegregation Focus

Underrepresentation is essentially linked to desegregation principles. The field is becoming more social simply by examining itself in terms of the peculiar ties it has with the desegregated school environment. Desegregation is the major social transformation of the times; therefore, it becomes a crux in most racial equity contexts. Desegregation has been a reality in schools for more than 4 decades. During those decades, changing educational, political, economic, and social perspectives have affected its intent and outcomes in various ways. The intent and outcomes of desegregation are not the focus of the desegregation discussion in this chapter. The focus is on its existence—particularly with regard to its peculiar relationship to the field.

Some proponents of desegregation, particularly African American proponents, view the field with trepidation regarding its purpose and realities. They believe the field is a leading opponent to desegregation. The field's current demographics sends a clear segregationist message because it continues to operate in the most segregated educational environments in education. Ford, Harris, and Webb (1995) note that abundant data suggest that gifted programs are the most segregated educational programs in the United States.

Minority children, particularly African Americans, the economically disadvantaged, and underachievers are severely underrepresented in gifted education and overrepresented in special education programs for children who are learning disabled, behaviorally disordered, and mentally retarded.

The field presents a multipart incongruity in terms of desegregation, its intent, social justice, and a democratic society. One part of the incongruity involves the passage of the Jacob K. Javits Gifted and Talented Students Act in 1988. The act provides federally funded resources to the field. The act places high priority on the identification of who are gifted racial minorities, economically disadvantaged, limited English proficient, or who have other disabilities in empowerment zones—usually urban, high-poverty areas eligible for United States Department of Education (USDE) intervention. As of this writing, the act has received congressional approval to be refunded at $11.25 million. This is the highest level of funding it has received in its 14 years. The Javits Act proved to be a significant element in desegregating the field, but it lacks the strength to maximize its effectiveness in terms of real equity. In order for real equity to happen and to transform present conditions, significant due process procedures must be part of an initiative.

Another part of the incongruity concerns the field's stakeholders, their message, and the audience. The stakeholders qualitatively speak and write cogently and prolifically about equity and underrepresentation concerns in the field, but their work is not embraced or supported to the degree and level that it deserves with the general African American educational community.

Each time the field's stakeholders, who are committed to equity, academic and cultural diversity, and excellence, express their views on identification and underrepresentation, they are essentially discussing desegregation in at least three of its major tenets—access, support, and the opportunity to learn. For decades, these stakeholders have addressed the field's segregationist-like practices and have developed strategies to rectify them. The strategies have proven useful for desegregating the field. When refocused, they may also be useful regarding general education's ongoing desegregation concerns. Few of the field's stakeholders, however, explicitly promote strategies that address underrepresentation in the field as desegregation strategies useful outside the field.

Also not enough of the field's stakeholders' views are expressed outside the field's literature, except for Ford, who posited her views on desegregating gifted education in her article *Desegregating Gifted Education: A Need Unmet* (1995) in *The Journal of Negro Education.* It is imperative for stakeholders committed to equity, academic diversity, cultural diversity, and excellence to develop relationships and to continue to associate frequently with general education. These connections and relationships are particularly critical to establish with general education's African American educational community.

Spreading the Message and Responsibility

Guaranteeing African American learners access, opportunity, and support to participate in high-level challenging curricula may go far to address the strong notion among many African American scholars that schools were not designed to, and are not intended to, realize each learner's high quality of life. Their notion is associated with the belief that many practices found in schools perpetuate the racial, cultural, and economic stratification that characterizes today's society. Education perpetuates underrepresentation by continuing to adhere to curriculum and instruction models that are not relevant for African Americans. Additionally, service delivery models may be too remote in terms of the African American response preferences. Tracking systems combined with standardized testing rather than ongoing assessment enhances and facilitates the perpetuation of underrepresentation. What can be done about this problem? As with any problem, communication is a key. The responsibility of overcoming an issue that affects such a precious resource is the problem and responsibility of all of society. Many social and educational organizations have limited awareness of this situation, but they could make great contributions to help remediate the problem given their scope, capacity, stated missions, and funding.

The National Association of Black School Educators (NABSE), the National Association for Gifted Children (NAGC), the Council for Exceptional Children (CEC), the equity assistance centers (EACs) and the regional educational laboratories (RELs) represent five groups who, through their stated missions, could be important collaborators with stakeholders in the field of underrepresentation. Each of these groups holds a prominent place in the educational system in the United States because of their unique purposes. The NABSE, NAGC, and CEC could be instrumental in overcoming underrepresentation. Each has a documented history that is directly or indirectly focused on such issues.

The EACs could play a vital role in assisting the field in overcoming underrepresentation. They are connected with the Office for Civil Rights (OCR), which supports and monitors equity issues in education. The OCR in recent years has become more proactive as concerns education rather than simply reacting to equity violations. The OCR and CEC TAG (The Association for the Gifted) Division have established a relationship to learn more about each other's functions. Perhaps this relationship will stimulate collaborative efforts. Such partnerships are critical in meeting the concerns of underrepresentation.

The work of the RELs tends to be narrowly focused and directed toward problems in education with less daunting challenges than those underrepresentation presents. Additionally, RELs tend to focus on problems that have a high level of success potential regarding solution finding.

Although their mission statements and funding sources might lead one to believe that they would welcome a concern, such as underrepresentation, they may hesitate because of the potential risk of failure. However, the RELs have reformulated their mission in recent years in terms of accountability, which is important for their political survival. This new accountability may affect their capacity for projects related to underrepresentation. It will be useful, therefore, to explore collaboration possibilities. If their apprehension proves to be an obstacle to direct collaborative initiatives with the field, they can at least provide indirect services because of their collaboration with other educational resources throughout the United States.

Using nonacademic organizations and federal educational agencies as new resources, and creative thinking in problem solving, some successes should be possible regarding eliminating underrepresentation practices. The agencies and organizations previously mentioned may or may not be ideal, but they are suggestions to stimulate thought about reducing underrepresentation.

Underrepresentation Relationships to Identification

Earlier in this chapter, it was suggested that the causes of underrepresentation are rooted in sociocultural political issues related to power, privilege, control, economic stratification, cultural attitudinal misalignment, confusion, conflict, and fear about differences in society. Each of these elements has significant bearings on school programs and vice versa. Most school programs and services are characterized by similar areas, including mission statements, a curriculum focus and delivery plans, staffing plans, staff development plans, and advocacy strategies. Additionally, programs and services have an administrative support staff; an assessment and evaluation services staff; goals, philosophy, and implementation plans; budget supports; and, with exceptional learners, an identification or referral area—the most disconcerting area for African American learners who are gifted. Each area, especially identification, must be carefully audited to determine its equity quotient (EQ). A deliberate, continuous, and systematic in-depth investigation of all areas must be a priority in program management schemes. For example, school and program mission statements generally make exalted, lofty proclamations on ideals and goals about "attaining academic success for all children." A better statement would contain wording focused on "each child," rather than all children, and address guarantees regarding access, the opportunity to learn, and support for each child in every facet of the school's operation.

Mission statements are discreet passive elements of programs and services, and they are rarely examined unless an equity problem occurs in the district, school, or programs and civil rights attorneys become involved. They should be examined for their EQ as concerns the student population and the program's implementation. Although mission statements are discreet and passive, they should have an active influence on programs and services and must be weighed against equity principles, fairness, and what is just and right for each individual and the groups she or he represents.

Because equitable identification is critical to the program's operation and has a significant bearing on sociocultural contexts of the greater society, extreme care and sensitivity must be used in planning, managing, enhancing, or, in this context, transforming identification. A primary reason that African American children, as well as other racial ethnic minorities, are underrepresented in the field is because most identification processes are, by nature, comparison processes. All identification processes should find and serve as many children as possible who have unique needs that cannot be met in a general classroom environment. Comparison elements of the process should be focused on discovering the level and degree of unique needs and to provide some "hints" as to how the unique needs can be met in the gifted classroom.

Equity problems arise when we compare across ethnicities, gender, and economic conditions. This is the quickest way to initiate underrepresentation. Identification processes must, therefore, be "renormed" to better represent the diversity in the population. The rationale for renorming, and not to compare children across ethnicities, is simple. Different groups bring different experiences to school.

The collective experiences within a group are likely to be more similar than dissimilar. This is not to suggest that variations do not exist in a group. This is far from true. As a group, however, it is likely that more similarities will be evident than dissimilarities; therefore, it makes sense to determine needs in consideration of ethnicity, gender, and economic status. In that regard, it is unfair to include (compare the needs of) affluent white children with African American children who qualify for free or reduced price lunch in an identification process, particularly if safeguards or interventions have not been designed to manage or factor out human and instrumental bias and other pitfalls associated with traditional identification procedures and diverse populations.

Implementation Process

The parameters of this chapter will not allow detailed information on all of the aspects of renorming for identification purposes, but an overview of the implementation process is provided.

- Focus on placing programming for African American learners in differentiated, required, subject-based areas of the gifted services. There, caregivers are more likely to support subject-based programming because they have a better understanding of the subjects than non–subject-based areas. Additionally, the subject areas probably include the greatest benefits in terms of the learners' postschool experiences.

Training/Teacher Preparation/Preparing for the ID Process

- Eliminate cut-off scores or points.
- Make sure all program staff are trained in areas focused on multicultural gifted education and are aware of the accommodations provided by renorming strategies. Make sure staff have at least a summary (but ideally, a comprehensive) accounting (differentiated educational plan [DEP]) of the information from the identification process for each child with whom he or she interacts.
- Provide general staff specialized training and opportunities for follow-up training on culture and its relationship to giftedness before the search (identification process) begins.

Parent Advocacy

■ Conduct parent meetings to clarify the process, to seek support, and to collect information about the child. The meetings should accommodate parents' schedules and comfort levels in terms of location. If the meetings can be conducted in their neighborhoods, locally, then conduct them there. This will help personalize the process, which is an important concept in terms of building trust and support.

Information Collection

■ It is important to emphasize an "information collection process" rather than a nomination, referral, or selection process.
■ Nominating, referring, and selecting tend to align with limiting, limits, and limited concepts rather than expansive concepts. When parents or teachers provide *information*, it tends to be richer and more indicative of learners' potential than that obtained from nominations, referrals, or selections. Additionally, better data regarding the learners' cultural connections to his or gifts may be a value added benefit for learner and program services. Eliminate the terms *nominate, refer,* and *select* from your program description. They have the tendencies to negate equity-based attitudes.

Program/Service Capacity

■ Determine enrollment capacity in the differentiated subjects. Make adjustments as needed. These may be as simple as a minor schedule adjustment or very complex, such as training or hiring staff.

Develop Subgroups/Renorm the Population

■ Determine the number of students across a grade level. Group them by gender, ethnicity, and economic status by grade level. Determine the percentage of students you can seek from each subgroup. For example, African American males not receiving free or reduced price lunch is one group, African American females not receiving free or reduced lunch is another group, African American males receiving free or reduced lunch is another group, African American females receiving free or reduced lunch is yet another group. Do this for each ethnicity across each grade level.

Data Analysis

■ Analyze balanced (subjective and objective) information collected from multiple data sources (parents, peers, self, community teachers, tests) and other information, especially if the information emerges from sources that are related to how intelligence among African American students is received, transmitted, and reflective of their learning styles, preferences, or characteristics. Some of those characteristics include a preference for relational, holistic, and visually stimulating activities and environments; social, cooperative, interactive grouping; and opportunities for kinesthetic and tactile expression. Analyze the information in terms of the group, that is, conduct an *in-group* analysis. *Do not compare information across groups.* The goal is to look for learners who demonstrate the greatest need within their cultural groups.

- Do not place high priority on teacher information, unless teachers have been trained and demonstrate high levels of cultural competence, using appropriate culturally relevant identification tools.
- Do not place high priority on information from tests. Test bias is a well-known reality. Many factors inhibit the performance of African American students on standardized tests of intelligence and achievement, specifically, environmental factors, psychological variables, cognitive styles, and problems with the tests themselves (Ford, 1996). Be careful: Some tests purport to be culture free. No test is culture free. A member or members of one or more cultures designed it; therefore, his or her cultural experiences are reflected in it.

Data Interpretation

- Ford and Harris (1999) suggest the following regarding how best to assess needs when using tests. Interpret test information after it has been

1. adapted or modified relative to the characteristics of the African American population;
2. renormed to reflect local norms and needs; and
3. modified in terms of cut-off scores.

Examine test percentile information on all students along with other collected data. If a group of African American advantaged students have scores in the ninety-ninth percentile and are the highest scoring among their group, they should be considered for services if other data indicators are complementary. If a group of African American disadvantaged students have scores in the sixty-ninth percentile and are the highest scoring students among their group, then these students should be considered for services because they are demonstrating the most different (highest) response to the learning environment with regard to their peers.

It is incumbent on those who are in charge of interpreting identification information to find strengths across the African American population, regardless of how their scores compare with other populations. Many useful program improvements can be made in the general environment as well as the gifted program environment with this information. There is more data than is needed from the investigations of the research base to eliminate underrepresentation. Considering another part of Edmonds's quote "Whether we do it...depend[s] on how we feel about the fact that we haven't so far."

Summary and Conclusion

This chapter focused on schools as social institutions, their roles as agents of social change, and their participation in the greatest social transformation in America—the desegregation of its schools and African Americans and gifted education. Social change is about quality in many areas including rights, privileges, and life. Most schools include many components to meet those ends, including a unique component generally termed *gifted education.* A composite description of gifted education was derived after an examination of dozens of gifted educational descriptions. The definitions generally stated that gifted education services help learners who demonstrate or have the potential to demonstrate high degrees of intellectual or creative behaviors.

These learners may also exhibit an exceptionally high degree of motivation, or may excel in specific academic fields. Gifted behaviors are apparent in certain people, at certain times, and under certain circumstances (Renzulli, 1986). Such potential or behavior requires unique instruction or services to help these learners achieve at the maximum levels of their potential. This description certainly does not focus on any one ethnic group and, therefore, is paradoxical to the underrepresentation issue.

For decades, gifted education has experienced equity problems in terms of underrepresentation of nonwhite students. This problem is associated with a society that demonstrates that its moral evolution is yet incomplete. That part of society continues to mock claims to fairness and justice. It continues to echo the willful ignorance and fears of its founding fathers. This continuity of ignorance, fear, and mockery to fairness and justice reflects schools' ill preparedness to fully accept the social transformation of which they have been a part since the mid-twentieth century. This ill preparedness is perpetuated in overt and covert ways, one of which is gifted education.

Gifted education has routinely functioned on the fringes of a transformed society because that society remains largely segregated and worse—the segregation is largely accepted. The acceptance of segregated gifted educational services has been so pervasive and persistent that it has attained *practice* status. A practice, or to practice, requires a course of actions be repeated to improve performance. The practice of segregated gifted education has, indeed, been practiced so long and so well that its performance has improved—in its continued underrepresentation of nonwhite students. It remains insulated and isolated to the desegregated school.

This has occurred despite decades of documented data concerning culture as related to conceptions of giftedness and underrepresentation, including its causes, obstacles, and strategies to overcome it. The problem has several dimensions. It includes problems at the highest levels of educational support maintaining that giftedness does not have the critical mass to be considered important in the greater scheme of educational servicing. On the day-to-day level, it includes problems of well-meaning administrators, sensitive to equity issues, turning their deaf ears and their blind eyes to gifted program issues because they are well aware of the personal occupational hazards associated with attempts to desegregate gifted education.

Concrete solutions to underrepresentation are not presented in the chapter. Currently, such solutions may not exist for a variety of reasons. Perhaps we are too embryonic in our stages of evolution in terms of a diverse world to develop the solutions. Perhaps the solutions will come because of honest, personal, and political reflections on the events of September 11, 2001. For many, those events helped solidify the realities that we cannot dispel others because they have different views and that open communication, access, support, and opportunities are key to a successful coexistence. What is presented is an array of perspectives on how to address underrepresentation and ideas to reduce its severity. Concrete solutions remain elusive because it will require not only an extensive knowledge base but also the opening of hearts among a preponderance of individuals dedicated to a just and fair world.

REFERENCES

Adderholdt-Elliot, M., Algozzine, K., Algozinne, B., & Haney, K. (1991). Current state practices in educating students who are gifted and talented. *Roeper Review, 14,* 20–23.

Allen, S., & Graden, J. (1995). Collaborative problem solving for intervention design. In A. Thomas & J. Grimes (Eds.), *Best practices in school psychology-III* (pp. 667–678). Bethesda, MD: National Association of School Psychologists.

Baldwin, A. Y. (1989). The purpose of education for gifted black students. In C. J. Maker & S. W. Schiever (Eds.), *Critical issues in gifted education: Defensible programs for cultural and ethnic minorities* (Vol. 2, pp. 237–245). Austin, TX: PRO-ED.

Baldwin, A. Y. (1999). *The many faces of giftedness: Lifting the masks.* Belmont, CA: Wadsworth.

Brown v. Board of Education, 347 U.S. 483 (1954).

Chalfant, J., & Pysh, M. (1989). Teacher assistance teams: Five descriptive studies on 96 teams. *Remedial and Special Education, 10,* 49–58.

Edmonds, R. R. (1979, March/April). Some schools work and more can. *Social Policy,* 28–32.

Elliott, S., & Fuchs, L. (1997). The utility of curriculum-based measurement and performance assessment as alternatives to traditional intelligence and achievement tests. *School Psychology Review, 26,* 224–233.

Feuerstein, R. (1979). *The dynamic assessment of retarded performers.* Baltimore, MD: University Park Press.

Ford, D. Y., (1996). *Reversing underachievement among gifted black students: Promising practices and programs.* New York: Teachers College Press.

Ford, D. Y., Grantham, T. C., & Harris, J. J., III. (1996). Multicultural gifted education: A wakeup call to the profession. *Roeper Review, 19*(2), 72–78.

Ford, D. Y., Harris, J. J., III, & Webb, K. (1995). Desegregating gifted education: A need unmet. *Journal of Negro Education, 64*(1), 52–62.

Ford, D. Y., & Harris, J. J., III. (1991). On discovering the hidden treasure of gifted and talented African-American children. *Roeper Review, 13*(1), 27–33.

Ford, D. Y., & Harris, J. J., III. (1999). *Multicultural gifted education.* New York: Teachers College Press.

Frasier, M. (1989). Identification of gifted black students: Developing new perspectives. In C. J. Maker & S. W. Schiever (Eds.), *Critical issues in gifted education: Defensible programs for cultural and ethnic minorities* (Vol. 2, pp. 213–225). Austin, TX: PRO-ED.

Frasier, M. M. (1979). Rethinking the issue regarding the culturally disadvantaged gifted. *Exceptional Children, 45*(7), 538–542.

Frasier, M. M., Garcia, J. H., & Passow, A. H. (1995). *A review of assessment issues in gifted education and their implications for identifying gifted minority students.* Storrs: National Research Center on the Gifted and Talented, University of Connecticut.

Frasier, M. M., Martin, D., Garcia, J., Finley, V. S., Frank, E., Krisel, S., & King, L. L. (1995). *A new window for looking at gifted children.* Storrs: National Research Center on the Gifted and Talented, University of Connecticut.

Fuchs, D., Fuchs, L., & Barr, M. (1990). Mainstream assistance teams: A scientific basis for the art of consultation. *Exceptional Children, 57*, 128–139.

Harry, B. (1994). *The disproportionate representation of minority students in special education: Theories and recommendations.* Project FORUM. Final report (pp. 8–11, 43–48). Alexandria. VA: National Association of State Directors of Special Education (ED 374 637).

Hilliard, A. (1999, September). *From custodial to beneficial practice.* Paper presented at the Conference of 100 Black Men of America, Inc., Washington, DC.

Jacob-Timm, S., & Hartshorne, T. S. (1998). *Ethics and law for school psychologists* (pp. 95–119, 226–228). New York: Wiley.

Kitano, M. K. (1991). A multicultural educational perspective on serving the culturally diverse gifted. *Journal for the Education of the Gifted, 15*(1), 4–19.

Lee, C. C. (1996). *Multicultural issues in counseling: New approaches to diversity.* Alexandria, VA: American Counseling Association.

Luft, P. (1995). *Addressing minority overrepresentation in special education: Cultural barriers to effective collaboration.* Paper presented at the 73rd annual International Convention of the Council for Exceptional Children, Indianapolis, IN, pp. 4–9.

Markowitz, J. (1995, September). *Disproportionate representation: A critique of state and local strategies.* Policy Forum Report (pp. 3–5, 8–140). Alexandria, VA: National Association of State Directors of Special Education (ED 392 195).

Markowitz, J. (1996). *Strategies that address the disproportionate number of students from racial/ethnic minority groups receiving special education services: Case studies of selected states and school districts.* Report prepared by Project Forum. Alexandria, VA: National Association of State Directors of Special Education.

National Academy Press, Commission on Behavioral and Social Sciences and Education. (2002). C. Cross & S. Donovan (Eds.), *Minority students in special and gifted education.* Washington, DC: Author.

National Association of School Psychologists. (1994a). *School psychologists' involvement in the role of assessment.* Position Statement adopted by NASP Delegate Assembly.

National Association of School Psychologists. (1994b). *Assessment and eligibility in special education: An examination of policy and practice with proposals for change.* Prepared for Project Forum of the National Association of State Directors of Special Education for the Office of Special Education Programs, U.S. Department of Education. Washington, DC: U.S. Department of Education/Office of Special Education Programs.

National Association of State Directors of Special Education. (1994). *Disproportionate representation of students from minority ethnic/racial groups in special education: A policy forum to develop action plans for high priority recommendation.* Final report, Project Forum: Proceedings of a Policy Forum in Disproportionate Representation (Pentagon City, August 1994). (ED 378 716).

National Association of State Directors of Special Education. (1995). *Disproportionate representation of culturally and linguistically diverse students in special education: A comprehensive examination.* Prepared by Project Forum. Alexandria, VA: Author (ED 379 812).

Orfield, G., & Yun, J. T. (1999). *Resegregation in American Schools.* The Civil Rights Project, Harvard University, Cambridge, MA.

Patton, J. M., & Baytops, J. L. (1995). Identifying and transforming potential. In A. Ford, F. E. Obiakor, & J. M. Patton (Eds.), *Effective education of African-American learners: New perspectives* (pp. 27–61). Austin, TX: PRO-ED.

Quinn, M., & Jacob, E. (1999, September). Adding culture to the tools of school psychologists. *Communiqué, 28*(1), 34, 38–39.

Renzulli, J. S. (1986). The three-ring conception of giftedness: A developmental model for creative productivity. In R. J. Sternberg & J. Davidson (Eds.), *Conceptions of giftedness* (pp. 53–92). New York: Cambridge University Press.

Reschly, D. (1997). Utility of individual ability measures and public policy choices for the twenty-first century. *School Psychology Review, 26,* 234–241.

Reschly, D., Kicklighter, R., & McKee, P. (1988a). Recent placement litigation, Part I. Regular education grouping: Comparison of Marshall (1984, 1985) and Hobson (1967, 1969). *School Psychology Review, 17,* 19–21.

Reschly, D., Kicklighter, R., & McKee, P. (1988b). Recent placement litigation, Part II: Minority EMR overrepresentation: Comparison of Larry, P. (1979, 1984, 1986) with Marshall (1984, 1985) and S-1 (1986). *School Psychology Review, 17,* 22–38.

Reschly, D., Kicklighter, R., & McKee, P. (1988c). Recent placement litigation, Part III: Analysis of differences in Larry P., Marshall and S-1 and implications for future practices. *School Psychology Review, 17,* 39–50.

Reschly, D., & Ysseldyke, J. (1995). School psychology paradigm shift. In A. Thomas & J. Grimes (Eds.), *Best practices in school psychology-III* (pp. 17–32). Bethesda, MD: National Association of School Psychologists.

Richert, E. S. (1985). Identification of gifted children in the United States: The need for pluralistic assessment. *Roeper Review, 13*(2), 68–72.

Richert, E. S. (1987). Rampant problems and promising practices in the identification of disadvantaged gifted students. *Gifted Child Quarterly, 31*(4), 149–154.

Shade, B. (1990). *Engaging the battle for African-American minds (commissioned paper).* Washington, DC: National Alliance of Black School Educators.

Shade, B. J., & Edwards, P. A. (1987). Ecological correlates of the educative style of Afro-American children. *Journal of Negro Education, 56*(1), 88–99.

Shade, B. J., Kelly, C., & Obeg, M. (1997). *Creating culturally responsive classrooms.* Washington, DC: American Psychological Association.

Shapiro, E., & Skinner, C. (1990). Best practices in observation and ecological assessment. In A. Thomas & J. Grimes (Eds.), *Best practices in school psychology-III* (pp. 507–518). Bethesda, MD: National Association of School Psychologists.

Shinn, M. (1995). Curriculum-based measurement and its use in a problem solving model. In A. Thomas & J. Grimes (Eds.), *Best practices in school psychology-III* (pp. 547–568). Bethesda, MD: National Association of School Psychologists.

Simone, N., & Irving, A. (1969). To be young, gifted and black. On *The Essential Nina Simone* [CD]. New York: RCA. (1993)

U.S. Department of Education. (1999). *OCR elementary and secondary school civil rights compliance report.* Washington, DC: Office for Civil Rights.

U.S. Department of Education/Office of Special Education Programs. (1996). *Meeting the needs of students with disabilities in inner cities, Chapter 4 of the 18th Annual Report to Congress.* Washington, DC: Author.

U.S. Department of Education/Office of Special Education Programs. (1998a). *Congressional findings excerpted from the Individual with Disabilities Education Act, Part A, Section 601(c).* Washington, DC: Author.

U.S. Department of Education/Office of Special Education Programs. (1998b). *The racial and ethnic composition of students with disabilities. The Twentieth Annual Report to Congress.* Washington, DC: Author.

Ysseldyke, J., & Christenson, S. (1993). *The instructional environment system-II.* Longmont, CO: Sopris West.

Ysseldyke, J., Dawson, P., Lehr, C., Reschly, D., Reynolds, M., & Telzrow, C. (1997). *School psychology: A blueprint for training and practice II.* Bethesda, MD: National Association of School Psychologists.

CHAPTER

5 Opportunities in Gifted Education for Haitian Students

JAIME A. CASTELLANO

The identification and education of culturally and linguistically diverse students for gifted education can perhaps best be described as intermittent and inconsistent. Across the United States these students are underidentified, underserved, or simply eliminated from the screening process that serves as the primary catalyst for inclusion into gifted education programming and opportunity. Some insiders in bilingual/ESL education, as well as gifted education, would consider this business as usual. The fact that there are millions of students in the public school system who are non-English or limited English speaking only exacerbates an already suspect gifted education system that is designed to identify only the best, brightest, and most able students.

The research in gifted education that targets underrepresented student populations typically addresses issues of culture and ethnicity. The little available research that specifically addresses linguistic diversity most often involves the Spanish-speaking population where the service is provided in their heritage language. And though there are programs, such as Mosaic 2000 in Chicago, that offer gifted education services in other languages, research as to the identification and education of other language groups as a focus of study is, for all practical matters, nonexistent. Surf the Net, search the stacks, contact any of the national centers for gifted education, do an ERIC search, call the U.S. Department of Education's Office of Educational Research and Improvement (OERI), and you will see.

In the southeast region of the United States, more specifically, in South Florida, Haitian Creole is the second most often spoken language by school-age students enrolled in programs for teaching English to speakers of other languages (ESOL) (Florida Department of Education, 2000). In the school district of Palm Beach County, Florida, approximately 8,000 Haitian students are receiving ESOL services (2000). Just as many, if not more, are being served in the school districts of Broward and Miami–Dade counties. There are thousands more enrolled as "regular curriculum" students. However, despite their large numbers, and classification, they are grossly underrepresented in gifted education programs. The purpose of this chapter is to expand the research base in gifted education for culturally and linguistically diverse students, to include the Haitian and Haitian American student.

Belanca: A Case Study

Belanca is a third grader. Her family immigrated to the United States from Haiti in 1996. After living 2 years in the United States, she speaks English very well. In reviewing her school file, Belanca's third-grade teacher saw that she received the highest possible marks in reading and math at the end of second grade. She also noted that Belanca grasped new concepts quickly and could apply them to other learning situations. In addition, she showed much creativity in her artwork. She is well liked by her peers and demonstrates leadership behavior and skills in cooperative learning groups. Belanca topped out on the reading running record for third grade. She has also shown great improvement in written composition, which is her weakest skill.

How could we document Belanca's eligibility for gifted education using this information? What gifted characteristics can we use to support her candidacy? Does she demonstrate the need for a gifted program?

Intellectual Assessment. The fact that Belanca has done so well academically after being in the United States for approximately 2 years is remarkable. As an English language learner, she scored at the top of her class in reading and math at both the second and third grade, and topped out on another diagnostic assessment in her third-grade reading program. Furthermore, when considering the predominant language functions of listening, speaking, reading, and writing, and how they are assessed in the public school system, Belanca has apparently surpassed grade-level expectations. Scholastically, does she have the intellectual ability to pursue placement in a gifted education program? Yes!

Gifted Characteristics. There is no question that Belanca manifests many of the gifted behaviors associated with Haitian students, other characteristics typically attributed to culturally and linguistically diverse students, and still others found in white middle-class gifted students. Based on the aforementioned scenario, the following gifted behaviors are or were evident in Belanca's behavior:

- Problem-solving ability
- Ability to code switch
- Highly motivated
- Easily adjusts to environment
- Curious/inquisitive
- Creative (high degree of musical or artistic ability)
- Demonstrates leadership behavior
- Balances appropriate behaviors expected of the heritage culture with the new culture

- Functions at language proficiency levels above that of nongifted LEP peers
- Demonstrates cross-cultural flexibility
- Learns a second or third language at an accelerated pace (formal or informal)
- Excels in math achievement tests

Need for a Special Program.   Based on a combination of factors, it is clear that Belanca has demonstrated a need to be considered for a special program. Input from the regular classroom teacher, past and present school performance, leadership behavior, checklists of gifted behavior, ability to apply new skills to novel situations, and creativity support the need for Belanca to be considered for gifted education.

Potential Barriers in the Identification of Underrepresented Student Populations

Despite efforts at the local school district level and by the State Department of Education in Tallahassee, Florida, students from low-socioeconomic status families and minority group communities, including those of Haitian descent, continue to be underrepresented in gifted programs throughout South Florida. During the 1997–1998 school year, the Sarasota Project sponsored by the University of South Florida developed a compendium of activities to improve services for students who are gifted.

Part of this report includes strategies and recommendations to assist in the recruitment and retention of African Americans in gifted education programs. To expand on these recommendations, and to include students in free or reduced lunch, ESOL students, and those from other culturally and linguistically diverse groups, the Working on Gifted Issues Project, also sponsored by the University of South Florida (1999), was created.

One division of this project included a group of gifted education administrators, teachers, and advocates from five South Florida counties whose primary responsibilities include the following:

1. Identifying barriers in the identification of low-SES and minority populations for gifted education programming.
2. Identifying strategies for recruiting low-SES and minority student populations into gifted education.
3. Identifying strategies for retention of low-SES and minority student populations in gifted education.

The combined efforts of this group, with more than 100 years of experience in gifted education, produced the following barriers in the identification of low-SES and minority populations for gifted education programming. The barriers are categorized as follows:

Perceptions/Stereotyping of Minority and Low-SES Students
- Low-SES students are often viewed as needing remedial education rather than being considered for programs of the gifted.
- Low-SES students are often stereotyped. Teachers often assume that because the student is African American, or Haitian, or Hispanic that he or she has grown up in poverty, lived in a ghetto, and could not be classified as gifted.
- Teacher's knowledge of students' IQ scores, SES, area of home location, and family structure contribute to stereotypes and low expectations of these students.
- Many educators are biased toward low-SES students, and those who have behavior problems are often placed in remedial or other compensatory programs.
- Some students who score consistently low on standardized measures of achievement may not be revealing their true ability.
- The social implications of low-SES students, as a group, include risk factors, such as poverty, neglect, and racial oppression. They are overrepresented among children with psychological problems. The perception is that they cannot be gifted.

Bias of Assessment Instruments and Checklists Used During Identification
- In many school districts current evaluation methods often do not make use of multiple criteria. Data should be gathered from multiple sources rather than a single criterion (e.g., IQ tests).
- Low-SES and other underachieving students may demonstrate their abilities more often in nontraditional fashions and in nonschool settings.
- Many diverse gifted students experience gaps of specific basic skills, which adds to the difficulty in getting these students nominated, let alone identified, for gifted programs.
- Quite often, the checklists used in identification show that characteristics of low-SES and underachieving students is noticeably absent. The primary focus tends to be on academic and cognitive characteristics of giftedness.

Parental Perceptions and Knowledge
- A lack of parental awareness exists in poor and minority communities regarding gifted education.
- The economic status of some families creates a sensitivity that leads to non-involvement in special school activities. The parents assume there is a cost associated with special programs.
- Some parents fear there will be a loss of culture, that is, tradition, customs, language.
- The possibility that the child will leave the neighborhood school is another concern that parents have, as well as the possibility that entering a gifted program may lead to a negative change in the child, for example, elitism, superior attitude.

English Language Proficiency
- Students with language barriers (limited vocabulary and experience) are often omitted for consideration for gifted programs.
- Students for whom English is a second language or who use nonstandard English may experience academic difficulty. They may be perceived as inarticulate or unintelligent.

Lack of Teacher Training
- Teachers are not necessarily good at identifying poor, minority, or other culturally and linguistically diverse children for gifted education.
- Staff development training is often neglected for teachers of the gifted, and regular education teachers are not provided training in the areas of identification, curriculum modification, and assessment.

Attitude of Psychologists, Administrators, and Counselors
- Counselors and psychologists may not be formally trained to evaluate poor, minority, and other culturally and linguistically diverse students for gifted education.
- With regards to testing, students are frequently taken to an unfamiliar environment and tested by an inexperienced or insensitive psychologist. As a result, students may not put forth their best efforts.

Lack of Early Identification
- Early identification of young gifted students is often neglected. When giftedness is neglected at an early age, it is vulnerable to extinction.

Fear of "Brain Drain"
- There are public schools that do not refer their potentially gifted underrepresented students because they want to keep their high-test scores, especially at low-performing schools.

The barriers outlined are not associated with one specific group but with all those who have been historically excluded from gifted education. For South Florida, these students include African American, Haitian or Haitian American, Hispanic, poor, limited English proficient (LEP), and other culturally and linguistically diverse student populations.

Characteristics of Giftedness or Potential Giftedness in Culturally and Linguistically Diverse Children

Persistent underrepresentation has led researchers and practitioners to call for substantive changes in identification procedures. Maker (1996) proposes four modifications to the process. First, identification practices should be congruent with contemporary conceptions of giftedness. Second, identification should focus on achieving equal representation of all cultural and ethnic groups. Third, such identification practices need to be developed for school districts, keeping in mind the resources available. Fourth, identification procedures should be developed that use valid and reliable measures of abilities that are valued by the student's ethnic and cultural group.

Connected to Maker's last modification are the actual gifted behaviors, or characteristics, manifested by students who are culturally and ethnically diverse. Those students who are also non–English or limited English speaking display many of the same characteristics.

From 1987 to 1996, project GOTCHA (Galaxies of Thinking and Creative Heights of Achievement) was designated a Title VII Academic Excellence Program by the U.S. Department of Education. GOTCHA is the only Academic Excellence program recognizing giftedness, or potential giftedness, in students enrolled in ESL or bilingual classrooms across the United States. The program focus was development of the English language by emphasizing the students' gifted or creative and talented abilities.

As of 2002, project GOTCHA continues to be implemented under the direction of International Educational Consultants, Inc., and includes multiple sites in Florida, Louisiana, Georgia, and other states. From 1996 to 1999, Norma E. Hernandez and Nilda Aguirre, project consultants and trainers, compiled data from program teachers identifying the behaviors or characteristics displayed by students enrolled in the program, many of whom qualify for their district's gifted education program after a period of participation in the GOTCHA program. It is important to reiterate that program teachers, those with the most contact with the target student population, have identified the following characteristics of giftedness or potential giftedness in the bilingual or ESL students they serve.

- Eagerness to share information about their heritage culture.
- A strong desire to teach peers words from their cultural heritage and ethnic background.
- Eagerness to translate for peers and adults.
- Ability to balance appropriate behaviors expected of the heritage culture and new culture.
- Advanced knowledge of idioms and native dialects with ability to translate and explain meanings in English.
- Ability to understand jokes and puns related to cultural differences.
- Ability to read in heritage language two grade levels or more above his or her grade level.
- Ability to function at language proficiency levels above that of nongifted LEP peers.
- Code-switching ability.
- Cross-cultural flexibility.

- Sense of global community and awareness of other cultures and languages.
- Ability to learn a second or third language at an accelerated pace (formal or informal).
- Excelling in math achievement tests.
- Exhibiting strengths in the creative areas of fluency, elaboration, originality, and flexibility.

Many of these behaviors are also characteristic of those Haitian students enrolled in the project GOTCHA program and are consistent with this author's work with the Haitian community in Palm Beach County, Florida.

Voices of a Community: How the Haitian Community Perceives Giftedness in Its Own Children

The Florida Department of Education (2000) has identified Hispanic and Haitian students as those most represented in programs for teaching English to speakers of other languages (ESOL) in the school districts of Palm Beach, Broward, and Miami–Dade. Research on how the Hispanic community perceives giftedness in its own children is available. However, virtually no research exists on issues of giftedness in Haitian school-age children, including how the adult Haitian community perceives giftedness in its own children.

In the school district of Palm Beach County, Florida, major initiatives have been undertaken to increase the number of underrepresented students in gifted education classrooms. Students of Haitian descent are one of the targeted populations for inclusion. As district staff outlined strategies to boost these numbers, it became evident that in order to develop a comprehensive plan for inclusion, input from the Haitian community was needed.

As a result, and under this author's direction, a town meeting was held with the Haitian community of Palm Beach County. The following information summarizes that meeting and is indicative of how South Florida Haitians perceive gifted and talented behavior in their own children. The meeting took place in February 1998 and included the following groups:

- Haitian Creole-speaking parents
- Bilingual (Creole/English) teachers
- Haitian Creole community language facilitators and translators
- Teachers of English to speakers of other languages (ESOL)
- Leaders of the Haitian business community
- Leaders of the Haitian religious community
- Building-level administrators (principals and assistant principals)
- District-level administrators (departments of multicultural education and federal programs personnel, and gifted education program administrators)

TABLE 5.1 Characteristics of Giftedness and Cultural Values of Haitians and the Behaviors Resulting from Their Interactive Influence

Absolute Aspects of Giftedness	Cultural Values Often Characteristic of Giftedness	Behavioral Differences
High level of verbal ability	Creole spoken at home and church	Strong communication skills, even when limited in the language; Creole spoken at home, English at school
Emotional depth and intensity	Strong physical and spiritual foundation	Takes others' problems personally; touching as a sign of affection; eye contact from child to adult may be considered "defiance" in culture
Unusual sensitivity to feelings and expectations	Male as head of the family, but does not dominate; strong matriarchal sense; women responsible for discipline	Children may assume adult roles with, or for, parents; high respect for friends, teachers, and peers
Ability to conceptualize solutions to social and environmental problems	Strong nuclear and extended family ties	Often assume responsibility for family, young siblings, and other relatives within the extended family
Unusual retentiveness; also an unusual capacity for processing information	Traditional culture; value of African ancestors	Successfully adapts to both mainstream and heritage culture; Americanized during the day at school, Haitian at home
Leadership	Sense of being competitive; capable of being collaborative	Can function equally well individually or in small groups

At the meeting participants identified the following primary characteristics of giftedness in Haitian and Haitian American students.

- Ability to problem solve (may not be able to articulate process in English)
- Ability to code switch (translate from one language to another at a high level of accuracy)
- High motivation
- Easy adjustment to environment
- Ability to learn quickly

- Curiosity/inquisitiveness (asks many questions)
- Creativity (high degree of musical or artistic talent)
- Strong memorization skills (related to the importance of rote learning in Haiti)
- Ability to perform multiple tasks at one time
- Demonstration of leadership behavior

Additionally, when cultural values and their behavioral differences were matched to what generally are perceived as absolute aspects of giftedness, the Haitian participants generated the information in Table 5.1. For those parents who spoke no English, translators were provided.

This information documents many of the same types of gifted behavior also found in other underrepresented groups of students identified as culturally and linguistically diverse. In attempts to validate the gifted behavioral characteristics generated by the Palm Beach County Haitian community, the research was shared with other Haitian educators from Broward County, Miami–Dade County, New York City, and Boston. The process was informal, consisting of oral interviews. There was a general consensus that the information was on target and did, in fact, reflect behaviors of gifted or potentially gifted Haitian and Haitian American students.

Strategies for Recruiting and Retaining Haitian and Other Culturally and Linguistically Diverse Students

Although many of the issues involving the education of gifted minority children revolve around the definition, identification, and assessment of giftedness, other issues exist. Among these are the emotional, social, and psychological concerns of underrepresented groups of students who have been recognized as gifted. It has been increasingly understood that gifted children do not automatically achieve in life and school. To illustrate, some gifted and talented students have been found to have special fears, anxieties, and stresses related to success (Ford & Harris, 1995). These findings support the view that additional considerations must be given to the social and emotional well-being of gifted minority students. Psychological tensions can often involve peer, cultural, and societal pressures. This is particularly true for African American students. Failure and underachievement of gifted African American students has been correlated to peer and cultural pressures. Peers who do not do well academically have been known to pressure their gifted peers to underachieve in school. This author contends that the same pressures faced by gifted and talented African American students enrolled in middle- to large-size urban school districts are also faced by many Hispanic, Haitian, LEP, and other socioeconomically disadvantaged students.

In addition, no single model or practice has been established for instructing minority students who are gifted although many have been researched and implemented (Hartley & Wasson, 1989). The type of instructional program depends largely on several issues related to the students and the school. Components, such as the talents of the students, the number of students, the background of the students, and the talents of the teachers, should all be considered when developing an individualized program for gifted students (Cohn, 1990).

Other strategies to recruit and keep gifted and talented Haitian and other underrepresented students in programs for the gifted once they enter include recruiting practices and retention ability.

Strategies for Recruiting

- Gather data from multiple sources rather than a single criterion.
- Use former students as ambassadors to assist in the recruitment process.
- Plan and conduct recruitment fairs in the local community, for example, at malls, grocery stores, and churches.
- Encourage newly identified underrepresented gifted students to participate in site visits to gifted classrooms with their parents or guardians.
- Use community resources for communication, such as newsletters, Web sites, and other multimedia resources, in the heritage language of the parents and community.
- Develop programs and activities both in and out of school to help students increase awareness of their own talents.
- Design and implement student mentorship programs to include shadowing, internships, and sponsorships.*
- Increase the diversity of teachers with gifted education experience.
- Implement effective results-driven professional staff development opportunities for all teachers, support staff, and administrators.*
- Collaborate with university preservice programs to design modules specific to identifying and nurturing underrepresented gifted student populations.
- Increase the selection pool of underrepresented students by using nontraditional measures, such as portfolios, performance-based projects and activities, and opportunities to demonstrate the student's unique skills and talents.
- Develop strategies as part of the school improvement plan designed to target and identify underrepresented students as part of the selection pool for gifted programming.
- Provide potential candidates with learning strategies to be successful in the transition to the gifted classrooms.
- Select relevant curriculum and instructional methods and models that are culturally sensitive and meet students' cognitive and academic needs.*
- Include after-school programming with academic components that support and nurture the achievement of poor and minority students.*

*These items can also be used as retention strategies.

Strategies for Retention

Once underrepresented students are enrolled in gifted education classrooms, it is imperative that program staff and administration implement initiatives in the areas of curriculum and instruction, staff development, counseling, assessment, and parental involvement, among others, which serve to keep the children in the program. In the area of curriculum and instruction, culture and equity issues are especially important. The gifted program should develop a culturally relevant curriculum that addresses the sensitive values, attitudes, and heritage of participating students. Books, videos, audiotapes, charts, software, games, and other educational and instructional materials in Creole are available through Educa Vision Inc. in Coconut Creek, Florida. Their Haitian/Creole educational resources also include material in the areas of reading; writing; poetry; survival English; dictionaries; literacy; social studies; culture; arts, sciences, and math; and health.

Instruction should be individualized to the child's learning style and modality, with accommodations provided to meet unique needs. It is also important that teachers consult the research for curriculum adaptations for underrepresented students. To showcase the talents of diverse gifted students, program teachers and administrators should consider having them participate in local, state, and national competitions. The positive aspects of competition will be a selling point to students and parents. For those unable to afford such experiences, partnering with other sponsors provides an equal opportunity to participate in these competitions without having to worry about where the money will come from. Finally, the use of bibliotherapy to enhance self-concept and to teach inquiry skills through content makes this approach an important part of the learning process.

Retaining diverse gifted learners in appropriate programs necessitates an improvement in the transition between elementary and middle, and middle and high school. Staff development opportunities that bring transition teachers together solidifies a continuous gifted education experience. During these transitional meetings, the focus is on the talents, not the deficits, of underrepresented students. Varied teaching strategies, assessing student work without bias, and adapting teaching styles to match students' learning styles should be at the core of staff development training. Of course, successfully retaining poor and minority students in gifted education classrooms requires that building-level and district-level administrators also be part of the staff development cycle.

The counseling of gifted students may include a mentorship program that offers internships and career awareness. Peer counseling in the form of meetings, conferences, tutoring, and the like are also viable options for consideration. Nurturing and fostering resilience in diverse gifted learners ensures that they adapt to the many barriers to achievement and the many stresses in their daily lives. Modeling and providing opportunities through daily planning, thinking about the future, and thinking creatively promote critical thinking and problem-solving behavior.

Developing comprehensive counseling services that employ strategies which promote high self-esteem within the gifted program are crucial to the retention of these students. If possible, recruit a diverse counseling staff to allow underrepresented students to feel comfortable when seeking counseling services. There is also a trend across the United States to promote same-gender classrooms across the curriculum, particularly in math and science where females continue to be noticeably absent. Extending this concept to same-gender support groups would be appropriate.

An important extension of any gifted education program with poor, minority, and other culturally and linguistically diverse students is the establishment of a parent network or parent support group. Recruiting parents to serve as volunteers, mentors, experts in residence, and resources in general adds to the overall gifted education experience. If the parents are non-English or limited English speaking, it is incumbent that the school district arrange for interpreters or translators to be present at any meetings with them.

Using formal and informal feedback from students allows teachers and administrators to modify the programs as needed. These forms of qualitative assessment procedures validates the fact that the ideas of students are appreciated and considered. With specific regard to assessment and evaluation of academic achievement and cognitive development, the use of portfolios, performance-based projects, and other alternative assessments helps determine the effectiveness of curriculum initiatives. Not all diverse gifted learners are logical/mathematical or verbal/linguistic. As a result, their learning styles must be taken into account as an appropriate, but challenging, curricular program is planned.

There is some indication that because of the field's historic inability to identify various forms of giftedness in culturally diverse groups, a paradigm shift is currently occurring in gifted education. In the emerging paradigm, giftedness is perceived as complex, multifaceted, and multidimensional (Maker, 1996; Passow & Frasier, 1996) and is considered developmental and process oriented, rather than static or equated to a score on an intelligence test (Maker, 1996). A theme central to this paradigm is that giftedness is nurtured in particular social and psychological contexts and, most important, that gifted behavior appears in many different forms in every cultural group (Passow & Frasier, 1996).

This underscores the importance of acknowledging the fact that, although the majority of Haitian students are poor, they are as capable and as deserving as any other group. The skills and talents of all, but most particularly the most talented children, must be nurtured. Furthermore, because giftedness can be viewed as multidimensional and process oriented, Haitian (Creole) and other culturally and linguistically diverse students stand a better chance of gaining access to nomination and identification processes.

Summary and Conclusion

Gifted and talented students come from all cultural, linguistic, and economic backgrounds. As far back as 1950, when the Education Policies Commission deplored America's "tragic waste" of talent and giftedness among minority children, the underrepresentation of these populations has been documented (Passow & Frasier, 1996). The greatest source of untapped talent lies within disadvantaged minority populations. Children from minority populations do not participate in gifted programs at a rate that reflects their presence in the general school population (Frasier, Garcia, & Passow, 1995).

When looking closely at the Haitian population of South Florida, this is certainly the case. They too are overlooked and go unrecognized by the schools that serve them. Additionally, when important school district data is disaggregated by demographics, they are considered and categorized as African American. From a cultural and linguistic perspective, African American and Haitian students are more different than they are similar. This author contends that, if anything, the cultural and linguistic background of Haitian students is more similar to that of Hispanics, specifically, the Caribbean Hispanic.

If this population of students is recognized for who they are, some with outstanding gifts and talents, only then will we be able to address issues of equal access and opportunity in gifted education programs. Until then, labeling them something they are not does a huge disservice to them as a people. Developing more inclusionary processes that target the strengths of Haitian and other students who have been historically "shut out" of these programs is essential.

In conclusion, all children have a right to an appropriate quality education. The goal of education should be to help all students maximize their capabilities. Gifted education programs should serve the needs of academically gifted students of all races, ethnicities, languages, and socioeconomic levels. Any identification procedure must be diverse and sensitive enough to allow students from a variety of cultures and backgrounds to demonstrate their highest level of ability.

REFERENCES

Cohn, L. (1990). *Meeting the needs of gifted and talented minority language students.* ERIC Clearinghouse on Handicapped and Exceptional Children. Reston, VA. (ERIC Document Reproduction Services No. ED 321 485)

Florida Department of Education. (2000). *Annual Report on Students Enrolled in English to Speakers of Other Languages (ESOL) program.* Division of Public Schools and Community Education, Bureau of Instructional Support and Community Services. Tallahassee, FL.

Ford, D., & Harris, J. (1995). Underachieving among gifted African-American students: Implications for school counselors. *The School Counselor, 42,* 196–203.

Frasier, M., Garcia, J., & Passow, A. (1995). *A review of assessment issues in gifted education and their implications for identifying gifted minority students.* The National Research Center on the Gifted and Talented. (ERIC Document Reproduction Services No. ED 388 024)

Hartley, E., & Wasson, E. (1989). An ounce of prevention: A case study of a migrant student. *Rural Special Education Quarterly, 10,* 26–30.

Maker, J. (1996). Identification of gifted minority students: A national problem, needed changes, and a promising solution. *Gifted Education Quarterly, 40*(1), 41–50.

Passow, A., & Frasier, M. (1996). Toward improving identification of talent potential among minority and disadvantaged students. *Roeper Review, 18*(3), 198–202.

School District of Palm Beach County, Florida. (2000). *Annual Report on Students Enrolled in English to Speakers of Other Languages (ESOL) program.* Department of Multicultural Education. West Palm Beach, FL.

University of South Florida, at Sarasota. (1999). Working on gifted issues (WOGI) project: Improving services for students who are gifted. *Serving underrepresented, low SES, and minority student populations.* Sarasota, FL.

6 Biracial and Bicultural Gifted Students

VIRGINIA GONZALEZ

This chapter provides a conceptual framework for understanding formal and informal contexts for learning and development that biracial and bicultural gifted or potentially gifted students are exposed to. Two central factors are analyzed: (1) poverty level and (2) quality of family environment. A second section discusses further family and schooling factors influencing biracial and bicultural gifted students' development, learning, and achievement.

A third section critically reviews the literature on the effect of home language and culture on biracial and bicultural gifted students' learning, developmental, and achievement levels. Emphasis is on continuities and discontinuities between home and school environments, including further review of the following topics: (1) the role of mainstream school culture in relation to (a) demographic data of minorities and immigrants, (b) the "new mainstream" student in U.S. public schools, (c) biracial and bicultural children, and (d) drop-out rates; and (2) the role of teachers as cultural mediators and mentors. Closure will be reached by discussing how educators can accept the challenge of responding to the needs of diverse gifted students.

Formal and Informal Contexts for Learning and Development Among Gifted and/or Potentially Gifted Diverse Students

In this first section a theoretical framework serves as a context for understanding what is presently known in how developmental, psychological, and sociocultural factors affect learning, development, and academic achievement in diverse children, such as biracial and bicultural students. When trying to discuss and synthesize results of studies of diverse children's development, as discussed by Cocking (1994), the dilemma is, "How to look for developmental commonalities and their variants without distorting the culture-specific" (p. 394). Then, we expect to find some continuities and discontinuities in how diverse children learn and develop when they have a biracial, bicultural, or bilingual background.

However, understanding the source of these continuities and discontinuities becomes challenging because there are many possible origins of variations, such as

1. Developmental factors that may present some universals and some culture-specific patterns across different groups of diverse children (e.g., ethnic differences present across cultural subgroups, such as within the Hispanic community—Mexican Americans, Puerto Ricans, etc.).
2. Psychological factors that signal individual differences and unique patterns found in specific children.
3. Sociocultural and environmental factors including their socioeconomic status (SES) and family and school contexts they are exposed to.

In relation to the latter cluster of factors, there are numerous related contextual variables affecting diverse learners that are present in the family structure (e.g., language used at home, educational level and occupation of parents, level of acculturation of parents, quality of the parent–child relationship, mental health of parents, number of siblings, birth order, etc.) as well as in the school culture (e.g., teachers' attitudes and beliefs, quality of educational programs, level of familiarity of educators with the child's language and culture, etc.).

The presence of developmental, psychological, and sociocultural/environmental factors results in the need for educators to understand that minority children may show potential for giftedness, but not necessarily an advanced degree of learned or acquired knowledge or information, as is the case for mainstream middle-class children. In addition, the uniqueness of each child and his or her particular ethnic and linguistic background affects the idiosyncratic characteristics of development, learning, and academic achievement. Expectations and perceptions of giftedness among mainstream and minority parents also differ in relation to intellectual, academic, emotional, social, and creative aptitudes. For instance, minority parents and teachers (of Mexican American background) may differ in their perceptions of giftedness because of their exposure to different sociocultural environments (Clark & Gonzalez, 1998; Gonzalez & Clark, 1999). As illustrated by a case study in Clark and Gonzalez (1998), Mexican American parents conceptualize giftedness as advanced emotional maturation and moral judgment (e.g., respectfulness, obedience, being helpful to siblings and parents). In contrast, this same case study presented a comparison with a minority teacher's perception of the same potentially gifted minority child from a mainstream cultural perspective (e.g., academic and intellectual abilities in verbal, reasoning, and leadership skills).

Then, different possibilities emerge in the complex interaction among developmental, psychological, and sociocultural factors influencing development, learning, and academic achievement in diverse children. In order to understand the origin of this complex interaction among variables, it is important to have a *process* approach and to control for cultural variations by analyzing educational methodologies (e.g., instructional tasks and materials) in terms of the relative cultural distance to the child. As asserted by Cocking (1994), "The task is labeled as *proximal* or *distal* to a culture based on where the task lies in the behavioral expectations in that culture.... Familiarity with the task and materials determine *relative* proximal or distal relationships with the task performers" (p. 404). Thus, educators need to use culturally appropriate (or proximal) instructional and assessment methodologies for better serving diverse children.

In addition, by understanding individual differences at a psychological level, educators can take into account cultural and sociocultural factors that affect learning, development, and achievement among biracial/bicultural students. Moreover, Cocking (1994), further asserts: "Flexibility in developmental timing may be due to variation in the environmental features of the child's culture and societal context or to factors within the individual" (p. 399). For the case of diverse gifted children, these individual differences may act as important mediating variables that could be related to, or independent from, their cultural and language characteristics. That is, individual differences, such as higher levels of cognitive potential, can affect significantly how gifted children develop and learn.

Another possible effect of sociocultural/environmental variables is that there are subtle differences within microsystems surrounding individuals living within the same cultural and language background, such as schools attended. This chapter discusses such subtle difference as mediating factors, such as the role of educators as mentors. It is also possible that linguistic factors present in the sociocultural environment affect developmental processes, as exemplified by "overall language competencies [that] are reached through different pathways and in terms of different language skills" (Cocking, 1994, p. 406). In addition, differences in development in relation to cultural factors can be present in "differences in performance; differences in encoding, storage, and retrieval of information; and differences that relate in the broadest sense to information processing and problem solving. These phenomena are chosen to represent developmental processes within specific cultural contexts and as interpreted by the individual cultures" (p. 407). Cocking presents culture as a construct or variable that mediates development differently, depending on whether it represents the particular culture of origin of children. He proposed that different cultural interpretations of developmental processes are possible; therefore, educators should interpret development within the culture of origin of the students. Thus, culture can mediate developmental processes, resulting in some general, universal, or continuous aspects; as well as in some unique, culture-specific, or discontinuous processes. For the case of bicultural learners, it is important for educators to understand how cultural realities are negotiated at home. For instance, what language is used by parents to communicate among themselves and with their children, what cultural traditions are followed and how they are adapted into behavioral patterns (e.g., food, holiday celebrations, dress codes, religious issues, etc.). In the next section this discussion on the role of home and school as a sociocultural context of development continues.

Family and Home Environmental Factors Influencing Biracial and Bicultural Gifted Students' Development, Learning, and Academic Performance

Poverty Level

Most minority children are at risk of suffering from developmental delays and underachievement because of the negative impact of poverty on their development. Alarming demographic data has been observed for the SES level of minority children and families. Based on demographic statistics from the U.S. Bureau of the Census (2000), as of 1999, 13.8 percent of all families of all races with children under 18 years of age had cash incomes below the poverty level. The percentage was lower for white, non-Hispanic families (8 percent), and it increased dramatically for minority families, with 28.9 percent for African Americans, and 25 percent for Hispanics. This report also indicated that in 1999 the below poverty percentage decreased for married-couple families when children under the age of 18 years were included, with 3.9 percent for white–non-Hispanic, 8.6 percent for African American, and 16.8 percent for Hispanic. Moreover, this report also showed that in 1999 the percentages were significantly affected by whether the household was headed by a single parent, and whether that parent was male or female. In comparison to all families counterparts, the percentage of those below poverty level increased for male households, with no wife present, with children under 18 years of age, which for all races was 16.2 percent; and 11.9 percent for white–non-Hispanic, 21.4 percent for African American, and 26 percent for Hispanic. However, the increment almost tripled in comparison to all families counterparts when the household was headed by a female, with no husband present, increasing to 35.7 percent for all races; and 25.4 percent for white–non-Hispanic, 46.1 percent for African American, and 46.6 percent for Hispanic.

Biracial/bicultural children are at a higher risk of living below the poverty level in comparison to mainstream children, especially when the household head is a single mother. Compounding the low-income level, there are many other associated social and environmental factors, such as quality of the community or neighborhood in which minority children and families live. As noted by McLoyd (1998), "African American and Puerto Rican children are more likely than non–Latino White children to experience persistent poverty and, if they are poor, to live in areas of concentrated poverty" (p. 186). Living in high-poverty communities presents major disadvantages for minority children, such as quality of public services and exposure to negative life threatening environmental stresses (e.g., street violence, homelessness, illegal drugs, etc.).

Another factor reported is the analysis of distinct aspects of poverty characteristics (i.e., age of onset of poverty, duration of poverty, initial disadvantage, and depth of poverty). As noted by Bronfenbrenner and others (1996; cited in McLoyd, 1998), poverty tends to occur more often during early childhood, affecting most children before they reach 6 years of age, primarily because of the higher likelihood of having younger parents with lower wages. Garrett, Ng'andu, and Ferron (1994) found that the proportion of the child's life lived in poverty, and whether the child was born into poverty, achieved a statistically significant effect on the quality of the home environment. As concluded by Garrett and colleagues (1994), the effect of poverty on the quality of children's home environments is complex, with an interacting pattern of many mediating variables (e.g., quality of family environment, poverty, and maternal and child's characteristics). As they stated, "The greatest responsiveness in the quality of the home environment occurred among the poorest households, those in which children experienced initial disadvantage or the greatest persistence of poverty" (p. 342).

In sum, demographic data supports the need to take into consideration the interacting effect of external (i.e., low-SES) and internal (i.e., psychological, developmental) factors affecting minority children's performance in school. There is a need to understand what mediating factors present in the family cultural environment and school setting can prevent diverse children from underachieving and dropping out of school. Thus, based on demographic data and research findings, the importance of conducting in-depth analysis of the characteristics of poverty can be documented, including (1) age of poverty impact, (2) duration of poverty, (3) degree of economic disadvantage in comparison to the U.S. poverty level, and (4) mediating factors present in the family cultural environment. The discussion of how poverty can be mediated by quality of family structure factors continues in the next section.

Quality of Family Structure Factors.

Quality family environments can mediate poverty and have a positive impact on diverse children's development. Following is a discussion of the interaction of low-SES factors and the protective mechanisms present in the family that support the development of the biracial/bicultural child. Family structure factors include the backgrounds of parents, such as

1. Level of formal education attained (i.e., cultural style of schooling).
2. Level of native and English language proficiency (both academic and social levels—i.e., degree of literacy).
3. Rural or urban living in home country and United States.
4. Reason for immigration (related to country of origin).
5. Number of years (or generations) in the United States (related to their degree of cultural adaptation to the United States).
6. Resourcefulness of parents to cover basic needs of children (connected to cultural adaptation).
7. Mental health of parents (emotional availability to respond to children's needs).

8. Occupation (professionals, white or blue collar).
9. Ethnicity (diversity within cultural and linguistic groups, e.g., Cuban American, Puerto Rican, Korean American, Japanese American).

Another cluster of factors refers to family characteristics, such as

1. Single or dual family household (e.g., mother and/or father present and relationship to family income).
2. Number of siblings.
3. Birth order (e.g., older siblings of immigrant or illiterate parents are at higher risk for underachievement).
4. Degree of native and English language proficiency of siblings (both academically and socially, especially degree of literacy skills).
5. Presence of extended family members in the household (e.g., grandparents, aunts and uncles who contribute with income and emotional/mentoring support).
6. Beliefs and value systems toward schooling and the education of children.

As defined by McLoyd (1998), "Unlike poverty status, SES signifies an individual's, a family's, or a group's ranking on a hierarchy according to its access to or control over some combination of valued commodities such as wealth, power, and social status" (p. 188). Many parental background characteristics, such as occupation, educational level, prestige, power, and lifestyle, denote a multidimensionality of mediating factors associated with SES that affect a child's development. For instance, the parents' SES strongly affects their behaviors and child rearing practices through some mediating variables, such as parental educational levels and occupational attainments; therefore, home language use in relation to academic or literacy activities is stimulated at home. It is important to note that these environmental factors can vary their mediating effects with age, gender, race, and ethnicity, and thus findings with majority populations cannot be generalized to minority groups. Even further, there is diversity within minority groups, so the effect of ecological factors needs to be analyzed in light of the confounding effect of race, ethnicity, SES, cultural, and linguistic factors, especially for the case of biracial and bicultural learners.

However, the presence of poverty does not mean that the cultural background of minority parents and children is also deprived or diminished. On the contrary, in many instances minority cultural values and goals are preserved within a bicultural identity and help to maintain high educational aspirations of parents for their children. As with any other family, minority, low-SES parents can stimulate and nurture successfully the development of their children within a well-structured family environment, providing strong moral values and ethnic pride in their children, helping to promote even gifted development (Clark & Gonzalez, 1998).

In addition, the parents' SES is also related to the number of years of residency in the United States, and, therefore, to whether they are immigrants or first, second, or third generation in the United States. Then, the level of acculturation can interact with the presence of poverty, which is also related to parental stress and whether parents are able to access mainstream resources, therefore, becoming fully fledged participants within the mainstream society. For instance, Wang (1993) studied Hispanic (first- and second-generation Caribbean families, including Cubans, Puerto Ricans, and Costa Ricans), African American, and Anglo second-grade children from low- and middle-class SES backgrounds living in Orlando, Florida. Wang found that cultural familial factors (e.g., family structure, such as family size, child's birth order, parents' marital status, parental divorce and separation, and language spoken at home; and parent–child interactions, such as whether parents assisted in their child's homework) related to SES were better predictors of the child's metacognitive developmental skills than the child's ethnicity. Thus, Wang concluded, "SES supersedes ethnicity as a predictor for a child's metacognitive development" (p. 87). Similar findings were also reported by Walker, Greenwood, Hart, and Carta (1994), who showed that differences found between Hispanic and African American children from low-SES backgrounds were attributable to their SES-related factors (the home, community, and school environments), rather than to their minority background.

Furthermore, some authors have found that household characteristics related to small family size can enable parents to develop higher-quality home environments and influence more positively their children's development, possibly resulting in giftedness (Blake, 1989; Zuravin, 1988; both cited in Garrett et al., 1994). Then, some household characteristics can impact the child's developmental outcome. For instance, the low-SES family composition can have an effect on the number of siblings and the presence or absence of a mother or father companion, and other adults (e.g., extended family member).

Poverty can be a high-risk factor for child development and could have a negative impact when significant mediating processes for successful adaptation are damaged, such as the quality of the attachment between minority parents and their children. The presence of committed, involved, caring, and competent parents provides a crucial and powerful adaptive system that serves to protect minority children's development. Well-adapted parents, or any other committed and effective adults, can function as scaffolds to provide opportunities, protective mechanisms, and emotional support for minority children exposed to at-risk ecological factors (such as poverty) to develop resilience. Masten and Coatsworth (1998) highlighted the importance of providing at-risk children (because of poverty factors) with a protective ecological environment, especially during infancy and early childhood because "there is no such a thing as an invulnerable child" (p. 216).

Understanding the dynamic way in which developmental and ecological factors influence adaptive, resilient processes (such as giftedness) in at-risk children is challenging, especially in the case of biracial and bicultural children. The next section sheds some light on understanding how the dynamic interaction of family structure factors and schooling factors influence development in potentially gifted, diverse children.

The Role of Home Language and Culture on Diverse Gifted Children's Development: Continuities and Discontinuities Between Home and School Environments

Traditional views of relating SES factors only to the income of parents as an indication of poverty level have been replaced with a multidimensional view. This contemporary perspective includes SES within sociocultural factors that analyze the multiple components present in the family structure and school environments. The omnibus variable of family structure represents social, cultural, and linguistic factors as communication and socialization tools for child rearing. This section discusses the importance of understanding the impact of the biracial/bicultural family's degree of acculturation on child development and, ultimately, on achievement levels attained in school. More specifically, this section considers how language and cultural practices at home relate to the degree of acculturation of parents and children, which are reflected in their bicultural or minority identities.

Depending on the degree of acculturation of biracial/bicultural families, various discontinuity or continuity approaches can be taken to explain underachievement problems, or the resilience or potential giftedness present in minority children. Thus, the discussion of family structure factors (e.g., home language use, degree of acculturation) becomes key for understanding development in potentially gifted, diverse children from low-SES backgrounds.

Several authors (see e.g., Delgado Gaitan, 1994; Ogbu, 1982; Suarez-Orozco, 1989) have studied the impact of language used at home by parents in the socialization process of minority children. These authors support the contemporary view that language is used as a major tool to transmit implicitly cultural values to children. Thus, the way in which language is used at home by parents also reflects different cultural ways of socializing children, which Shatz (1991) calls "communicative modes," or styles related to transmitted cultural content. For instance, some socialization practices transmit cultural patterns of social and linguistic interactions among individuals as well as in relation to social institutions. Moreover, Ochs and Schiefellin (1984) concluded that language used by adults also carried implicit information about how to function within a particular social system. Given that the U.S. public school system is also a social institution, the continuity or discontinuity of language and cultural practices at home and school may explain the degree of adaptation present in minority parents and their children.

For instance, different patterns of home-language use present among different-generation Hispanic families reflect a variation in degrees of acculturation. In the case of Mexican American immigrant parents, the primary use of Spanish by children affects positively the family structure and quality of communication with parents. In contrast, first-generation Mexican American parents participating in Delgado Gaitan's (1994) study spoke English as their primary language, with Spanish spoken only with relatives who were monolingual Spanish (typically of a previous immigrant generation, such as grandparents). As Delgado Gaitan (1994) observes, "not only had English become the first language in one generation but Spanish language loss was significant in most cases" (p. 79).

Interestingly, even though language loss occurs after only one generation, the traditional Mexican American values survive across intergenerational socialization practices even when using English but only in relation to the context of interpersonal family relations (Delgado Gaitan, 1994). For instance, the practice of traditional Mexican American values, such as respect for elders, was observed by Delgado Gaitan (1994) in how parents ask their children not to interrupt when adults chat at home. All the children participating in this study were from Mexican American backgrounds, and these findings are relevant for this population. However, it is important to note that these language and cultural patterns studied among Mexican American, low-SES families may be different among other Hispanic subgroups (e.g., Puerto Ricans, Cubans, Central and South Americans) representing other SES levels. Ethnic groups, such as Hispanics, tend to be very heterogeneous in racial, SES, cultural, and linguistic characteristics. I would also consider a child born to Hispanic parents from different ethnic groups (e.g., Puerto Rican mother and Mexican American father) as a biethnic child (but not a bicultural one) because of dialectal variations of Spanish and different ethnic behavioral patterns (e.g., food, holiday celebrations, etc.).

Thus, the more traditional view of considering language the only tool for the transmission of cultural values to children (e.g., see Ochs & Schiefellin, 1984) is too simplistic. There is a need to consider that even monolingual English first-generation parents can transmit the duality of traditional minority values as well as mainstream cultural values, even though they are using English or a second language as a communication and socialization tool. Native speakers of English, then, who come from minority backgrounds, can use the mainstream language with minority modes of communication. For instance, parents using *code mixing, code switching*, and culturally appropriate minority nonverbal behaviors at home may transmit implicitly minority cultural values to their children. That is, in reality, mainstream English and culture are not modeled by parents within the family environment, but a new bicultural identity is created within a minority family with a specific degree of acculturation.

Minority families trying to integrate two cultural systems also stimulate in their children a greater cognitive and social flexibility, which may result in potential for giftedness. Then, bicultural children can also adapt to the discontinuities of home and school cultures because they can successfully accomplish situational problem-solving processes. Finally, as discussed in the previous section, to the extent that ethnicity and sociocultural adaptive strategies are independent from SES, the fact of being poor should be an independent factor on the quality of the home structure.

The Role of Mainstream School Culture

Stereotypical images of minority students can negatively impact educators' attitudes and beliefs. In turn, these stereotypes and negative attitudes in the mainstream school culture can play a negative role in minority students' academic performance and ethnic identity. Language minority students immersed in mainstream school environments that stereotype their cultural and linguistic diversity start internalizing these stereotypical images, resulting in low self-esteem and self-concept; emotional factors that inhibit their cognitive potential (i.e., potential for giftedness); and delays in development and learning, which lead to further delays in academic achievement.

These stereotypical images result from mainstream and middle-class educators' lack of knowledge and personal contact with minority students and their families and communities. These stereotypes also result from sociohistorical, economic conditions, and political conflicts between mainstream and minority groups. For the case of immigrant groups, these stereotypes reflect myths such as "immigrant children can learn English and adapt to the mainstream culture within a very short period of time." The philosophy of assimilation and acculturation into mainstream U.S. society, and the "sink or swim" educational approach of an English-only curriculum reflect these stereotypes within the mainstream school culture. In an effort to dispel these stereotypes and myths, this discussion is continued later in relation to the dramatic increase of minority and biracial/bicultural children in the U.S. public schools during the past two decades because of immigration trends.

Demographic Data on Minorities and Immigrants.   Based on 1990 U.S. census data, Ovando and Collier (1998) reported that between 1980 and 1990, the U.S. population increased by 9.8 percent. However, minority groups grew at a much larger percentage than the mainstream white population. Whites increased by 6 percent, whereas Hispanic Americans grew by 53 percent, Asian and Pacific Islanders by 107.8 percent, African Americans by 13.2 percent, and Native American by 37.9 percent. The much higher rate of growth of nontraditional (i.e., Hispanic and Asian/Pacific Islanders) groups is because of high legal and illegal immigration trends, and a higher fertility rate. The second-highest growth rate of traditional (i.e., African American and Native American) minority groups was also because of a higher fertility rate.

In addition, population estimates of the foreign born done by the U.S. Census Bureau (2000), consistent with the 1990 population estimates report that Hispanics of any race would account for the larger percentage (43 percent), followed by white–non-Hispanic (25.3 percent), and by Asian/Pacific Islander–non-Hispanic (24.5 percent). According to the U.S. Bureau of the Census (1992), the 1990s (7.3 million) and 1980s (4.4 million) show the largest number of immigrants legally admitted since the 1920s (4.1 million), 1910s (5.7 million), and 1900s (8.7 million). In addition, as reported by the U.S. Department of Justice (1999), the decade of the 1990s showed the largest percentage of immigrants admitted through the family-sponsored program (e.g., 72 percent in 1998), with a much smaller percentage admitted through the employment-based preferences (e.g., 11.7 percent in 1998) and other categories (e.g., refugees and those seeking asylum at 8.3 percent in 1998). These numbers include both aliens who were previously living abroad and those who were already living in the United States.

According to an Immigration and Naturalization Service Report (2000), immigration trends from 1981 through 1996 show a total of 13.4 million legal immigrants admitted, with the largest proportion represented by Mexico (3.3 million), Asian/Pacific Islanders (i.e., Philippines, Vietnam, China, and Korea, with less than 1 million each), and Latin Americans (i.e., Dominican Republic, El Salvador, and Cuba, with less than 1 million each). In contrast, immigration trends from 1820 through 1996 show a total of 63.5 million legal immigrants admitted, with European countries showing the highest numbers (i.e., Germany at 7.1 million, Italy at 5.5 million, the United Kingdom at 5.2 million, Ireland at 4.7 million, the former Soviet Union at 3.7 million, Austria at 1.8 million, and Hungary at 1.6 million), followed by Mexico (5.5. million), Canada (4.5 million), and the Philippines (1.4 million). However, it is interesting to note that most of the Mexican immigrants entered the United States from 1981 to 1996 (3.3. million out of 5.5 million from 1820 to 1996). This new reality of immigration trends has also increased dramatically the number of language minority or English as a second language (ESL) students in U.S. public schools. For an extended discussion of immigration and ESL students, see Gonzalez (2001).

"New Mainstream" Students in U.S. Public Schools.   Gonzalez, Brusca-Vega, and Yawkey (1997) discuss the "new mainstream student," who represents the sizable segment of the school-age population who are culturally and linguistically diverse. As national reports have indicated, during the first decade of the twenty-first century, one third of the United States will be individuals of color and for whom the English language and traditional Anglo American ways will not be primary (Commission on Minority Participation in Education and American Life, 1988; Hodgkinson, 1992).

Data during the 1990s already illustrated these trends. Of the 45 million students enrolled in public school and private elementary and secondary schools, more than 30 percent were from groups designated as racial or ethnic minorities (i.e., African American, non-Hispanic, 16 percent; Hispanic 12 percent; Asian/Pacific Islander, 3 percent; and Native American/Native Alaskan, 1 percent). As reported by the Western Interstate Commission for Higher Education (WICHE) and the College Board (1998), the proportion of white–non-Hispanics in U.S. public elementary and secondary schools was expected to decline from 65 percent in 1995–1996 to 62 percent by 2000–2001. The enrollment of Hispanic students will increase from 13 percent to 16 percent and Asian/Pacific Islanders will grow from 3.8 percent to 4.3 percent, with a constant representation of African Americans (13 percent) and Native Americans/Native Alaskans (1 percent). Moreover, this diversity will increase as the total U.S. population moves toward the 50 percent division between non-Hispanic whites and other groups that is expected by 2050.

In addition, a large percentage of the Hispanic, Asian/Pacific Islander, and Native American/Native Alaskan populations are from cultural and linguistically diverse backgrounds. About 6.3 million (or 14 percent) students in grades K–12 speak languages other than English at home, including 2.3 million, or 5 percent, who receive bilingual or ESL services. Of the latter group, the most common native languages are Spanish (72.9 percent), Vietnamese (3.9 percent), Hmong (1.8 percent), Cantonese (1.7 percent), Cambodian (1.6 percent), and Korean (1.6 percent). The number of students in bilingual or ESL programs has nearly doubled from the mid-1980s to the late 1990s, and it is expected to continue growing as the number of native-born and foreign-born home speakers of languages other than English increases in the twenty-first century. Moreover, the academic needs of ESL students are compounded by the fact that a larger portion of the U.S. population is not only becoming minority but also biracial and bicultural because of intermarriage trends between mainstream and minority groups and among minority groups.

Biracial and Bicultural Children and Families. It is important to understand that even though national statistics report growth of ethnic groups, the racial diversity comprised of intermarriages, resulting in biracial children, may not be accounted for accurately in census data. Sociologists typically look at the intermarriage rate as one of the key indicators of assimilation between ethnic groups. As reported by Rodriguez (1999) in the *Houston Chronicle,* "nationwide, interracial unions now account for about 4 percent of all marriages" (p. A12). More than 2 million children have been born to multiracial couples, showing similar intermarriage rates between today's minorities and those of the second-generation offspring of European immigrants at the turn of the 1900s.

However, the intermarriage trends show differences across ethnic groups. As cited in the *Houston Chronicle,* "According to a Census analysis by Harrison [from the Washington DC Center for Demographic Policy] and demographer Reynolds Farley for the Russell Sage Foundation, one-third of US born Hispanics ages 25 to 34 today are married to non-Hispanic whites. Thirty-six percent of US-born Asian Pacific men, 45% of Asian-Pacific women and more than 70% Native-Americans also have married whites" (p. A12). However, it is interesting to note that most of these intermarriages take place in diverse states (e.g., California, Texas, Florida, and New York) and that about 30 states remain predominantly white (e.g., Utah, Wyoming, Michigan, and the New England states). For instance, "one of every 6 multiracial children is California-born" (Rodriguez 1999, p. A12), and the intermarriage rate in California is twice as common than in other states. An interesting illustration of this demographic trend in California is the fact that "In 1998, 'Jose' was the most popular boy's name on birth certificates in California, and in 1997, it topped the list in Texas" (Rodriquez, 1999, p. A12).

However, the 1990 census also showed that fewer than 10 percent of African American males and 4 percent of females aged 25 to 34 had married white spouses; a much lower rate in comparison to Hispanics and Asian Pacific U.S.-born individuals. Thus, so-called minority groups based on their cultural and linguistic diversity, such as Hispanics and Asian Pacific, are assimilating with mainstream white U.S. citizens at a much faster rate than racial minority groups, such as African Americans. This intermarriage trend is exacerbating the white–black separation in the United States with an "in between" mass of multiracial individuals that can more easily access mainstream U.S. society (because they are half white and half minority).

Adding to the growing intermarriage rate in the United States is the fact that Hispanics and Asian Pacific minorities are originally multiracial in nature, resulting from historical interracial blends produced by immigration and colonization trends present for centuries in their countries of origin. For instance, the establishment of Spanish (Spain), French, Portuguese, and Dutch colonies in Latin America from the early 1500s until the late 1800s brought intercultural contact and intermarriage with different indigenous groups. This colonial period in Latin America was followed by heavy European, African, and Asian voluntary and involuntary (slavery) immigration during the 1800s and 1900s. This heavy immigration period of Europeans into Latin America during the late 1800s and early 1900s was motivated by the same political, economic, and social factors that brought millions of immigrants to the United States through Ellis Island (see Gonzalez, 2001, for more on this topic). Thus, Hispanics are a multiracial "creole" blend, represented by all kinds of racial combinations and intermarriages. Hispanics intermarrying in the United States does not represent a new phenomenon but simply a continuation of their multiracial and multicultural background.

Even though the intermarriage rates have increased dramatically in some U.S. states, interracial children still attend segregated schools and live in communities in which the majority of students are minority and from low-SES backgrounds. Increments in demographic trends favoring minority and multiracial groups do not necessarily mean changes in social power associated with socioeconomic trends. Increments in numbers also carry with them an increase in tension and anti-immigrant and antiminority sentiments. An example of this increased tension would be the public urge to assimilate southern European immigrants into U.S. culture and the English language that developed during the early 1900s as a response to the changes in Ellis Island immigration trends (Gonzalez, 2001). Today, this tension is illustrated by the changing political ideology in states in which minorities will out number whites by the year 2015, such as California's initiatives against immigration, affirmative action, and bilingual education.

As declared by Tanton, founder of the Federation for American Immigration Reform, "the flurry of California initiatives on immigration, affirmative action, and bilingual education were really about whites wanting to protect what they have;

about not wanting to disappear into history" (cited in *Houston Chronicle*, 1999, p. A12). Thus, the issue of demographic and immigration trends is clearly an issue of power and SES in America. This tension present in society also has spread to the reality of U.S. public schools as illustrated by the high dropout rates of minority, low-SES youngsters. Diverse students can be denied access to middle-class professional U.S. society, and therefore to social power, when contextual factors (i.e., SES backgrounds, education) prevent genuine access to high-quality education.

Dropout Rates.   One of the major educational problems creating tension in U.S. public schools, and triggering the announcement of an educational crisis during the 1990s, has been the alarming increase in dropout rates among minority students (U.S. Department of Education, 1996). Mainstream public education in the United States is currently experiencing tensions and conflicts, formally announced as the "educational crisis" that the "school reform movement" of the early 1990s and the "school restructuring movement" of the late 1990s is responding to. The movement of the early 1990s called for changes in the educational approaches to become more inclusive in order to meet the educational needs of the increasing number of diverse children (e.g., to increase the representation of minority children in gifted education). As discussed in the previous section, the immigration trends of large numbers of Latin American and Asian groups since the 1980s is now changing the student population in U.S. public schools. The late 1990s movement calls for raising educational standards for *all* students, including the poor and diverse (see Holmes & Duron, 2000), by providing (1) high-quality instructional programs linked with alternative assessments and development of critical thinking and problem-solving skills and (2) professional development for pre- and inservice teachers in issues of diversity (e.g., ESL development, methodology, and assessment; and multicultural education). The school restructuring movement calls for systemic change in higher education for training teachers, and for developing a new "diverse" mainstream school culture to represent the diversity found in regular classrooms.

The National Center for Educational Statistics (NCES) reported in 1999 that during the 1990s between 347,000 and 544,000 students in grades 10 through 12 left school each year without successfully completing a high school program. In 1999, the proportion of dropouts between the ages of 16 and 24, young adults who have not earned a high school credential and are out of school, was much higher for Hispanics (28.6 percent) than for African Americans (12.6 percent), whites (7.3 percent), and Asian/Pacific Islanders (4.3 percent). In addition, white and Asian/ Pacific Islander young adults in 1991 were more likely than their African American and Hispanic counterparts to complete their high school studies. Statistics that bring good news report that about 85.9 percent of all young adults not enrolled in high school (ages 18 through 24) completed high school through 1999. On the negative side, 11.2 percent of the 34 million 16- through 24-year-olds were dropouts (NCES, 1999), and the majority of them consisted of underrepresented minority students in higher education (i.e., Hispanics and African Americans).

Teachers as Cultural Mediators and Mentors

In the contemporary climate of demographic and systemic change experienced by U.S. public schools, and with the need to reverse the dropout rates for minority, biracial/bicultural students, educators need to value and respect the diversity brought by minority students' backgrounds. Educators are key agents in affirming students' cultural and linguistic identity (most likely of a bicultural and biracial nature) by (1) celebrating and nurturing their bicultural backgrounds (e.g., their native languages, and their family value and belief systems), (2) believing in their potential for development (including potential for giftedness), and (3) mentoring and advocating for their academic success.

Achieving learning success will be accomplished when educators and students develop a healthy emotional rapport in which trust and respect is reciprocal. Stereotypes need to be dispelled by educators who acknowledge that each child will have individual differences in personality, as well as variations in cultural patterns present across racial, ethnic, SES, and family and community characteristics. Educators need to become aware of the powerful influence of their expectations for nurturing students' learning and developmental potential. This reflection process is called an "awakening experience" (Gonzalez et al., 1997). As part of their professional development, educators need to undergo a personal reflection process in order to examine their beliefs and value systems, expectations, and attitudes and stereotypes toward minority students. Educators can benefit from this personal reflection by discovering the individuality in each biracial/bicultural child by interacting and developing trusting relationships with them, their families and communities. Learning emphatically about how to foster a meaningful educational environment for the uniqueness of each bicultural child will liberate educators of stereotypes and myths.

Functioning as an effective mediator between the inner child's world and the bicultural sociocultural settings represented by families and communities, is both a challenge and an imperative for educators. The challenge is for educators to discover and link personal and school lives of bicultural students to a meaningful and high-quality instructional program. The imperative is to reduce dropout rates of these students, and to increase their achievement and representation in gifted programs, by developing their potential for critical thinking and problem-solving skills.

Implications for Gifted Education Programs and Classrooms

It is important to highlight the fact that teachers have a key social role as mediators and mentors for helping diverse bicultural and biracial students adapt to the school culture, and to thrive and achieve at their highest learning and developmental potential. Teachers continue to face a dramatic change in the demographic reality of their classrooms during the first decade of the twenty-first century, with diverse students representing one third to one half of the students in their class-rooms, depending on their geographic location. As mentors, teachers need to serve as advocates for uncovering gifted potential in their diverse students, a developmental trend that will have continuities and discontinuities in comparison with mainstream students. That is, diverse students express their potential for giftedness in relation to the unique bicultural or bilingual backgrounds and styles of adaptations and identities they have developed during their daily social interactions and negotiations between their family and school environments.

Teachers acting as mentors can respond to these unique adaptations by creating a high-quality academic curriculum, stimulating problem-solving and critical-thinking skills, and by cultivating an emotionally supportive atmosphere in the classroom. By establishing a positive emotional rapport with diverse students, the teacher can transmit implicitly cultural values and communicative modes or styles of social interaction, and therefore model a positive social adaptation to academic environments. Teachers can also establish emotional rapport with their diverse students' families and community members by modeling sociocultural adaptive strategies and healthy bicultural or bilingual identities. It is vital, therefore, for teachers to model positive attitudes, cultural value systems, and social adaptation strategies because the school culture itself still may reflect numerous stereotypical images of minority students. These images may reflect myths; historical, social, and economic conditions; and political conflicts between minority and main-stream groups.

Gifted education programs need to be accessible for diverse students, and classroom teachers can help increase their representation by valuing and helping identify their gifted potential, increasing their resilience, and decreasing their vulnerability to exposure to at-risk ecological factors. As shown by demographics, most diverse students would come from low-SES backgrounds, and therefore, the cultural and linguistic uniqueness in their patterns of learning and development need to be uncovered and nurtured by a high-quality diverse curriculum implemented by the regular classroom teacher. Genuine access to an enriched and diverse curriculum can provide biracial and bicultural students with equal educational opportunities to actualize their gifted potential into skills, abilities, and higher-knowledge levels. Only by giving these diverse students genuine opportunities to develop their gifted potential can we help reduce their dropout rates and increase their representation in gifted education programs.

Summary and Conclusion

No one method of assessment and instruction can be prescribed for educators to meet the challenge of educating all diverse students. Such a panacea would be the easiest solution that most teachers seek. However, educators must discover their own approaches by engaging in "soul-searching" processes: a critical thinking and problem-solving process in relation to the needs arising every day in their classroom practice. Each teacher must understand the unique "chemistry" that develops when he or she encounters the uniqueness of each bicultural child. Teachers must discover the learning styles and practices to which they respond best. That is to say that classrooms develop "personalities," and each cohort of new students brings idiosyncratic differences creating, for teachers, the need for a new adaptation.

As this chapter has documented, environmental, family, and schooling factors all affect diverse students' learning, development, and achievement. It is important for educators to mediate between the students' cultural and linguistic identity and the mainstream school reality. Even though most diverse learners come from low-SES families, parents can effectively structure the home environment to nurture their development. Ideally, parents and teachers should communicate and collaborate to create a meaningful transition between home and school environments. Educators need to respond to the challenge of providing high-quality and meaningful education for diverse gifted children by creating a bridge between the parents' and the children's experiences for a successful adaptation.

Demographic data and research findings support the notion of the "new mainstream student" in U.S. public schools, who is becoming not only minority but also biracial and bicultural. These new demographic trends create social and educational tensions represented in the school system in high dropout rates among diverse students. Avoiding stereotypic views and myths of minority students is important, as is recognizing developmental discontinuities between majority and minority learners. As educators, we can make a significant difference in recognizing potential for giftedness among students who are biracial and bicultural. They are worth the effort.

REFERENCES

Clark, E. R., & Gonzalez, V. (1998). *Voces* and voices: Cultural and linguistic giftedness. *Educational Horizons, 77*(1), 41–47.

Cocking, R. R. (1994). Ecologically valid frameworks of development: Accounting for continuities and discontinuities across contexts. In P. M. Greenfield & R. R. Cocking (Eds.), *Cross-cultural roots of minority child development* (pp. 393–409). Hillsdale, NJ: Erlbaum.

Commission on Minority Participation in Education and American Life. (1988). *One third of a nation.* Washington DC: American Council on Education, Education Commission of the States.

Delgado Gaitan, C. (1994). Socializing young children in Mexican-American families: An intergenerational perspective. In P. M. Greenfield & R. R. Cocking (Eds.), *Cross-cultural roots of minority child development* (pp. 55–86). Hillsdale, NJ: Erlbaum.

Garrett, P., Ng'andu, N., & Ferron, J. (1994). Poverty experiences of young children and the quality of their home environment. *Child Development, 65,* 331–345.

Gonzalez, V. (2001). Immigration: Education's story past, present, and future. *College Board Review, 193,* 24–31.

Gonzalez, V., Brusca-Vega, R., & Yawkey, T. (1997). *Assessment and instruction of culturally and linguistically diverse students with or at-risk of learning problems: From research to practice.* Needham Heights, MA: Allyn & Bacon.

Gonzalez, V., & Clark, E. R. (1999). *Folkloric* and *historic* views of giftedness in language-minority children. In V. Gonzalez (Vol. Ed.), *Language and cognitive development in second language learning: Educational implications for children and adults* (pp. 1–18). Needham Heights, MA: Allyn & Bacon.

Hodgkinson, H. H. (1992). *A demographic look at tomorrow.* Washington, DC: Institute for Education Research.

Holmes, D., & Duron, S. (2000). *LEP students and high-stakes assessment: Approaches/strategies to accommodate LEP students.* Washington, DC: National Clearinghouse for Bilingual Education, Center for the Study of Language and Education.

Immigration and Naturalization Service Report. (2000). *Immigration statistics by country of origin.* Washington, DC: U.S. Government Printing Office.

Masten, A. S., & Coatsworth, J. D. (1998). The development of competence in favorable and unfavorable environments. *American Psychologist, 53*(2), 205–220.

McLoyd, V. C. (1998). Socioeconomic disadvantage and child development. *American Psychologist, 53*(2), 185–204.

National Center for Education Statistics. (1999). *The condition of education* (NCES 99-022). Washington, DC: U.S. Government Printing Office, Indicators 11 and 12.

Ochs, E., & Schiefellin, B. B. (1984). Language acquisition and socialization: Three developmental stories. In R. Shweder & R. LeVine (Eds.), *Culture theory: Essays on mind, self, and emotion* (pp. 276–320). New York: Cambridge University Press.

Ogbu, J. (1982). Cultural discontinuity and schooling. *Anthropology and Education Quarterly, 13*(4), 290–307.

Ovando, C. J., & Collier, V. P. (1998). *Bilingual and ESL classrooms: Teaching in multicultural contexts.* Boston: McGraw-Hill.

Rodriguez, L. (1999, September 26). Multiculturalism may hold key to future racial harmony. *Houston Chronicle,* pp. A1, A12.

Shatz, M. (1991). Using cross-cultural research to inform us about the role of language in development: Comparisons of Japanese, Korean, and English, and of German, American English, and British English. In M. H. Bornstein (Ed.), *Cultural approaches to parenting* (pp. 139–153). Hillsdale, NJ: Erlbaum.

Suarez-Orozco, M. (1989). *Central American refugees and US high schools: A psychological study of motivation and achievement.* Stanford, CA: Stanford University Press.

U.S. Bureau of the Census. (1992). *Statistical abstract of the United States: 1992.* Washington, DC: U.S. Government Printing Office.

U.S. Bureau of the Census. (2000). *Projections of the resident population by race, Hispanic origin, and nativity.* Washington, DC: U.S. Government Printing Office.

U.S. Department of Education, National Center for Education Statistics. (1996). *Dropout rates in the United States, 1994* (NCES 96-863) Washington, DC: U.S. Government Printing Office.

U.S. Department of Justice, Immigration, and Naturalization Service. (1999). Legal immigration, fiscal year 1998. *Annual Report, 2,* May. Office of Policy and Planning: Statistics Branch. Washington, DC: U.S. Government Printing Office.

Walker, D., Greenwood, C., Hart, B., & Carta, J. (1994), Prediction of school outcomes based on early language production and socioeconomic factors. *Child Development, 65,* 606–621.

Wang, A. Y. (1993). Cultural-familial predictors of children's metacognitive and academic performance. *Journal of Research in Childhood Education, 7*(2), 83–90.

Western Interstate Commission for Higher Education (WICHE) & the College Board. (1998). *Knocking at the college door: Projections of high school graduates by state and race/ethnicity for 1996–2012.* Boulder, CO: WICHE.

7 Gifted and Talented Females

The Struggle for Recognition

VALENTINA KLOOSTERMAN
KEITH SURANNA

> *If a [woman] does not keep pace with [her] companions, perhaps it is because [she] hears a different drummer. Let [her] step to music which [she] hears, however measured or far away.*
>
> —Henry David Thoreau

Throughout history, females have consistently experienced inequalities that males traditionally have not. This, of course, is not breaking news. There is an abundance of documentation regarding women's struggles to be viewed and accepted as equals with their male counterparts. However, the struggles of gifted and talented females in particular have not always been at the forefront of our collective consciousness. Often, as the stories of gifted women that have transcended their particular situations throughout history are told, the assumption is made that their success would be self-evident. Surely, their giftedness alone would guarantee their success, it is often assumed. Digging a bit deeper, however, it becomes apparent that not only do these misconceptions impede and often damage the lives of gifted females but they can also have lasting negative effects on society at large. Thus, in order for gifted females to thrive in the world, their struggles for recognition must be examined.

This chapter begins with a discussion of the multifaceted and complex struggles of gifted females. Aspects that should be considered when serving gifted females are then offered. Finally, we close with some reflections on gender equity and eminence.

The Struggles of Gifted Females

Historically, men have written pedagogical, psychological, historical, and political treatises and doctrines, and these works have often neglected or dismissed the female experience. For example, although Thomas Jefferson is widely considered one of the greatest champions for universal education, he "didn't consider the possibility of female geniuses; his plan allowed for three years of schooling for girls, enough to prepare them for marriage and motherhood" (Mondale & Patton, 2001, p. 24). Jefferson's conception of women's education is only one example throughout U.S. history reflecting unequal gender opportunities. The struggle for females in education continued to the point that a federal law needed to be enacted in order to prevent them from being discriminated against. It was not until 1972, when this law, Title IX, stated that

> No person in the United States shall, on the basis of sex, be excluded from participation in, be denied the benefits of, or be subjected to discrimination under any program or activity receiving Federal financial assistance. (U.S. Department of Education, 1998, p. 1)

When considering examples such as these, coupled with the fact that insufficient research has focused on the development of female talent, it takes little effort to realize how our educational system, as well as our entire society, has historically neglected and stymied gifted females. Recognizing the limited amount of information on gifted females, some researchers and practitioners in gifted education, as well as women's studies, have, over the past 20 years, carried out new inquiries that focus on the uniqueness of gifted girls and women.

Gender Differences

As human beings we cannot escape our biology. Most 3-year-olds, of course, can easily differentiate between males and females. However, the achievements of gifted females can be sorely minimized when using simple biologically determined roles to perceive gender differences. In fact, studies of the changing role of women in society provide documentation that many differences are indeed not biologically, but socioculturally based. The media is one clear example of how gender differences are influenced by sociocultural factors that have a sociological explanation. Stereotypical images of boys and girls in cartoons and commercials, toys, and boy-centered print material continue to portray boys as active thinkers and physically oriented and girls as passive and home or beauty oriented. New technology, such as the Internet, didactic software, and some video games usually offer the possibility of enriching learning, but this does not always mean less biased products on the market.

"The expectations of docility and conformity for girls throughout early childhood initiate the gifted girl to her eventual underachieving role in society"

(Davis & Rimm, 1989, p. 348). When children are constantly bombarded with images such as these, often well before they even begin school, it may take years before they begin questioning them. Furthermore, if adults have not been equipped with tools to question these misconceived roles, it is realistic to think that children will not be provided with these tools either.

There is evidence, however, that when adults and children are given the opportunity to become aware and question stereotypical sociocultural gender differences, positive results can certainly be observed. In fact, the correction of these misconceptions may not only free women to achieve equally with men but also free men of their stereotypical views of women. Unfortunately, until this occurs on a consistent and global scale, continued differential socialization of girls and boys will remain.

Family: Gender and Expectations

The development and education of gifted females begins in the home. Parental attitudes and behavior can have a lasting, often indelible, influence on females' achievements. Some indications suggest that although gifted girls may continually face stereotyping in school and society, their family life greatly impacts, both positively and negatively, their achievement and goals (American Association of University Women [AAUW], 1992; Reis, 1987, 1998; Sadker & Sadker, 1994).

Many parents and elementary teachers, unconsciously or not, often equate boys' performances to ability and girls' performances to effort (Dickens & Cornell, 1993; Fenneman, Peterson, Carpenter, & Lubinski, 1990; Heller & Ziegler, 1996). On the contrary, parents who express appreciation and encouragement toward their daughters' talents may positively contribute to girls' self-images and accomplishments. Reis (1998) found that

> talented girls with career-oriented mothers tended to develop a variety of talents and interests early in life and feel less conflict about growing up and becoming independent, autonomous women. Girls...whose mothers had been at home, however, struggled with ambition and conflicts about work and home. (p. 38)

Thus, when gifted girls do not receive acceptance early on at home, they feel hindered in their path to success, and their achievements and goals may never be realized, or they may never even be given the opportunity to achieve.

The Influence of Society, Culture, and Diversity

The notion that women are naturally inferior to men pervades ancient religious texts, laws, and even some modern cultures (Silverman, 1995a). Views of females' roles and responsibilities, as well as behaviors and looks, are ubiquitous in U.S. society. One need only watch television, listen to the radio, or read books and magazines to easily garner these societal attitudes and opinions. Value conflicts about women's roles permeate society, and, as a result, the education of gifted girls is also conflicted. These value conflicts are greatly exacerbated when gifted females are also culturally and linguistically diverse (CLD); from urban, rural, or low socioeconomic environments; as well as lesbians and women with disabilities (Fox, Sadker, & Engle, 1999; Noble, Subotnik, & Arnold, 1999; Reis, Hébert, Díaz, Maxfield, & Ratley, 1995).

The little work that has been done in this area does not paint a particularly positive future for these unique populations of gifted females. Fox and colleagues (1999) discuss how CLD girls are not only less likely than boys to be identified for gifted programs but they also tend to drop out of gifted programs at higher rates than boys, particularly in high school. The plight of gifted CLD girls from particular racial and ethnic groups, such as Asian American and Hispanic, often stems from deeply rooted patriarchal families in which traditional gender roles are pervasive (Kerr, 1994; Lashaway-Bokina, 1996). Kerr (1994) states that

> Gifted Native American girls may be reluctant to show their intellectual abilities because of a strong wish not to stand out, which is not just a preference but a cultural imperative. Many bright girls simply cannot do anything which brings attention to themselves as individuals, for in the extremely communal Native American culture, focus on the individual is not just in bad taste: it is wrong. (p. 179)

Furthermore, not only are gifted women who are lesbians or have a particular disability subject to sexism, they are often hindered by racism, homophobia, and other damaging assumptions (Noble et al., 1999). Hence, regardless of with what particular population gifted women are identified, Reis (1995b) reminds us that "as a society, we must offer an encouraging message to gifted females: that ambition is not only acceptable but also a desirable trait in females, and that a female model of productivity should include work that is personally exciting and stimulating" (p. 170).

Education: Opportunities and Challenges

Educators at all levels, often without being aware of it, discourage females from developing their talents equally with males. Little research is available regarding gender differences between bright boys and girls in early childhood education. However, it is known that although girls and boys have similar participation rates in activities that may prepare them for school, girls ages 3 to 5 are more likely than boys in this age group to demonstrate early literacy and small-motor skills, such as writing their own names or holding pencils correctly, that are essential to the accomplishment of many academic tasks (National Center for Education Statistics, 2000a, p. 2).

Gifted and talented students are usually found equally among both genders in elementary school, with young girls often outperforming boys in both grades and standardized test scores. Beyond the fifth grade, however, boys begin to outperform girls in both math and science. Thus, as they progress in their education and enter the workforce, the number of gifted males greatly outweighs the number of gifted females. Some researchers (Arnold, 1995; Hany 1994; Kline & Short, 1991; Reis & Callahan, 1989) have found that, beginning in elementary school, girls' self-confidence progressively dissipates. Discouraged by lower test scores, especially in the fields of math and science, gifted girls are not encouraged to continue in these areas of study. Fox and colleagues (1999) write, "It is also likely that they will not be encouraged to pursue majors and careers in mathematics and science by parents, teachers, and counselors who interpret lower test scores as indicative of girls' lower ability in these areas" (p. 68).

Boys receive more attention from teachers than girls throughout their education. They are listened to more often in class because they call out answers more frequently than girls do. Boys also receive more informative responses and precise remediation from teachers, and they are also both praised and criticized more than girls (Eccles, 1987; Fox et al., 1999; Gaskell & Willinsky, 1995; Hansen, Walker, & Flom, 1995; Heller & Ziegler, 1996; Sadker & Sadker, 1994; Silverman, 1995b).

Schools, along with families, must now be proactive leaders in improving the education and waning self-esteem of gifted girls in order to combat these eschewed values. Professional educators at all levels need to be reflective practitioners, aware of their own biases they bring to the job in order to begin to address gender equality in the classroom.

Self-Perception: Construction of Identity

Gifted females begin to lose their self-confidence in elementary school and continue to do so as they progress in their education (see also AAUW, 1992; Klein & Zehms, 1996; Orenstein, 1994). As gifted girls enter adolescence, they become hypersensitive to societal views, regarding the roles and responsibilities of women via popular television, movies, music, and print. The idea of "being feminine" becomes an important value for girls, whereas educational achievement and productivity are often thought to be masculine characteristics. This, coupled with the fact that even bright males consider attractiveness more important than intelligence when it comes to the opposite sex, contributes to the prevailing lack of self-confidence in young gifted women.

Research conducted over the past 20 to 30 years has identified particular phenomena that contribute to gifted females' poor self-image. Many bright young females experience what has come to be known as the "perfection complex" (Brown & Gilligan, 1993; Reis, 1987, 1998), which causes them to set unreasonable goals for themselves, and, as a result, when they feel they have not achieved "perfection" in a particular endeavor, their self-esteem suffers. Along with other researchers, Horner (1972) discusses the "fear of success syndrome." This syndrome inhibits young gifted women when they fear that success and competence may lead to rejection by their peers and families. Named after the character in *Gone with the Wind*, the "Scarlett O'Hara syndrome" refers to the phenomenon when females use their appearance or other means to manipulate and gain particular favors and special considerations from others. Reis (1998) states, "Instead of relying on their own skills and strengths to reach a goal, individuals who experience this syndrome rely upon manipulation to achieve" (p. 90).

Hansen and colleagues (1995) discuss some important factors that will contribute to the improvement of bright young women's self-perception and esteem: "respecting girls as key players; connecting girls to caring adults; ensuring girls' participation and their success; and empowering girls to believe they can realize their dreams" (p. 6). Perhaps only then will we not only perceive but also celebrate gifted females' positive self-perceptions and achievements.

The Means Toward Positive Change

Once the unique struggles of gifted females are identified and understood, the means through which these struggles can be challenged and, ultimately, eradicated must be considered. While considering these means to positive change, it must be understood that if society as a whole shares in the culpability of the struggles of gifted females, it also must take responsibility for implementing and facilitating the changes. Thus, we have identified six major aspects that should be considered and carefully analyzed in order to respond to the unique socioemotional and educational needs, interests, and abilities of gifted females: (1) assessment and test performance, (2) school programs and services, (3) counseling, (4) higher education, (5) career choice and workforce, and (6) teacher preparation.

Assessment and Test Performance

Limited information is available regarding the accuracy of assessment procedures, such as psychometric and academic tests, with respect to gender differences. Most identification procedures in gifted programs do not discriminate students' academic performance by considering gender differences. However, the educational system has rewarded and condemned students' educational opportunities mostly based on test results. Studies have shown, however, that girls seem to score ahead of boys on most academic measures at the elementary level, but that scores gradually decrease by middle school and high school (College Entrance Examination Board, 1998; Fox et al., 1999; Reis & Callahan, 1989). Issues of gender bias and fairness in testing are areas in the field of gifted education that still need to be carefully explored and described by researchers and practitioners. Only when gender issues that are linked to testing are fully understood will we cease fostering erroneous views of both boys and girls, especially at the upper educational levels.

We recommend an ongoing multidimensional assessment approach to identify potential talents and high abilities in girls and young adolescents. Among others, this assessment approach may include classroom observations, autobiographies, parent interviews, student interviews, student portfolios and reports, anecdotal logs, interest surveys, student journals, and exploratory enrichment activities. This type of assessment should always take into account the personal characteristics of each girl, as well as her cultural and linguistic background.

School Programs and Services

Despite the urgent necessity for school programs and services that focus on the unique characteristics of gifted girls, effective instructional services and educational interventions are relatively rare. To respond to this need, some school districts have implemented single-sex classrooms, for example, in the areas of math and science. There certainly exist outspoken critics to this approach, especially because there is insufficient data to support this practice. However, it has been noted that girls are provided with more individualized attention in settings such as this.

In addition, a select number of educational programs have been recognized as exemplary or promising programs in promoting gender equity in mathematics, science, and technology: ASPIRE (Alabama Supercomputing Program to Inspire Computational Research in Education); EQUALS, Family Tools and Technology, National Science Partnership for Girl Scouts and Science Museums; and Playtime in Science: An Equity-Based Parent/Child Science Program (U.S. Department of Education, 2001). These programs, albeit not specially designed for gifted girls, certainly provide them the opportunity to explore and develop their high abilities. Thus, these programs are a step in the right direction.

As explained previously, the experience of the gifted female is rarely taken into account in the regular classroom. Reis and Callahan (1989) have noted that gender bias is common in both accelerated instruction and enrichment for gifted students. Austin (1998) explains that both boys and girls benefit in mathematics when gifted programs integrate it with other subject areas, such as language arts.

When working with high-ability girls, one important recommendation for educators and gifted specialists to consider is using a differentiated curriculum that promotes an awareness of different student learning style preferences. With this in mind, Renzulli and Reis (1985, 1994, 1997) created a model for the talent development of all students, The Schoolwide Enrichment Model (SEM). A major component of the SEM, the Total Talent Portfolio, plays an important role in assessing interests, abilities, and learning style preferences. The latter includes instructional style preferences, learning environment preferences, and thinking and expressive style preferences of each individual student. Table 7.1 represents the major dimensions of the Total Talent Portfolio. Although it is beyond the scope of this chapter to delve deeply into the Total Talent Portfolio, it is strongly believed that this tool may provide relevant information about the style preferences and abilities of underrepresented culturally and linguistically diverse students (Kloosterman, 2001) as well as gifted girls (Purcell & Renzulli, 1998).

In the regular classroom or gifted program, opportunities for girls in reading biographies and reading literature that depicts girls as heroines, leaders, and inventors; seeing and working with high-achieving women and older talented girls;

TABLE 7.1   Dimensions of the Total Talent Portfolio

Abilities	Interests	Style Preferences			
Maximum Performance Indicators	Interest Areas	Instructional Style Preferences	Learning Environment Preferences	Thinking Style Preferences	Expression Style Preferences
Tests Standardized Teacher-made Course grades Teacher ratings **Product evaluation** Written Oral Visual Musical Constructed (Note differences between assigned and self-selected products) Level of participation in learning activities Degree of interaction with others	Fine arts Crafts Literary Historical Mathematics/logical Physical sciences Life sciences Political/judicial Athletic/recreation Marketing/business Drama/dance Musical performance Musical composition Managerial/business Photography Film/video Computers Other (specify)	Recitation and drill Peer tutoring Lecture Lecture/discussion Discussion Guided independent study* Learning/interest center Simulation, role-playing, dramatization, guided fantasy Learning games Replicative reports or projects* Investigative reports or projects* Unguided independent study* Internship* Apprenticeship*	**Inter/Intrapersonal** Self-oriented Peer-oriented Adult-oriented Combined **Physical** Sound Heat Light Design Mobility Time of day Food intake Seating	Analytic (school smart) Synthetic/creative (creative, inventive) Practical/contextual (street smart) Legislative Executive Judicial	Written Oral Manipulative Discussion Display Dramatization Artistic Graphic Commercial Service
Ref: General Tests and Measurements Literature	Ref: Renzulli, 1977b	*With or without mentor Ref: Renzulli & Smith, 1978	Ref: Amabile, 1983; Dunn, Dunn, & Price, 1975; Gardner, 1983	Ref: Sternberg 1984, 1988	Ref: Renzulli & Reis, 1985

104

and participating in extracurricular activities, associations, and academic and sport competitions further enhance the possibility for girls to develop positive self-images and leadership capabilities. This also provides them with the opportunity to learn about achieving women and understand the training and personality characteristics needed for high career achievement. These opportunities can also benefit boys in promoting awareness of the accomplishments of bright females.

Counseling

To avoid or cope with many of the syndromes previously described that could be present or potentially so in gifted females, counseling is one of the most important strategies recommended by experts in gifted education. Counseling also serves as a systematic approach for educators, school counselors, and parents seeking new ways to assist gifted girls in the planning and preparation of their education and future career choices.

Each individual has needs and a personal style, and individual or group counseling should be a choice for each gifted girl. Currently, there exist a few guidance programs, such as group discussions, counseling services, and seminars, to attend to the unique needs of gifted girls. One of the most critical aspects that many girls, especially gifted girls, confront and learn is the stereotypical assumption that the causes of their success are because of luck and effort, and their failure because of a lack of ability (Callahan, Cunningham, & Plucker, 1994; Dickens & Cornell, 1993; Dweck, 1986; Reis 1998; Rimm, 1991). This phenomenon is also described as "the impostor syndrome."

The value of mentoring and counseling cannot be underestimated when working with gifted females. Gifted girls and adolescents may benefit by interacting with mentors, qualified counselors, and other advocates in order to recognize their abilities, personal goals and expectations, and possible career choices. In an already socioculturally demanding atmosphere, these professionals and caring people might help gifted females to be better prepared socially and professionally.

Higher Education

For both genders to compete freely and equal in the workforce, academia must offer females an equally rigorous and preparatory course of study. Regarding female enrollment, great improvements have been noted on college campuses throughout the United States. In fact, women now make up the majority of college students in the United States. "College enrollment in the fall of 2000 was 15.1 million. Of the fall 2000 students, 6.5 million are men and 8.7 million are women" (National Center for Education Statistics, 2000b).

In many professional schools, especially medical and law schools, the rise in female enrollment has been dramatic. According to the Education Development Center (1999), the percentage of law degrees earned by women increased from 7 percent in 1971 to 43 percent in 1994. The percentage of medical degrees granted to women also increased from 9 percent in 1972 to 38 percent in 1994. Perhaps, nowhere is the presence of women more increasingly apparent than in intercollegiate athletics (Fox et al., 1999). The number of female college athletes has risen from 25,000 in 1971 to 100,000 in 1994 (Education Development Center, 1999). Considering the high profiles of successful women's athletic programs at such Division I schools as the University of Connecticut, the University of Tennessee, and Notre Dame, there is no indication that this trend will subside anytime soon. However, despite these advances, the traditional gender patterns remain, "with women earning a majority of the master's and doctoral degrees in education and health, and men earning nearly three-quarters of the degrees in computer science and a higher proportion in engineering" (National Center for Education Statistics, 2000a, p. 9).

Although women have made impressive strides on U.S. college campuses, the fact remains that men have historically dominated higher education in the United States, and, in general, this bias continues. Males lead in numbers, salary, and rank. For example, the National Center for Education Statistics (2000b) reports that the average salaries of full-time instructional faculty "for men in 1998–99 ($58,048) were considerably higher than the average for women ($47,421)" (p. 30). This clearly hinders gifted women in all disciplines who lack available female faculty members to serve as mentors. As Kerr (1994) notes, "The recognition of giftedness, identification with one's chosen field, leadership and maturity, and the presence of mentors all foster the achievement of gifted women in college. Yet these qualities and commodities are in short supply on the typical campus" (p. 135). A gifted woman, who is provided with higher education, solid career orientation, and strong role models, enjoys a positive self-concept and a general satisfaction with her professional life.

Career Choice and Workforce

Traditionally, an abundance of women have been found working as teachers, nurses, social workers, librarians, and in home economics. However, more than any other time in history, large numbers of women are now experiencing a certain amount of equity pursuing work traditionally and exclusively reserved for men. Despite this recent development, women still remain relatively rare in the highest spheres of such domains as the sciences, economics, and politics. For example, at the time of this writing, less than 5 percent of the National Academy of Sciences members were women, and only 10 women scientists are Nobel laureates. Only 24 women have been elected heads of state or government in the past century, and of the 185 highest-ranking diplomats to the United States, only seven are women (Reis, 1998). We can also see such trends in the arts. Reis (1998) reports, "Within the 21 highest budgeted orchestras in the United States, there are no female musical directors or conductors in permanent positions" (p. 29). Middle-class, male, white, heterosexual values, practices, and assumptions have traditionally defined most professions. Hence, Noble et al. (1999) write,

The long-standing tradition of excluding women from public life meant that women's experiences were largely overlooked in studies and theories of talent development. Thus, the process of turning potential talent into actual achievement has been generally explicated for men but not for women. (p. 141)

The "queen bee syndrome" describes a woman who is able to succeed in her career while also succeeding as a mother and wife. However, even when a woman experiences this syndrome, she often finds herself in a conundrum, consistently trying to do everything and do it well. When focusing on her career, she may feel as if she is abdicating her family responsibilities, and conversely, when focusing on her family, she may be criticized for neglecting her employment duties. This situation becomes doubly difficult when societal opinion differs so greatly. On one hand the independent woman, or superwoman, is thought to be the desired role, and on the other particular religions and overly moralistic social commentators tout traditional values. "This intensely personal struggle to try to develop their personal talents while they also try to meet the needs of those they love causes gifted women the most conflict, guilt, and pain" (Reis, 1998, p. 114). However, when women believe their achievements and career goals are supported by their families and significant others, they are better able to handle this societal schizophrenia.

Teacher Preparation

Despite the fact that the overwhelming majority of the teaching force in public schools is female, the concept of gender equality is just beginning to be addressed in both preservice and inservice teacher training. However, this concept is usually presented in an extremely superficial fashion, often viewed as "add on" course work or simply used to fulfill state certification requirements. If children are to be educated by professionals in environments that foster and encourage both boys and girls to develop and realize their talents and abilities, teachers must be taught to provide such an education. Teachers at all levels must be discerning consumers of curriculum material that is often biased in language, content, or illustrations. Neophyte teachers need to reflect on their teaching to understand that the education they provide, the biases they bring to the classroom, the language and material they use, and the ways in which they assess all impact, however subtly, children's perceptions of themselves and their world.

As an imperative aspect of quality education, gender equity must be discussed in theory and manifested in practice. If teacher educators wish to encourage an understanding of gender equity, it will be through these two dimensions. Only then will the full power of this concept be realized for service in our public schools. Thus, for a teacher education program to be successful in this aspect, gender equity needs to be ingrained and explicit in every aspect of the program. This must begin with professors and administrators possessing a common understanding of what gender equity actually entails. On acceptance into their teacher education program, students should be made fully aware of its emphasis on gender equity. Both university and public school teachers and administrators must model the concept for them throughout their education. For example, during a science methods class, professors should not only discuss ways to teach science but also the reasons young girls often show a lack of interest and sometimes fail in science. Furthermore, in student teaching placements, gender equity should be modeled by cooperating teachers who implement excellent practice in the classroom and serve as advocates for students in PPTs. If they are provided with a preservice program such as this, beginning teachers will be much better prepared to serve their students, both boys and girls, and in a more equitable manner (Suranna, 2000).

Equity and Eminence

Throughout this chapter, relevant developmental, sociocultural, and educational factors that promote or impede equal opportunities for gifted girls and women to explore and develop their potentials have been described. Via gender inequity at all educational levels, females continue to struggle for recognition in the workforce. As society moves toward a more equitable situation, positions of power should also be analyzed and promoted as a catalyst for change.

In order to provide educators with tools in serving gifted girls, some researchers have reviewed and documented the lives and accomplishments of eminent women. Some important personality traits were found in studies of eminent women: commitment, determination, motivation, creativity, solitude, refusal to acknowledge limitations of gender, and patience (Callahan & Reis, 1996; Filippelli & Walberg, 1997; Kerr, 1994; Piirto, 1998; Reis 1995a). In her research study of 12 older women who achieved eminence in their respective fields beyond the age of 50, Reis (1995a) writes, "Determination was clearly exhibited by every subject throughout most of her life" (p. 67).

Considering the many struggles that gifted females continually confront, it must be noted that only a small fraction of women throughout history have attained eminence in the world. However, there will always remain countless gifted girls and women in our families, schools, universities, places of worship, and workplaces who go unnoticed. They deserve and must be provided not only our respect and admiration but also fixed means and opportunities in all spheres of society that will assist them in their being and realization.

Summary and Conclusion

In the field of gifted education, gifted females are identified as a special population. Culturally and linguistically diverse children, children with disabilities, and poor children are other groups whose talents and abilities have been traditionally underestimated, unrecognized, and, consequently, undeveloped. Significant issues impacting gifted females in their struggle for equal educational opportunities for the expression of creative thinking and achievement have been described. For bright women, the struggle continues in the workforce.

Educators and families have a major responsibility to create environments and opportunities in which girls, as well as boys, can explore their potential talents and develop their abilities. The fruits of these efforts can be experienced only when a major shift in societal values occurs. As we strive toward this end, we will most certainly, and in a profound way, provide the kind of futures our bright students so richly deserve. This is especially important for our gifted and talented females.

REFERENCES

Amabile, T. (1983). *The social psychology of creativity.* New York: Springer-Verlag.

American Association of University Women. (1992). *The AAUW report: How schools shortchange girls.* Washington, DC: The American Association of University Women Educational Foundation.

Arnold, K. D. (1995). *Lives of promise.* San Francisco: Jossey-Bass.

Austin, S. (1998). *Transactional writing: Empowering women and girls to win at mathematics.* Arlington, VA: National Science Foundation.

Brown, L. M., & Gilligan, C. (1993). *Meeting at the crossroads: Women's psychology and girls' development.* New York: Ballantine.

Callahan, C. M., Cunningham, C. M., & Plucker, J. A. (1994). Foundations for the future: The socio-emotional development of gifted, adolescent women. *Roeper Review, 17,* 99–105.

Callahan, C. M., & Reis, S. M. (1996). Gifted girls, remarkable women. In K. Arnold, K. D. Noble, & R. F. Subotnik (Eds.), *Remarkable women: Perspectives on female talent development* (pp. 171–192). Cresskill, NJ: Hampton Press.

College Entrance Examination Board. (1998). *Profile of 1998 college bound seniors.* Princeton, NJ: Educational Testing Service.

Davis, G. A., & Rimm, S. B. (1989). *Education of the gifted and talented.* Needham Heights, MA: Allyn & Bacon.

Dickens, M. N., & Cornell, D. G. (1993). Parent influence on the mathematics self-concept of high ability adolescent girls. *Journal for the Education of the Gifted, 17,* 53–73.

Dunn, R., Dunn, K., & Price, G. E. (1975). Diagnosing learning styles: Avoiding malpractice suits against school systems. *Phi Delta Kappan, 58*(5), 418–420.

Dweck, C. S. (1986). Motivation processes affecting learning. *American Psychologist, 41,* 1040–1048.

Eccles, J. S. (1987). Gender roles and women's achievement-related decisions. *Psychology of Women Quarterly, 11,* 135–171.

Education Development Center. (1999, Spring). Promoting equity for girls and women. The women's educational equity act resource center. *Mosaic,* 18–19.

Fenneman, E., Peterson, P. L., Carpenter, T. P., & Lubinski, C. A. (1990). Teachers' attributions and beliefs about girls, boys, and mathematics. *Educational Studies in Mathematics, 21,* 55–69.

Filippelli, L. A., & Walberg, H. J. (1997). Childhood traits and conditions of eminent women scientists. *Gifted Child Quarterly, 41*(3), 95–104.

Fox, L. H., Sadker, D., & Engle, J. L. (1999). Sexism in US schools: Implications for the education of gifted girls. *Gifted and Talented International, 14,* 66–79.

Gardner, H. (1983). *Frames of mind: The theory of multiple intelligences.* New York: Basic Books.

Gaskell, J., & Willinsky, S. (Eds.). (1995). *Gender in/forms curriculum.* New York: Teachers College Press.

Hansen, S., Walker, J., & Flom, B. (1995). *Growing smart: What's working for girls in school.* Washington, DC: American Association of University Women Educational Foundation.

Hany, E. A. (1994). The development of basic cognitive components of technical creativity: A longitudinal comparison of children and youth with high and average intelligence. In R. F. Subotnik & K. D. Arnold (Eds.), *Beyond Terman: Contemporary longitudinal studies of giftedness and talent* (pp. 115–154). Norwood, NJ: Ablex.

Heller, K. A., & Ziegler, A. (1996). Gender differences in mathematics and the sciences: Can attributional retraining improve the performance of gifted females? *Gifted Child Quarterly, 40,* 200–210.

Horner, M. S. (1972). Toward an understanding of achievement related conflicts in women. *Journal of Social Issues, 28,* 157–175.

Kerr, B. A. (1994). *Smart girls. A new psychology of girls, women, and giftedness.* Scottsdale, AZ: Gifted Psychology Press.

Klein, A. G., & Zehms, D. (1996). Self-concept and gifted girls: A cross sectional study of intellectually gifted females in Grades 3, 5, 8. *Roeper Review, 19*(1), 30–34.

Kline, B. E., & Short, E. B. (1991). Changes in emotional resilience: Gifted adolescent females. *Roeper Review, 13,* 118–121.

Kloosterman, V. I. (2002). The schoolwide enrichment model: Promoting diversity and excellence in gifted education. In E. I. Diaz & J. A. Castellano (Eds.), *Reaching new horizons: Gifted and talented education for culturally and linguistically diverse students.* Boston: Allyn & Bacon.

Lashaway-Bokina, N. (1996). *Gifted, but gone: High ability, Mexican-American, female dropouts.* Unpublished doctoral dissertation, University of Connecticut, Storrs.

Mondale, S., & Patton, S. B. (2001). *School. The story of American public education.* Boston: Beacon Press.

National Center for Education Statistics. (2000a). *Trends in educational equity of girls and women.* (NCES 2000-030). Washington, DC: U.S. Government Printing Office.

National Center for Education Statistics. (2000b). *Digest of education statistics, 2000.* (NCES 2001-034). Washington, DC: U.S. Government Printing Office.

Noble, K. D., Subotnik, R. F., & Arnold, K. D. (1999). To thine own self be true: A new model of female talent development. *Gifted Child Quarterly, 43,* 140–149.

Orenstein, P. (1994). *Schoolgirls: Young women, self-esteem, and the confidence gap.* New York: Doubleday.

Piirto, J. (1998). Themes in the lives of successful contemporary U.S. women creative writers. *Roeper Review, 21*(1), 60–70.

Purcell, J. H., & Renzulli, J. S. (1998). *Total talent portfolio: A systematic plan to identify and nurture gifts and talents.* Mansfield Center, CT: Creative Learning Press.

Reis, S. M. (1987). We can't change what we don't recognize: Understanding the special needs of gifted females. *Gifted Child Quarterly, 31*(2), 83–89.

Reis, S. M. (1995a). Older women's reflections on eminence: Obstacles and opportunities. *Roeper Review, 18*(1), 66–72.

Reis, S. M. (1995b). Talent ignored, talent diverted: The cultural context underlying giftedness in females. *Gifted Child Quarterly, 39*(3), 162–170.

Reis, S. M. (1998). *Work left undone. Choice and compromises of talented females.* Mansfield, CT: Creative Learning Press.

Reis, S. M., & Callahan, C. M. (1989). Gifted females: They've come a long way—or they have? *Journal for the Education of the Gifted, 12,* 99–117.

Renzulli, J. S. (1977a). *The enrichment triad model: A guide for developing defensible programs for the gifted.* Mansfield, CT: Creative Learning Press.

Renzulli, J. S. (1977b). *Interest-a-lyzer.* Mansfield, CT: Creative Learning Press.

Renzulli, J. S., & Reis, S. M. (1985). *The Schoolwide Enrichment Model: A comprehensive plan for educational excellence.* Mansfield, CT: Creative Learning Press.

Renzulli, J. S., & Reis, S. M. (1994). Research related to the schoolwide enrichment model. *Gifted Child Quarterly, 38,* 2–14.

Renzulli, J. S., & Smith, L. H. (1978). *Learning styles inventory: A measure of student preference for instructional techniques.* Mansfield, CT: Creative Learning Press.

Rimm, S. B. (1991). Underachievement and superachievement: Flip sides of the same psychological coin. In N. Colangelo & G. A. Davis (Eds.), *Handbook of gifted education* (pp. 328–343). Boston: Allyn & Bacon.

Sadker, M., & Sadker, D. (1994). *Failing at fairness: How America's schools cheat girls.* New York: Scribner's.

Silverman, L. K. (1995a). Why are there so few eminent women? *Roeper Review, 18*(1), 5–13.

Silverman, L. K. (1995b). To be gifted or feminine: The forced choice of adolescence. *The Journal of Secondary Gifted Education, 6,* 141–156.

Sternberg, R. J. (1984). Toward a triarchic theory of human intelligence. *Behavioral and Brain Sciences, 7,* 269–287.

Sternberg, R. J. (1988). Mental self-government: A theory of intellectual styles and their development. *Human Development, 31*(4), 197–224.

Suranna, K. J. (2000). *The nature of teacher leadership: A case study of elementary school teachers from a five-year teacher education program.* Unpublished doctoral dissertation, University of Connecticut, Storrs.

U.S. Department of Education. (1998). *Title IX and sex discrimination.* Washington, DC: Office for Civil Rights.

U.S. Department of Education. (2001). *The U.S. department of education's gender equity expert panel. Exemplary and promising gender equity programs 2000.* Jessup, MD: Education Publications Center.

8 Gifted Education for the Native American Student

KEVIN FOLEY
OLIVIA SKENANDORE

There is no simple formula for providing appropriate education for gifted Native American students. This is a very culturally, socially, and racially diverse group within itself, making it by nature a complex group to deal with as a whole. No other ethnic group has been so consistently underrepresented in gifted education programs in the United States as the Native American.

The Indian Nations at Risk Task Force (1991) has articulated an Indian Student Bill of Rights that, although not specifically mentioning gifted Native Americans, certainly by implication addresses the needs of this population. This bill of rights includes the following:

- A safe and psychologically comfortable environment in school.
- A linguistic and cultural environment in school that offers students the opportunity to maintain and develop a firm knowledge base.
- An intellectually challenging program in school that meets community as well as individual academic needs.
- A stimulating early childhood educational environment that is linguistically, culturally, and developmentally appropriate.
- Equity in school programs, facilities, and finances across native communities, and in schools run by the federal government and in public schools in general.

This chapter discusses the diversity of the Native American population, briefly summarizes the history of Native American education, and offers suggestions for identifying and dealing with gifted Native American children. Curriculum and instruction from a Native American perspective is reviewed and suggestions for making parental connections are provided.

Issues that affect the education of gifted Native Americans are related to the nature of the identification process, including the instruments selected for identification and the types of program services that are offered, as well as the largely unmet need for a curriculum that is culturally relevant to individual tribal groups.

Diversity of the Indian Population

Almost 2.5 million Native American/Native Alaskan individuals live in the United States today, comprising less than 1 percent of the population. Of these, 67 percent do not live on reservations, most live west of the Mississippi, with high concentrations in cities such as Dallas, Minneapolis, Denver, Rapid City, Chicago, Los Angeles, and New York (Brown, 1970).

Because of the diverse socioeconomic and living situations of urban Native Americans, most statistical data on them in the United Sates comes from those living on reservations (Banks, 1995). The 328 federally recognized tribes vary in size from the Cherokee, with a population of nearly 1.9 million, and the Navajo, who number 369,000, to the Sioux nation (Dakota and Lakota) of 107,000, the Haudenosaunee (Iroquois) of 52,000, and numerous small tribes on tiny reservations throughout the United States, such as the several Luiseno tribes in southern California with fewer than 500 members each (U.S. Census Bureau, 1990).

These different tribes, or nations, have each developed their own techniques for maintaining cultural identity, and a visit to several reservations would reveal as many differences as similarities in the ways that they have found to be culturally persistent in the face of the influences that have sought to assimilate and acculturate them into the mainstream (Spicer, 1971).

Native Americans had developed complex societies over the thousands, or in some cases, tens of thousands, of years before European settlers arrived. Sophisticated patterns of social folkways, mores, and laws evolved in tribal societies and came to govern all aspects of political, economic, and ecumenical matters (even though most Native American societies would not divide their cultures into separate elements such as these). Passing on their culture and history through oral traditions rather than written ones, most native societies developed an emphasis on cooperation within the group (Bradley, 2001; Skenandore & Taradash, 1994) expressed in a reliance on the clan or extended family. In order to adequately serve this population, an understanding of the importance of the group, as opposed to an emphasis on individual achievement valued by the larger U.S. society, becomes a primary concern.

The History of Native American Education

Although the first Native American/non–Native American contacts were made centuries ago, the history of formal Native American education is little more than

100 years old. Historically, Native American education has been complex because of the unique relationship each tribe developed with the U.S. government over the past several hundred years. For some tribes, the treaty-making processes that established their rights and clarified their relationships with U.S. society extend back to the 1600s, when the eastern tribes encountered the Dutch, French, and English empires on the East Coast of the United States. Later, southwestern Native Americans came under the influence of the Spanish empire, while on the central plains, and many Native Americans were not confronted by the Europeans, or their descendents, until after the U.S. government had been established (Brown, 1970).

In the late 1800s Native American education emerged in the United States as a function of the U.S. War Department. Christian missionaries, whose presence was sanctioned by the government, made an effort to "civilize" Native Americans, which included teaching English to students and forcing religious conversion. Early formalized education for Native Americans in the United States was, therefore, both authoritarian and Eurocentric. The Christian churches that established schools frequently became the owners of prime parcels of land on which their schools, and their churches, were built, even though the Non-intercourse Act of 1790 forbade the acquisition of Native American land by others (Cohen, 1945).

In 1879 in Carlisle, Pennsylvania, Colonel Richard Henry Pratt founded a school to teach Native Americans how to live off the reservation. Pratt believed that all men were created equal and did not understand segregation, but he believed that Native Americans needed to become proficient in the European-based culture of the United States in order to progress. Pratt's purpose in founding his boarding school, which followed a military model, including the use of uniforms for boys and Victorian style dresses for girls, was to totally assimilate Native Americans into the dominant culture so that his graduates would achieve success outside the reservation. Assimilation meant that no Native American languages could be spoken, ever, and Native American dress and traditions were prohibited. Pratt convinced leaders of the Dakota tribes to enroll their children in his school for the opportunities they would receive, and the school educated more than 8,000 Native Americans in its 39-year history. Pratt's philosophy, however, did not allow for his students to retain any vestiges of their cultural heritage, and because the school lacked job placement services, many of its graduates returned to their reservations as members of neither their own cultures nor of the U.S. culture. Pratt's school became a model for many to follow (U.S. Indian Bureau, 1928).

The education of Native Americans for many years followed Pratt's simple philosophy of "kill the Indian, save the man." Elements of Native American culture thousands of years old were for many tragically destroyed when students had their cultural identities stripped away by their teachers as they were denied their language, religion, culture, and rituals. Only in 1993, with the passage of the Religious Freedom Act, were Indians legally protected from this happening (Cohen, 1945).

Today, a majority (90 percent) of Native American and Native Alaskan students attend public schools across the United States, as opposed to attending

Bureau of Indian Affairs (BIA) or tribal schools. Based on the 1990 census, there are approximately 600,000 Native Americans attending K–12 public schools, whereas approximately 50,000 (or fewer than 10 percent) are enrolled in the U.S. Department of the Interior BIA schools, organized under the Office of Indian Education Programs (OIEP). The 185 BIA schools are located in 23 states, and many are located on Native American reservations (National Indian Education Association, 2000).

Gifted and Talented Programs

Gifted and talented programs within the BIA system were established in 1988, but the bureau did not strongly support this type of program until the advent of the Jacob Javits Gifted and Talented Education Program, which began in 1994 to target underrepresented minorities in gifted education. Its highest priority was "the identification of and the provision of services to gifted and talented students who may not be identified and served through traditional assessment methods, including economically disadvantaged individuals and individuals of limited-English proficiency" (Gibson, 1998).

Several special grant projects, such as Project Spring, which investigated gifted students of low-socioeconomic status, including the Mescalero Apache of southern New Mexico, and Project Discover, which examined methods for more appropriate identification of both rural and urban Navajos in Arizona, have specifically targeted gifted Native American students (Spicker, 1995).

Identifying Gifted and Talented American Indians

Gifted and talented individuals exist in all racial groups and cultural settings, of course, but Native Americans tend to be underrepresented in programs for the gifted mostly for two reasons:

1. The traditions of oral language and cooperation rather than competition in the society.
2. The lack of selection criteria that take into account the unique culture of Native Americans (Bradley, 2001).

Most states use multiple criteria for identifying gifted students, but the use of an intelligence test is almost always one of these, and intelligence tests tend to favor heavily the groups on which the tests were normed in the first place. The Weschsler Intelligence Scale for Children—Revised Edition (WISC-R), for example, which is heavily verbal, logical, and scientific, is biased against Native Americans, whose communication is often nonverbal or undetailed (Florey, Nottle, &

TABLE 8.1   Characteristics of Gifted Native American Students

High Verbal Ability
- May have high verbal ability in native language
- May exhibit rapid acquisition of English once exposed to the language

Early Reading
- Advanced storytelling ability
- Ability to read environmental print

Questioning Attitude
- Sense of analysis, synthesis, and evaluation in asking questions
- *Note:* Some tribes raise children not to question authority

Keen Power of Observation
- Possible high levels of visual or auditory memory; some cultures learn predominantly by observation before demonstrating mastery
- Persistent, intense concentration

Learns Basic Skills Quickly and Easily
- May require more repetition at primary level until English is mastered

Wide Range of Interests
- May include culturally relevant activities

Unusual or Highly Developed Sense of Humor
- May be displayed through unique use of language or responses

Willingness to Take Risks
- May be influenced by familiarity of situation based on cultural experience

From Skenandore & Taradash, 1994.

Dorf, 1986). Performance-based tests, such as the Kaufman Assessment Battery for Children, are fairer, though timed tests in general are biased against Native Americans whose society does not value speed. Intelligence batteries by nature emphasize individual performance, which conflicts with the values of Native Americans of group cohesiveness and collective decision making.

Giftedness in Native Americans may be masked by students who have been trained to exhibit diplomacy, quiet individualism, and self-effacing behavior. Because 25 percent of Native Americans begin school speaking little or no English, and those who do often have Spanish influences (Pueblo Indians of the Southwest) or speak nonstandard dialects learned at home, Native Americans who do not speak standard English proficiently may not be recognized as verbally or linguistically gifted. Once exposed to the language, however, many of these students demonstrate high levels of verbal abilities in English. It is necessary, therefore, for educators to look for giftedness in Native Americans in other ways. Table 8.1 lists some characteristics of giftedness and the ways they may be demonstrated by culturally diverse (CD) populations, such as the Native American. Developed by

Skenadore and Taradash (1994), it may be used when looking for characteristics of giftedness in Native American children.

Native Americans often possess traits that are highly valued in their own cultures but are in almost direct opposition to the traits traditionally thought of as being characteristic of giftedness. The list of traits shown in Table 8.2 may be characteristic of some, but not all, Native Americans. This fact needs to be taken into consideration by teachers and others who are charged with referring students for possible inclusion in gifted programs (Callahan & McIntyre, 1994).

TABLE 8.2   Cultural Behaviors, Values, and Beliefs of Native American Students: Implications for Giftedness

Cultural Behaviors, Values, Beliefs	Implications for Giftedness
Tendency to be nonassertive	May not volunteer answers, therefore may be more competent than in-class participation may indicate
Values the group over the individual	May not respond in competitive environment where achievement results in individuals being singled out
Is not materialistic	May find material rewards unmotivating
Is less language dependent	Verbal expressions may not be used for demonstrating knowledge, skills, and abilities as much as nonverbal expressions
Is not facially expressive	May appear unmotivated or lacking in curiosity
Shows reticence	May appear uninvolved or unknowledgeable
Responds to custom	May appear uncreative or unoriginal
Has a different sense of time	May not work well under time pressure; speed may be valued over results
Is a holistic learner	May not respond well to linear or analytically presented learning activities
Is encouraged to learn from mistakes	May not see the correct response as the ultimate goal of a problem-solving activity
Values modeling as a mode of instruction	May wait to see how others perform before becoming involved
Uses auditory and visual learning strategies	Knowledge and skills might be more accurate in visual and auditory modes
Values memory in learning	May focus on memory tasks rather than those requiring higher-level skills

From Callahan and McIntyre, 1994.

Any assessment of intelligence should be tempered by an understanding that the traits listed in Table 8.2 might work against Native Americans when using traditional scales. Callahan and McIntyre (1994) recommend that intelligence assessments be accompanied by other data collection techniques, such as portfolio assessments.

Curriculum and Instruction

Because of Native American culture's high valuation of group effort and the esteem accorded an individual who works toward a group goal with little motivation for personal glory, teachers of gifted Native Americans need to design group activities as often as possible and to be keenly aware of the contributions to the group goal of all participants, even those who are not demonstrably leadership oriented. The Native American group member may seem quiet and uninvolved but will contribute where possible in a meaningful way, perhaps unobtrusively. Teachers can also look for knowledge to be demonstrated in ways other than verbal, perhaps in activities or visually.

Furthermore, teachers should be as aware as possible of the cultural heritage of all children in the classroom, Native Americans included. Sensitivity to Native American culture can result in lessons that the gifted Native Americans may be able to relate to wholeheartedly, and in assessments that take into consideration these cultural differences. The do's and don'ts listed in Table 8.3 for teachers of Native Americans in gifted situations may prove useful.

Davidson (1997) lists several caveats that educators need to be aware of when dealing with Native American students who have been placed in gifted classroom settings. First, gifted Native Americans should be expected to perform at the same levels as others, but this may not be easily achieved at first, and individual attention and encouragement may be needed to coax performance. Second, gifted Native Americans, like all children, have varied interests and may benefit from enrichment activities that focus on their cultural heritage. Finally, the gifted student may need individual emotional support and encouragement in dealing with the fact that the school culture and the home culture value different traits.

Parental Involvement

Parental involvement is important at the very early stages of identification of gifted Native Americans because one of the problems with getting this population properly identified in the first place is that traditional methods of judging giftedness may not be so readily appropriate for Native Americans. The Hardin, Montana, school system, which is 55 percent Native American, accounts for cultural variations from the start by making its parental assessment inventory culturally sensitive. Traits such as imagination and humor are included, but the inventory

TABLE 8.3 Do's & Don'ts for Teachers of Gifted Native American Students

Do	Don't
Present native peoples as appropriate role models with whom a native child can identify	Single out native children, asking them to describe their family's traditions
Avoid arts and crafts activities that trivialize native dress, dance, or ceremony	Assume that you have no native children in your class
Accurately know the history of native peoples, past and present, before attempting to teach it	Do or say anything that would embarrass a native child
Present native peoples as separate from each other, with unique cultures, languages, spiritual beliefs, and dress	Use ABC books that have an I for Indian or an E for Eskimo
Teach native history as a regular part of U.S. history	Use counting resources that count Native Americans
Use materials that put history in an objective perspective	Use stories that show non-native children "playing indian"
Use materials that present native heroes who fought to defend their people	Use picture books that show animals dressed as Native Americans
Discuss the relationship between native people and the colonists and what went wrong with it	Use books that show native people as savages, primitive craftspeople, or simple tribal people, now extinct
Use materials that show respect for and understanding of the sophistication and complexities of native societies	Have children dress up as Native Americans, with paper bag costumes or paper feather headdresses
Use respectful language when teaching about native peoples	Let children play with Native American artifacts borrowed from a museum or library
Use primary source materials—speeches, songs, poetry, writings—that show the linguistic skills of people who come from oral traditions	Teach about Native Americans only at Thanksgiving
Use materials that show native women, elders, and children as integral parts of native societies	Use insulting terms, such as squaw, papoose, brave, Indian giver, wild Indians, Indian blankets, or wagon burners
Talk about lives of native peoples in the present	Use books that portray native women and elders as subservient to warriors
Read and discuss good poetry, suitable for young people, by contemporary native writers	Assume that any native person knows details of other native nations

suggests ways for parents to recognize these traits as they might be specifically evidenced by a Native American child (Davidson, 1997).

Given that the culture of a gifted classroom might value or tend to emphasize traits that are at odds with those most valued by Native Americans, the teacher of gifted Native Americans must also be prepared to do some public relations with parents who would rather their children not develop some of these mainstream culture characteristics, such as competitiveness and an emphasis on speed in problem solving. Just as the teacher must offer emotional support to the students who are dealing with this juxtaposition of values, so must the teacher explain to the parents the value and purpose of these characteristics in their children.

Native American parents can also serve as a resource for the gifted classroom teacher, just as the parents of any child may serve this purpose. With Native American parents, however, the teacher has an opportunity to get involvement from firsthand sources when teaching about Native Americans in American history and culture. Firsthand, direct contact with parents can also help the teacher's cultural awareness level improve.

Summary and Conclusion

As with any special population, serving the needs of Native American students comes down to an awareness of cultural differences and how these differences may be manifested in the classroom behavior of the child. If more Native Americans are to be included in gifted programs, then at every level of the process, beginning with referral and leading to testing, curriculum design and implementation, assessment, and integration of the family into the educational experience, teachers and administrators must simply make themselves aware of the culture of this group and consider these cultural characteristics when making judgments and decisions. Underrepresentation of this group in gifted programs likely has much to do with the lack of referrals made and the use of rigid standards of acceptance based on what are perhaps culturally biased instruments. If administrators and classroom teachers in general can be given training in basic aspects of Native American culture in general, and in the cultures of certain Native American groups in particular who might be found in a particular region, then this lack of early identification of gifted Native Americans may be soon overcome.

REFERENCES

Banks, J. (1995). *Teaching strategies for ethnic studies.* Boston: Allyn & Bacon.
Bradley, C. (2001, Spring). *Conceptual Foundations Newsletter.* National Association for Gifted Children publication, p. 5. Washington, DC: National Association for Gifted Children.
Brown, D. (1970). *Bury my heart at wounded knee: An Indian history of the American west.* New York: Random House.

Callahan, C. M., & McIntyre, J. A. (1994, April). *Identifying outstanding talent in American Indian and Alaska Native students.* U.S. Department of Education, Office of Educational Research and Improvement. Washington, DC: U.S. Government Printing Office.

Cohen, F. S. (1945). Handbook of federal Indian law. U.S. Government Office of Indian Affairs. Washington, DC: U.S. Government Printing Office.

Davidson, K. (1997, Fall). What works. *Northwest Education Magazine* [On-line]. Available: http://www.nwrel.org/nwedu/fall_97/article7.html [2002, February 12].

Florey, J. E., Nottle, D., & Dorf, J. H. (1986). *Identification of gifted children among the American Indian population: An inservice model.* (ERIC Document Reproduction Service No. ED 273 399)

Gibson, K. L. (1998). Recognizing gifted minority students: A research-based identification approach. http://www.nexus.edu.au/Teacherstud/gat/gibson.htm.

Indian Nations at Risk Task Force. (1991). *Indian nations at risk: An educational strategy for change.* Washington, DC: U.S. Department of Education.

National Indian Education Association. (2000). *Transition paper.* Alexandria, VA.

Skenandore, O., & Taradash, G. (1994). *Best practices manual for gifted education in New Mexico.* New Mexico State Technical Assistant Document, pp. 11–12. Santa Fe, NM: New Mexico State Department of Education.

Spicer. E. (1971, November). Persistent cultural systems. *Science, 174,* 795–800.

Spicker, H. (1995). *Project Spring: Identifying rural disadvantaged gifted children.* Bloomington: Gifted and Talented Programs, Indiana University.

U.S. Census Bureau. (1990). *Top 25 American Indian tribes in the United States.* 1990 Census of the Bureau.

U.S. Indian Bureau. (1928). *The Merriam report.* Institute for Government Research. Washington, DC: U.S. Government Printing Office.

CHAPTER

9

The Gay Gifted Learner

Facing the Challenge of Homophobia and Antihomosexual Bias in Schools

SANDY COHN

For students in U.S. middle schools and high schools, homophobia and antihomosexual bias are simply painful facts of life (Bowman, 2001; Horowitz, 2001; Human Rights Watch, 2001). According to data collected in a yearlong study by students in one midwestern high school, the average public high school student hears an antigay remark every 7 minutes (Carter, 1997). According to the same study, teachers were found to intervene only 3 percent of the time.

In its provocative report, *Hatred in the Hallways: Violence and Discrimination Against Lesbian, Gay, Bisexual, and Transgender Students in U.S. Schools*, the Human Rights Watch (2001) spelled out in meticulous detail the serious threat that verbal harassment and physical violence has become in the school lives of gay, lesbian, bisexual, or transgender (GLBT) youths. This institutionalized prejudice not only affects gay students but also straight students who deviate in any way from rigid, stereotypic sex roles and modal gender expression. It is when these straight students who are mistaken for gay become targets of homophobic harassment that school administrators respond to homophobic acts of verbal and physical abuse, if they do so at all.

Although it is certainly the most extensive account of antigay harassment in schools, the Human Rights Watch report is only the most recent in a long series of studies, reports, and explications about the prevalence and destructiveness of homophobia in our nation's schools (Lipkin, 1999; Plummer, 1999; Unks, 1995). What is undeniably apparent is that homophobia serves to shape the school experience of students in U.S. schools. Homophobia has become a major component of the covert curriculum to which young learners are exposed on a daily, even hourly, basis in school, and to and from school.

The impact homophobia and antihomosexual bias has on gifted students can be profound particularly if a student is talented in a way that differs from sexual stereotypes. Regardless of his actual sexual orientation, a boy who is extremely gifted verbally and whose interests include writing poetry and participating in theater is very likely to hear from his schoolmates that he is not boy enough for them. Similarly, a girl who is an extraordinarily gifted mathematical reasoner or whose interests lean toward the mechanical or athletic will quickly learn that she is not girl enough for her classmates, either.

What Is Homophobia?

Homophobia was first defined as "the dread of being in close contact with homo-sexuals" (Weinberg, 1972, p. 4). This definition is consistent with the formal meaning of phobia as described in the psychological literature, "an intense, illogical, or abnormal fear of a specific thing" (American Psychiatric Association, 1994, p. 171). Since its introduction, however, the term has come to include a much wider range of negative emotions, attitudes, and behaviors toward homosexual persons. Haaga (1991) argues that homophobia is distinguishable from true phobias in the following five ways.

1. Although fear is the emotion most formally associated with phobias, homophobia is distinguished by intense hatred or anger.
2. Although phobias are typically perceived as excessive or unreasonable fears, homophobic reactions are more often considered justifiable, understandable, and acceptable.
3. Although phobias usually trigger avoidance, homophobia frequently results in hostile and aggressive expression.
4. Although phobias do not appear in political agendas, homophobia often includes calls for institutionalized prejudice and discrimination.
5. *Unlike* homophobia, people who have phobias tend to recognize them as disabling conditions and usually are motivated to seek help to change them.

School boys report (Plummer, 1999) that they start to use antigay epithets, such as "fag," "faggot," or "gay," when they are in primary school, well before they approach puberty. They typically use them as derogatory terms, general insults implying difference or "otherness," but they are also aware of the characteristics associated with the terms. Increasingly, the terms have come to denote "stupid" or "very un-cool."

By fourth and fifth grades, there is widespread use of these terms, which are unquestionably regarded as weapons of serious insult. Prepubescent use of homophobic epithets can be traced typically to role-modeling behavior of and mentoring by older children. With the approach of puberty, the words take on an unambiguous homosexual meaning.

The use of homophobic words evolves as children develop. It appears that new connotations do not simply replace earlier notions, rather they successively accumulate in overlapping layers of meaning. Plummer (1999) catalogs these developmentally evolving meanings in the following ways.

- *Being a baby:* Maturing boys should not act like babies. A boy who cries in school, who is vulnerable, and who is a "mommy's boy" is likely to be called "gay" or a "fag."
- *Being soft and weak, like a girl:* Boys should not exhibit feminine attributes. Beginning in the primary grades, boys and girls increasingly stay apart from one another on school grounds. Boys who do not honor this segregation, who are effeminate, girlish, sissies, pale, or wear pink are often called "gay." Boys should not betray boys' groups by joining girls or by separating from them to become loners.
- *Being unmasculine:* Boys who betray mainstream standards of masculinity are frequently targeted for abuse. These are youths who do not play group sports (especially those with higher status, such as football), are loners, conform to adult authority in preference to that of peers, or seek the company of girls' groups.
- *Being academic:* Boys are expected to demonstrate increasing maturity and physical competence. Boys should not be weak or cowardly. The labels "fag" and "gay" attach to boys who do not succeed in sports, do not fight, are academic and nonphysical, are sedentary, lose contests, are weak, or are late to develop physically. Of course, the sanction against being academic immediately targets any boy who is intellectually or academically talented and who chooses to honor and express his abilities in his actions.
- *Sexuality:* Young men should not "deviate" from what is considered "normal" sexuality. After puberty, there is a strong expectation for expression of "compulsory heterosexuality." Young men who refuse to refer to girls as sex objects, do not boast of sexual exploits in the locker room, or are not in a heterosexual relationship are often suspect.

Young males are exposed to homophobia and learn its implicit negative connotations in a variety of ways: by observation, deduction, and being personally targeted (Plummer, 1999). They observe the treatment of their classmates and learn quickly what could happen to them if they appear to be even a little different. The smarter they are, the more quickly they learn to develop the masking behaviors they think they need to survive (Kerr & Cohn, 2001). They ascertain the significance of homophobia from the reactions of others, their peers as well as those in authority. When issues related to homosexuality are raised in discussions, most people typically go quiet. The power of such silences imparts a special, often terrifying, status to homophobia (Plummer, 1999).

Children also learn the significance of being labeled "gay" after becoming the targets of teasing, verbal harassment, and physical violence themselves.

Although boys are more frequently the target of homophobia and antigay harassment in schools, girls who differ from feminine stereotypes also suffer attacks. This is especially true for girls who appear to be too tough, independent, and instrumental; who engage in rough and tumble activities; and who evidence talent in areas typically deemed masculine in character, such as mathematics, engineering, mechanics, and athletics (Kerr, 1994). It is more acceptable for girls, however, to show affection for other girls than for boys to demonstrate feelings for other boys.

Homophobia in School Settings

Specific subjects in school are believed to be more for boys and others more for girls. Far too often teachers and school counselors cooperate in the persistence of this mythology (Unks, 1995). In actuality, science, mathematics, and shop are not necessarily male domains, nor are art, literature, music, and home economics singularly female pursuits. In spite of this reality, in the often hyperintense and surreal school environment, what the students and teachers believe assumes the character of truth (Unks, 1995). As a result, most students stick to the gender defined subject groups. Only a few boys risk homophobic labels by diving wholeheartedly into poetry writing or theater or home economics (Kerr & Cohn, 2001). The impact of gender stereotypic academics on girls, causing them to avoid mathematics and quantitative science and thereby self-selecting themselves out of the most prestigious and lucrative career paths, has been widely documented over the past three decades (Benbow, 1988; Fox, Brody, & Tobin, 1980; Kerr, 1994). A number of studies have been undertaken in the past decade or so that attempt to establish the reliability and validity of these subject matter, gender stereotypes. The results of these studies are rather equivocal.

The Relationship Between Sexual Orientation and Cognitive Abilities

Sex-typical behaviors have been well documented in nearly every field in the social and behavioral sciences (Halpern, 1992). Examples range from sex-typical psychiatric diagnoses to selection of college majors. Some cognitive behaviors demonstrate no sex differences, others show relatively small differences, and still others reveal substantial and persistent sex differences. One of the largest sex differences, favoring males, is shown on tasks involving spatial–visual reasoning, particularly those tasks that involve transforming images in visual working memory and mental rotation (Halpern & Wright, 1996). In the context of mathematical reasoning, males have been disproportionately represented in the highest ranges of the mathematics section of the Scholastic Aptitude Test (SAT) (Benbow,

1988). Some differences, favoring females, have been found in verbal fluency tasks; synonym generation tasks; reading; and performance on college tests in English composition, literature, and foreign languages (Stanley, 1993).

Differences in cognition among persons of differing sexual orientation yield more complex patterns of results than those demonstrated in studies of sex differences. The most consistent pattern of differences between heterosexual males and homosexual males has emerged in studies of spatial–visual abilities. Heterosexual males repeatedly outperformed homosexual males on these tasks, and homosexual males outperformed females (orientation unspecified) (Gladue, Beatty, Larson, & Staton, 1990; Sanders & Ross-Field, 1986; Tuttle & Pillard, 1991; Willmott & Brierly, 1984). McCormick and Witelson (1991) found that heterosexual males demonstrated better visual–spatial ability than verbal ability, just the opposite pattern as that shown by heterosexual females. They also found that homosexual males tended to do equally well on tasks of both verbal and visual–spatial abilities.

Findings about verbal abilities varied widely from study to study, depending in large part on the measures used. Homosexual males were shown to perform better than heterosexual males and females (Tuttle & Pillard, 1991; Willmott & Brierly, 1984), somewhere between heterosexual males and females (McCormick & Witelson, 1991), or no different from heterosexual males (Gladue et al., 1990). The inconsistency of these results is understandable because verbal ability is a heterogeneous construct, so measures of different subtasks would not be expected to yield similar results (Halpern, 1992); different measures of verbal ability assess different cognitive processes that are only slightly correlated with one another (Halpern, 1992); each of the studies contained very small numbers of subjects; and the subjects are not representative of the population at large.

In spite of the lack of clarity in these findings, there appears to be an emergent pattern of differences in certain specific cognitive abilities among individuals of different sexual orientation, particularly between heterosexual and homosexual males.

The Effects of Homophobia and Antihomosexual Bias on Adolescents

Students who differ from local norms of gender expression are most frequently targeted for verbal and other forms of nonphysical harassment in situations remarkably near their classroom environments but just out of direct sight of their teachers, typically in the hallways and bathrooms (Human Rights Watch, 2001). Sexual minority youth populations report staying out of these areas as much as possible.

Physical harassment takes place most frequently on the way to and from school or at off campus events (c.f., Human Rights Watch, 2001). Boys are more frequently the targets of homophobic physical attacks. The attacks themselves are often characterized by extraordinary brutality and result in serious injury and even death (Franklin, 1998). Girls, however, especially same-sex oriented girls are more frequently the target of sexual harassment and sexual assault (Human Rights Watch, 2001).

Whether homophobic attacks result in injury or not, the psychological damage that results profoundly affects the lives of everyone involved. More than 20 studies have been undertaken to examine the relationship between sexual orientation and suicide among adolescents. In each case the frequency of suicide among gay, lesbian, or bisexual youths has been found to be much greater than for their straight counterparts. Incidence of suicide among gay subjects has been reported as high as six times that found for straight youths (Gibson, 1989; Human Rights Watch, 2001). Most of these studies suffer from the same flaw that severely limits their generalizability to the population at large. That flaw rests in the sample of subjects comprising the study. In each case the study was conducted on a "convenience" sample, that is, youths who identified themselves as gay and who were willing to take part in a study that included questions about sexual orientation. Even in the few studies that did use random samples of adolescents, the focus was on sexual identity (that is, identifying oneself as straight or gay)—something most adolescents rarely do.

The first study to use a nationally representative sample drew from the National Longitudinal Study of Adolescent Health (Russell & Joyner, 2001). It was also the first to include questions about same-sex romantic attractions and same-sex romantic relationships, as well as questions of sexual identity. The investigators also used audio computer-aided self-interviews to collect sensitive information, in which respondents listened to questions delivered via laptop computers through earphones, in order to reduce the influence of interviewers and parents on their responses. The results of this study indicate that same-sex-oriented young people are more than twice as likely as their same-sex peers who are opposite-sex oriented to attempt suicide. These findings persist regardless of the subject's age and family background characteristics. The study also reported increased likelihood of same-sex-oriented youths to feel hopeless and depressed, to abuse alcohol and other substances, and to have experienced an attempted suicide by a family member or a friend. For all of the youths in this study, victimization experiences were associated with suicidality (suicidal thoughts and suicidal attempts). The researchers note, "it is our hope that this study can put to rest any doubt that while most youths reporting same-sex sexual orientation make it through adolescences with no more problems than heterosexual youths, a significant number are at risk for suicide. These youths deserve intervention and prevention that they only rarely receive" (p. 1280).

Sexual minority youth face other developmental challenges that their heterosexual peers do not. Self-awareness of same-sex erotic feelings tends to occur during early adolescence, becoming increasingly crystallized at the start of and throughout puberty (D'Augelli, 1998). This is at least in part because of progress in cognitive development. Gay gifted learners may experience such personal awareness earlier than their agemates at least in part because of their relatively accelerated cognitive development. Increasing social awareness and acceptance of same-sex sexual orientation will likely result in more gay, lesbian, and bisexual youths acknowledging their sexual orientation to themselves and others (Savin-Williams, 1990, 1998). One result of the increased openness among the generation of present-day youth is greater support from similar young people, family members, and other adults. Alternatively, the same openness allows for increased vulnerability to victimization from more traditional social institutions, such as church and school. The HIV epidemic exacerbates the risks these youths face in profound ways.

Sanctions against expressing same-sex romantic feelings in any context typically result in loss of developmental opportunities to explore relationships and experience intimacy. D'Augelli (1998) identifies such loss as the first type of victimization sexual minority youth experience. Second, he notes, is the self-doubt induced by heterosexism, the internalization of the cultural assumption that heterosexuality is natural and good, whereas homosexuality is shameful. A strong sense of "otherness" results from isolation from others like themselves and from strident social assertions that homoerotic feelings are morally reprehensible. Because they feel so different (often not understanding why), sexual minority youth become reclusive or try to act "straight." Two personas emerge: a public one and a private one. The energy spent on maintaining a mask of gender-conforming behavior is energy that is not spent on the tasks of positive cognitive and social development. The distinction between the public and private personas can strengthen and persist to such a degree that the self fragments, a serious psychological disorder that interferes with the ability to work and to experience intimacy in relationships. The internalization of feelings of inferiority often results in experiences of alienation from family, school, and society in general (Savin-Williams, 1990, 1998). Such individuals become marginalized in the following ways.

- Sexual minority youth have school problems because of harassment from other students, which can result in excessive absences from school, poor academic performance, and even dropping out.
- Gay, lesbian, and bisexual adolescents run away from home, often having to live on the streets. They become homeless and bereft of educational opportunities.
- Many gay and bisexual males engage in criminal behavior to survive, which brings them into contact with authorities.
- Sexual minority youth abuse alcohol, drugs, and other substances to relieve the anxiety they experience from their daily stressors and their limited future as members of a stigmatized group.

The absence of support from parents, siblings, and extended family members (the support youth from most historically disenfranchised groups have relied on in the face of social stigmatization) exacerbates the problems faced by gay, lesbian, and bisexual young people. Fears that their families will reject them cause these youths to remain secretive. These fears appear to be well founded (D'Augelli, 1998).

The emergence of the HIV/AIDS epidemic has added enormously to the risks faced by sexual minority youths. Feelings that one's sexual orientation exposes one to the risk of a deadly infection further burden a person's sense of value. Such diminished sense of self only increases the likelihood of risky sexual behavior out of enhanced needs for companionship and intimacy (Human Rights Watch, 2001).

In light of the developmental challenges sexual minority youth face in their daily lives, one can only marvel at the resiliency of the vast majority of them who survive into adulthood.

Experiences of Gay Gifted Learners

Three articles have been published to date that address the experiences of adolescents who are both gifted and gay, lesbian, or bisexual (Friedrichs, 1997; Peterson & Rischar, 2000; Tolan, 1997). In his survey study of 53 GLB youths who were members of support groups from eight different metropolitan areas, Friedrichs (1997) found more than a third of them to have been in special programs for gifted students in their schools. Even though the sample of respondents was small, the large proportion of gifted youths in this GLB group indicates an urgent need for educators of the gifted to become attentive to the circumstances faced by those gifted GLB youths who might be in their charge.

Peterson and Rischar (2000) conducted a qualitative study of 18 GLB college students, focusing on their high school experiences, and identified three themes. Being twice different did appear to create additional emotional burdens related to depression and feelings of social isolation. Coming to terms with being different from the majority of their agemates in both ability and sexual orientation often resulted in attempts to deny one or the other of these central aspects of their identity, or, more frequently, in social isolation and loss of self-esteem. The school climate experienced by some of these teenagers seemed unsafe, because of psychological and physical harassment. In some cases, individuals sought to handle these uncertainties by academic or athletic overachievement, perfectionism, or overinvolvement in extracurricular activities; or, in other cases, by self-destructive behaviors such as dropping out of school, running away, substance abuse, or suicide. None of the participants reported turning to adults when they were experiencing such internal turmoil. Peterson and Rischar urge parents and teachers to become more alert to such issues; to create a school climate in which students with all kinds of differences are safe and accepted; and to make themselves available to listen, support, and help solve problems.

Tolan (1997) offered descriptions of several psychological challenges that might be faced by highly gifted adolescents and young adults. These descriptions were not based on empirical data, however. Tolan noted that premature self-labeling and premature developmental foreclosure of sexual identity might occur among highly gifted adolescents because they become aware earlier than their agemates of the complex issues surrounding sexuality and sexual stereotypes.

The Human Rights Watch (2001) study estimates that there are more than 2 million students in the United States who are gay, lesbian, or bisexual. If 10 percent of this population is identifiable as gifted, creative, or talented (a conservative estimate), there are more than 200,000 gay gifted learners in U.S. schools—gay gifted learners at serious risk of threats ranging from psychological injury to death.

Helping Gay Gifted Learners

Consider Dabrowski's theory that intellectual talent is sometimes accompanied by what he termed "overexcitabilities," hypersensitivities, inordinate degrees of response intensity, and extremely sensitive response triggers that are expressed as emotional, physical, and relational syndromes (Piechowski, 1975), which, he argues, potentiate creative productivity in various domains of human behavior. Add being gay to this equation and there is much about which to be sensitive, even oversensitive.

Conscious awareness of threats to the self and family often come earlier than usual for gifted learners. They have the capacity to place situations—national news, regional crises, local emergencies—into personally meaningful perspectives. They can try the horror on their own condition or on that of their families and friends. The threats can become personal and very real to them.

When they listen to members of the religious right condemn homosexuality and homosexuals, they have a hard time dodging thoughts about the terror of exposure and humiliation. When they hear that a gay college student has been murdered simply because he is gay, they can feel the horror of strangers, and even friends and family, turning against them. The fear and loathing that media messages perpetrate reaches them clearly. And for some of them, there simply is no "off" switch.

One of the first, foremost, and most important things that can be done for these youths who feel isolated, alienated, and threatened beyond belief is to reach out to them with the message that it is okay to be exactly who they are. This is something that individuals can do—as acquaintances, friends, family members, teachers, coaches, counselors, school administrators, members of the clergy, and even as political leaders. People can demonstrate tolerance in their own attitudes toward others who are different.

People can amplify the expression of that tolerance and inclusiveness to society in general by examining how schools create policies of nondiscrimination and inclusion, of protection based on sexual orientation and gender identity (Human Rights Watch, 2001). People can go much farther by recognizing the academic needs these intellectually gifted youths (and young people talented in a myriad of ways) have and how these needs might interact with issues of sexual orientation and gender identity. Such recognition can take the form of learning opportunities that tap into their uniquenesses and special qualities. Moreover, policies of "one-size-fits-all" education can be eschewed and attention can be paid to what the art and science of education informs us about how people learn (Bransford, Brown, & Cocking, 1999). Focus can be tuned away from the classroom as the unit of instruction and toward the individual as the unit of learning. In this way, the gifted student becomes the beneficiary of opportunities to learn in ways that support appreciation for individual differences and benefits from the expression of unique talents and gifts regardless of whether they fit into preconceived rigid notions of gender-appropriate attitudes, thoughts, and behaviors.

Summary and Conclusion

In very practical terms, we can make sure that our school districts have policies of nondiscrimination based on sexual orientation and gender identity, *and* that those policies are put into rigorous practice (Human Rights Watch, 2001). State legislatures should be urged to enact legislation to protect students from discrimination, harassment, and violence based on homophobia and antihomosexual bias. If current legislators cannot or choose not to do so, legislators need to be elected who can and will (Human Rights Watch, 2001).

State universities should ensure that all programs leading to teacher certification in elementary, secondary, and special education (and endorsements for teaching the gifted) provide training in working with diverse students, including those who are gay, lesbian, bisexual, transgendered, or even simply questioning their sexual orientation and sexual identity (Human Rights Watch, 2001). Federal and state governments must pass bills designed to protect educators and school staff from discrimination in employment based on sexual orientation and gender identity (Human Rights Watch, 2001).

In all school settings, students should have access to up-to-date and accurate information about issues of sexual orientation and gender identity. This information should include works produced by gay youths themselves. Gay–straight alliances and other school-based support groups should be encouraged, placed on equal footing with other school groups, and publicized in such a way that students know about them and are comfortable participating in them. Age-appropriate discussions should be integrated into relevant subjects areas, such as history, literature, and current affairs.[1]

Only when schools model and teach respect for all will society truly benefit from the gifts and talents of all its members, all of whom are born free and equal in dignity and human rights (Human Rights Watch, 2001).

---

[1]For a detailed listing of practical and immediate actions that can be taken by all levels of government in U.S. society, the reader is directed to pages 5–16 of the Human Rights Watch (2001) report.

REFERENCES

American Psychiatric Association. (1994). *Diagnostic and statistical manual of mental disorders* (4th ed.). Washington, DC: American Psychiatric Association.

Benbow, C. (1988). Sex differences in mathematical reasoning ability in intellectually talented preadolescents: Their nature, effects, and possible causes. *Behavioral and Brain Sciences, 11,* 169–232.

Bowman, D. (2001). Report says schools often ignore harassment of gay students. *Education Week, 20*(39), 1.

Bransford, J., Brown, A., & Cocking, R. (Eds.). (1999). *How people learn: Brain, mind, experience, and school.* Washington, DC: National Academy Press.

Carter, K. (1997, June). Gay slurs abound. *Des Moines Register,* p. 1.

D'Augelli, A. (1998). Developmental implications of victimization of lesbian, gay, and bisexual youths. In G. Herek (Ed.), *Stigma and sexual orientation: Understanding prejudice against lesbians, gay men, and bisexuals* (Vol. 4, pp. 187–210). Thousand Oaks, CA: Sage.

Fox, L., Brody, L., & Tobin, D. (Eds.). (1980). Women and the mathematical mystique: *Proceedings of the eighth annual Hyman Blumberg Symposium on Research in Early Childhood Education.* Baltimore: Johns Hopkins University Press.

Franklin, K. (1998). Understanding motivations: Contextualizing the narratives of antigay assailants. In G. Herek (Ed.), *Stigma and sexual orientation: Understanding prejudice against lesbians, gay men, and bisexuals* (Vol. 4, pp. 1–23). Thousand Oaks, CA: Sage.

Friedrichs, T. (1997). Understanding the educational needs of gifted gay and bisexual males. *Counseling and Guidance, 6*(3), 8.

Gibson, P. I. (1989). Gay male and lesbian youth suicide. In *Report of the secretary's task force on youth suicide* (pp. 110–142). Washington, DC: U.S. Department of Health and Human Services.

Gladue, B., Beatty, W., Larson, J., & Staton, R. (1990). Sexual orientation and spatial ability in men and women. *Psychobiology, 18*(1), 101–108.

Haaga, D. (1991). Homophobia? *Journal of Social Behavior and Personality, 6*(1), 171–174.

Halpern, D. (1992). *Sex differences in cognitive abilities* (2nd ed.). Hillsdale, NJ: Erlbaum.

Halpern, D., & Wright, T. (1996). A process-oriented model of sex differences in cognitive sex differences. In D. F. Halpern (Ed.), Psychological and psychobiological perspectives on sex differences in cognition. *Learning and Individual Differences, 8,* 3–24 [Special double issue].

Herek, G. (Ed.). (1998). *Stigma and sexual orientation: Understanding prejudice against lesbians, gay men, and bisexuals.* Thousand Oaks, CA: Sage.

Horowitz, A. (2001). Addressing homophobic behavior in the classroom. *Education Week, 20*(39), 38.

Human Rights Watch. (2001). *Hatred in the hallways: Violence and discrimination against lesbian, gay, bisexual, and transgender students in U.S. schools.* New York: Human Rights Watch.

Kerr, B. (1994). *Smart girls: A new psychology of girls, women, and giftedness* (Rev. ed.). Scottsdale, AZ: Great Potential Press.

Kerr, B., & Cohn, S. (2001). *Smart boys: Talent, manhood, and the search for meaning.* Scottsdale, AZ: Great Potential Press.

Lipkin, A. (1999). *Understanding homosexuality, changing schools.* Boulder, CO: Westview Press.

McCormick, C., & Witelson, S. (1991). A cognitive profile of homosexual men compared with heterosexual men and women. *Psychoneuroendocrinology, 15,* 459–473.

Peterson, J., & Rischar, H. (2000). Gifted and gay: A study of the adolescent experience. *Gifted Child Quarterly, 44*(4), 231–246.

Piechowski, M. (1975). A theoretical and empirical approach to the study of development. *Genetic Psychology Monographs, 92,* 231–297.

Plummer, D. (1999). *One of the boys: Masculinity, homophobia, and modern manhood.* New York: Harrington Park Press.

Russell, S., & Joyner, K. (2001). Adolescent sexual orientation and suicide risk: Evidence from a national study. *American Journal of Public Health, 91*(8), 1276–1281.

Sanders, G., & Ross-Field, L. (1986). Sexual orientation and visual–spatial ability. *Brain and Cognition, 5,* 280–290.

Savin-Williams, R. (1990). *Gay and lesbian youth: Expressions of identity.* New York: Hemisphere.

Savin-Williams, R. (1998). *"…And then I became gay:" Young men's stories.* New York: Rutledge.

Stanley, J. (1993). Boys and girls who reason well mathematically. In G. R. B. K. Ackrill (Ed.), *The origins and development of high ability* (pp. 119–138). Chichester, England: Wiley.

Tolan, S. (1997). Sex and the highly gifted adolescent. *Counseling, 6*(3), 2, 5, 8.

Tuttle, G., & Pillard, R. (1991). Sexual orientation and cognitive abilities. *Archives of Sexual Behavior, 20*(3), 307–318.

Unks, G. (Ed.). (1995). *The gay teen: Educational practice and theory for lesbian, gay, and bisexual adolescents.* New York: Rutledge.

Weinberg, G. (1972). *Society and the healthy homosexual.* Boston: Alyson Publications.

Willmott, M., & Brierly, H. (1984). Cognitive characteristics and homosexuality. *Archives of Sexual Behavior, 13*(4), 311–319.

10 Serving the Economically Disadvantaged in Gifted Education

The Palm Beach County Story

JAIME A. CASTELLANO
ANNE FAIVUS
WILL WHITE

Economically disadvantaged students are among the most underserved in gifted education. In results obtained by the National Educational Longitudinal Study (NELS), students from the bottom quartile in family income made up only 10 percent of gifted and talented program participants, whereas students from the top quartile made up 50 percent (Resnick & Goodman, 1997). Certainly, since the 1950s, there has been a recognition that this underrepresentation of minorities and the poor in talent pools constituted a waste that society simply could not afford. Efforts have been made to reverse this pattern, but they have been sparse and unsustainable (Passow, 1991). Is there a difference 10 years later? Certainly, the number of students identified and served in gifted education programs has grown substantially during this time period. However, the research is clear. Students from economically disadvantaged families continue to be excluded.

This chapter outlines how one Florida school district developed a program to serve economically disadvantaged gifted students found in 10 of their most poverty stricken (elementary) schools and communities. Highlighted are events leading to the expansion of program delivery models, or continuum of services, professional development and training, curriculum and instruction, and parent/community involvement, among others. The results of this effort validates the fact that gifted and talented students can be found in every school and in every community if an organized process is put in place with appropriate supporting infrastructure. By working collaboratively, primary stakeholders can make a difference in the lives of the most poverty stricken students who are gifted.

Gifted Education for the Economically Disadvantaged: What the Research Says

The reasons for underrepresentation of certain student groups from gifted education are well documented, despite the fact that gifted children can be found in every racial, ethnic, economic, and linguistic group (Castellano, 1998; Stephens & Karnes, 2000). The identification of gifted characteristics, and criteria used to identify and evaluate student potential, is at the bottom of the problem. This problem is most evident in the assessment phase of students considered for gifted education programming. The majority of early gifted programs consisted of white students who attained the needed IQ score that assured their entrance and subsequent participation. IQ scores, however, continue to serve as an exclusionary measure shutting out large percentages of poor and other culturally and linguistically diverse students. Ultimately, this practice exacerbates issues of inequity and often eliminates any opportunity of gifted placement for many of these students.

Gifted students can be found in all segments of society. Socioeconomic status (SES), race, and being disadvantaged are typically discussed together because they tend to confound each other (Coleman & Cross, 2001). Compounding issues of underrepresentation is the focus on homogeneity rather than heterogeneity in identifying poor and minority gifted children. Group stereotypes are perpetuated because of the tendency to characterize all members of a minority group with the attributes of group members who perform the least well (Banks, 1993; Kitano & Kirby, 1986; Tonemah, 1987; in Davis & Rimm, 1998).

In a study conducted by VanTassel-Baska, Olszewski-Kubilius, and Kulieke (1994), 147 gifted seventh and eight graders, of whom 97 were considered middle SES and 50 lower SES, and 56 were African American and 91 Caucasian, the following conclusions were made: (1) Self-esteem tends to be high among gifted students regardless of ethnicity, gender, or socioeconomic class; (2) the greatest differences were found between advantaged and disadvantaged students, supporting the concept that class may be more important than ethnicity in impending achievement (disadvantaged students believed they had less support from classmates; they also felt less academically and socially competent); and (3) gender differences were found, with females feeling less academically and socially competent and believing they received less social support from classmates than did their male counterparts.

From a program perspective, the conflict in values that often exists between the school and the home and community is a real one. What was true in 1970 is still true today. That is, disadvantaged students must sometimes deal with problems of at least two different value systems. As the Housing, Education, and Welfare Urban Education Task Force put it:

> Daily, the disadvantaged child must thread his way through the set of values that the school espouses and the set that he lives with and has learned from his family

and neighborhood. He must develop and carry out strategies that permit him to survive in both worlds without being overwhelmed by the conflict diverse value systems can produce. The extent to which he survives as a whole with a strong and stable self-concept and a sense of worth will be dependent on the quality and reality orientation of the strategies he employs. (p. 39)

The conflict in values is further compounded if the student is gifted. Often, gifted students who are disadvantaged, poor, or minority are ostracized by their peers for demonstrating advanced cognitive and academic ability.

Events Leading to the Expansion of Services: School District of Palm Beach County, Florida

Along with the poor, other groups of students that were, and continue to be, underrepresented in the gifted education programs of the school district of Palm Beach County include African Americans, Hispanics, Haitians, Native Americans/Indigenous, and the limited English speaking. As a result, in 1994 an official complaint was submitted to the Office for Civil Rights (OCR), which concurred with the plaintiff that the school district was excluding certain student groups. The district was then mandated to correct past practices.

At the time of the federal OCR complaint, the Department of Exceptional Student Education (ESE) requested administrative support and school board approval to have the gifted education program evaluated by a team of nationally recognized experts. In December 1997, the evaluation team directed a school board workshop on the importance of program evaluation and outlined the process that would be used. In January 1998, a team of four evaluators with expertise in gifted education visited elementary, middle, and high school classrooms and interviewed students, teachers, administrators, and parents. An evening meeting was held in the boardroom to explain the process to parents and to solicit their questions and concerns. The final report validated what was already known about underrepresentation in the district: Poor, culturally, and linguistically diverse students were being excluded from programs serving the gifted.

In July 1998, an independent report written by the National Coalition of Advocates for Students titled A Gathering Storm accentuated the need to increase the number of underrepresented students in the gifted education program. Coupled with the OCR complaint and the problems documented in the final program evaluation report, the superintendent issued a directive that a writing team would be selected representing the ethnicity and diversity of the school district to develop a continuum of services for gifted students. This writing team met over a 4-month period to review the identification and evaluation procedures.

To address the issues documented by the OCR, the program evaluation final report, and the Gathering Storm report, 10 elementary schools with high numbers of poor and minority students were chosen in March 1999 to participate in a program designed to increase their numbers in the district's gifted education program. Finally, in May 1999 the Department of Exceptional Student Education formed a second writing team to develop a specific implementation plan for a continuum of services to be implemented in the 2000–2001 school year. The plan would address staff development needs and the creation of a feeder pattern system to improve and expand gifted services in Palm Beach County. The 10 elementary schools chosen to be part of the gifted education program continuum would be priorities of both the writing team and gifted education program administrators.

Choosing the Schools Participating in the Expansion of Services

The school district of Palm Beach County is the fourth-largest school district in Florida and the fourteenth-largest in the United States. The district, which covers a geographic area approximately the size of Rhode Island, is currently serving more than 155,000 kindergarten through grade 12 students and 3,000 prekindergarten students in its 150 schools. There are approximately 19,000 employees and the annual budget is more than $2 billion. Furthermore, approximately 35,000 students are being served through Title I programs in kindergarten through twelfth grade with a budget for the 2001–2002 school year totaling $13.87 million. The overall poverty rate of students is about 50 percent.

The choice of schools to participate in the expansion of services was a difficult one. Senior level administrators needed to consider the demographics of the school district, to ensure that all ethnic groups and geographic areas were included. Members of the gifted education program writing team and district administrators were lobbied by special interest groups and principals, who were promoting their own school centers for selection. The stakes were high. Selected schools would be able to house and service their own gifted students identified as part of the expansion of services. Prior to the expansion, students identified as gifted at these schools were transferred to another school housing a full-time gifted program. This meant the sending school was losing their brightest students and potentially high standardized test scores to another school center.

In March 1999, each of five area superintendents selected two elementary schools from each of their respective areas to be part of the expansion of services. The criteria used for the selection of schools included number of African American, Hispanic, and limited English proficient (LEP) students, in addition to the school's poverty rate. Table 10.1 lists the selected schools and the percentages of students in each area. In addition, selected schools had histories of low-test performance, high percentages of at-risk students, high mobility rates, and frequent teacher turnover. All are further classified as Title I schools.

TABLE 10.1   Gifted Education Program Pilot Schools, 1999–2000

Schools	African American (percentage)	Hispanic (percentage)	LEP (percentage)	Low SES Free/ Reduced Lunch (percentage)
Area 1				
Plumosa	45.19	15.01	18.9	66.72
Forest Park	56.71	10.53	32.7	71.86
Area 2				
Rolling Green	52.64	28.28	43.6	82.94
Barton	60.47	28.51	46.5	90.59
Area 3				
Palmetto	9.53	67.73	52.1	84.11
Westward	80.17	5.91	17.6	81.71
Area 4				
Pahokee	72.15	24.88	18.9	94.92
Rosenwald	69.56	28.32	14.9	94.56
Area 5				
Lake Park	76.26	3.65	29.9	89.02
West Riviera	92.55	2.63	7.7	83.73

In Florida, each public elementary school is assigned a grade of A, B, C, D, or F, based on how well students enrolled in grade 4 perform on a state assessment in reading and writing, and how students in grade 5 perform on a state assessment in mathematics. The test results of each school are front-page material for the local newspapers. School centers cannot afford to lose their best and brightest students to other schools. The stakes are too high. This message was repeated time and again by principals. Some of them suggested that, in schools with large numbers of poor and minority students, losing the most talented students creates a brain drain of sorts and puts them at a disadvantage when they are graded by the state based on how well their students perform on state assessments of academic achievement.

Professional Development and Training

The implementation of any new program necessitates short-term and long-term staff development and training to ensure its success. Once the schools were selected it was decided that, initially, training would occur for all teachers of students in kindergarten through second grade, in addition to all teachers of English language learners. In April 1999, 230 teachers of kindergarten through second grade, ESE school-based contacts, and teachers of English language learners participated in a 1-day training program on characteristics and identification of students from historically underrepresented populations. This was only the beginning.

Additional staff development training was provided to parties involved in the process of implementing the continuum of services for the gifted. Persons receiving information and training included the following groups:

1. School-level personnel: ESE school-based contacts, administrators, and teachers (especially staff at full-time cluster sites and part-time resource sites, including the newly selected schools).
2. Area office staff: ESE team leader, resource teachers, administrators, and school psychologists.
3. District office personnel: Program planners, curriculum specialists, and resource teachers.
4. Individuals outside of the school system: Parents, private psychologists, preschool and other private school personnel, the media, and the general public.

Because of the great diversity found among the groups, including their experience, or lack of experience, regarding gifted education, staff development training was delivered to appropriate persons or groups based on their level of need in the following areas:

1. General information about gifted characteristics, indicators of giftedness, eligibility criteria, and program delivery.
2. Specific detailed information about identification, eligibility criteria, and state or district requirements and procedures.
3. Specific information about the child study team, eligibility staffing, development of a student's gifted educational plan (EP), and determination of the need for gifted program services.
4. Design and implementation of gifted programs.

Furthermore, the following training was also provided:

August, 1999. Fifty K–2 and English to speakers of other languages (ESOL) teachers from the new gifted centers participated in a 1-week summer institute that was arranged as a cooperative effort by the departments of ESE, federal programs, and multicultural awareness. Three national consultants provided additional information to the institute participants.

February–May, 2000. Workshops on the implementation plan for the new gifted centers, including long-term plans for gifted education were held for all elementary principals, area resource teachers, school psychologists, and school-based ESE contacts.

June, 2000. A 5-day summer institute, equity and excellence, was offered for teachers in the gifted pilot schools. Presentations included state and district policies, state academic standards (Sunshine State Standards), implementing the resource room model, and curriculum differentiation. Concurrent workshop sessions included alternative assessments, interest inventories, learning styles, grouping, curriculum compacting, problem solving, creative thinking, and higher-order thinking skills.

June, 2001. An opportunity for continued training was offered to both teachers of the gifted pilot schools and those teaching in other gifted education program delivery models. Focus topics included state and district policies, curriculum and instructional differentiation, curriculum compacting, problem solving, creative thinking, and higher-order thinking skills.

Finally, gifted courses for Florida endorsement in gifted education were offered to any district teacher for a nominal fee during the fall, spring, and summer. The five courses leading to the gifted education endorsement include (1) Nature and Needs of Gifted Students, (2) Special Populations of Gifted Learners, (3) Guidance and Counseling Gifted Students, (4) Creativity, and (5) Meeting the Curricular and Instructional Needs of Gifted Students. As of June 2001, more than 200 teachers have received endorsement in gifted education.

From Nomination and Screening to Assessment and Eligibility

After months of planning and implementing a strategic staff development agenda the district was ready to initiate a process to identify a talent pool of students at each of the 10 elementary schools being considered for their new gifted education programs. Every student enrolled in kindergarten through second grade would be academically screened with the Otis-Lennon School Abilities Test (OLSAT). Non-English or LEP students in these grades would be screened with the Raven's Standard Progressive Matrices. A joint recommendation was made by the school district's manager for psychological services, gifted education program administrators, and other building- and area-level staff to use a "cut score" to determine which students would move forward in the eligibility process. The following decision was made:

Otis-Lennon School Abilities Test (OLSAT)
In order to move forward in the identification process, students screened in grades K–2 needed a minimum standard score of 100 on the verbal or performance subtests of the OLSAT.

Raven's Standard Progressive Matrices
In order to move forward in the identification process, LEP students in grades K–2 needed to score 90 percent or higher on the Raven's Standard Progressive Matrices.

The screening of all kindergarten through second-grade students at each of the new gifted pilot schools accomplished its goal of identifying a talent pool. The evidence in Table 10.2 clearly demonstrates a dramatic difference when compared to the previous year when no screening instrument was administered. It is important to note that because these were new gifted programs, the school district assumed the total cost of every facet of the testing and scoring process.

Students who met the cut scores on the screening instruments were further evaluated with the math and reading subtests (subtests 22–25) of the Woodcock–Johnson Tests of Achievement or the Kaufman Test of Educational Achievement (K-TEA). The results, in the form of percentile ranks, were then placed accordingly on a matrix and the respective number of points was awarded. The gifted characteristics checklist used was one specific to historically underrepresented students. The checklist's place on the matrix is determined by the calculated score received after having added the totals and dividing it by the total number of items checked. If the characteristic was deemed unobservable it was not calculated in the total.

The district was legally required to use the matrix in Table 10.3 as per their Special Programs and Procedures Manual for Exceptional Students, which has been in effect since 1995. However, one change was made. Students of participating gifted pilot schools who totaled 21 points prior to the administration of an IQ test were determined eligible for the school's new gifted program and thus exempt from the IQ testing experience. Components of the Plan B Matrix for students enrolled in the gifted pilot schools are listed in Table 10.3.

The district's gifted education program administrators provided continued assistance to schools in the screening and evaluation process. They also worked with the ESE contact at each school in the administration of achievement tests.

TABLE 10.2   Otis-Lennon School Abilities Test (OLSAT): Administered in Pilot Schools (K–2)

Pilot School	1998–1999 Referrals for Gifted Education (K–5)	2000 OLSAT Screening (K–2)
Plumosa	16	124
Forest Park	13	116
Rolling Green	6	75
Barton	17	64
Palmetto	27	136
Westward	18	83
Pahokee	19	28
Rosenwald	12	71
Lake Park	14	75
West Riviera	20	130

TABLE 10.3 **Plan B Matrix for Pilot Schools**

	3 Points	4 Points	5 Points
Test scores			
Reading achievement	60–77	78–89	90–99
Math achievement	60–77	78–89	90–99
Gifted Behavioral Checklist	2.5–3.4	3.5–4.4	4.5–5.0
Classroom Performance (Average of Past 4 Quarters)			
Reading Grade	C(S)	B(VS)	A(E)
Math Grade	C(S)	B(VS)	A(E)
IQ Test by Licensed Psychologist	114–118	119–123	124 and Above
Totals			

Gifted Education Program Eligibility = 21 points

Once the tests have been scored, further assistance is given to the teachers of the gifted in the planning and scheduling of students for instruction.

One of the strengths of the identification and assessment process used at the new gifted pilot schools was the fact that students were tested by either an adult at the school center who knew and identified with the student or by a gifted program administrator with vast experience in testing culturally diverse students. A common observation by those involved with the testing of these economically disadvantaged students was that many of them did have high intellectual ability but fewer educationally nurturing experiences.

The adjustments made to the matrix for the new gifted pilot schools did, in fact, increase the number of students eligible for gifted education. However, many issues were discussed, debated, and scrutinized throughout the planning, organizing, and implementation of the pilot school program. With specific regard to the identification and assessment process, the concerns included the following:

1. Arguably, OLSAT is seen by many as an inappropriate screening instrument for identifying potential candidates from poor, minority, and other culturally and linguistically diverse student populations for gifted education. However, the commitment to purchase this instrument was made. Furthermore, many of the testing coordinators indicated the importance of having additional adults present during the actual testing of kindergarten, first, and second graders because these students are not well versed in taking standardized tests. Nonetheless, as seen in Table 10.2, it did provide each school with a substantial talent pool of students to further consider.

2. The Raven's Standard Progressive Matrices was administered to kindergarten students who were identified as possible candidates for gifted education

and who were also LEP. This practice was contrary to the information found in the test administration manual. Specifically, norms for interpreting results are based on a chronological age beginning with an age of 6 years, 6 months (p. SPM74). As a result, it can only be speculated how many LEP kindergarten students were eliminated for consideration.

3. Communication between teachers who share LEP students, in most cases between the ESOL and regular education teacher, was inconsistent in some of the gifted pilot schools. When a nomination was made by an ESOL teacher, he or she was responsible for completing the appropriate gifted characteristics checklist. In some instances the regular education teacher did not agree with the final checklist result, thus negatively affecting the matrix score.

Expanding the Continuum of Services

The pilot program model was implemented in the 1999–2000 school year in 10 elementary schools to identify and serve poor, minority, and other culturally and linguistically diverse groups of students who had not been served in existing gifted programs. The pilot program model addresses specific academic strengths of gifted students through instruction in a resource room model. In the Pilot School Model

1. All kindergarten through second-grade teachers and ESOL teachers received extensive training in the identification of gifted students and strategies for developing academic talent in diverse gifted learners.
2. Teachers implementing the model received ongoing technical assistance to ensure the success of the program.
3. Enrichment and acceleration were provided for resource room students to support their curriculum program.
4. Flexible grouping patterns (performance, interest, and multiage) was used to optimize learning.

Furthermore, certain advantages are offered through this send-out type of resource model. Gifted students, for example, are grouped with their intellectual peers, an integral component of high-quality programming for this population of students. The model is flexible enough to tailor curriculum and instruction to the abilities and interests of individual students. It also offers the opportunity for cooperation between regular classroom teachers and gifted education teachers. Of particular importance is the fact that this model allows students with uneven academic development to participate in regular education classrooms for grade-appropriate skills and in the resource room for skill-area strengths.

To further prepare for the students in this new program delivery model, implementation goals were established. After much discussion, the consensus was that an effective resource room should provide the following:

1. Enrichment activities that both enhance the grade-appropriate curriculum and reflect students' interests.
2. Accelerated learning opportunities that challenge students' strengths appropriately.
3. A learning environment that requires the application of higher-level thinking skills and develops divergent and creative thinking essential to problem-solving life experiences.
4. Activities that stimulate students to extend learning well beyond the regular classroom and that are commensurate with their abilities.

With the implementation of this pilot program model, the school district has expanded its range of options for students who are gifted in order to support each student's level of educational need, as determined by their education plan (EP). Besides the Pilot Program Model, other models include the following: (1) inclusive education model, which is implemented in the regular classroom with the teacher providing a number of curricular options including curriculum compacting, alternative assignments, independent study, and grouping for instruction (this model is appropriate for students who are identified as gifted but have only one or two areas of strength); (2) the resource room model, which is implemented as a send-out program from the regular classroom for a portion of the day for students who are excelling at a level the classroom teacher cannot easily challenge; and (3) the gifted center model, which groups gifted students together in classes for the entire school day (this model is appropriate for students who need the challenge of a comprehensive curriculum above the level of need for their age peers).

Curriculum and Instruction

To meet the special needs of students enrolled in the pilot program model, qualitatively different instruction was planned. Qualitatively different instruction refers to those learning experiences that reflect the development of critical and creative thinking skills, content acceleration, and affective education. Mere quantity of work is not desired.

According to Burnette (1999), there are many school factors that affect the success of culturally diverse students: the school's atmosphere and overall attitudes toward diversity, involvement of the community, and culturally responsive curriculum, to name a few. Of all of these factors, the personal and academic relationships between teachers and their students may be the most influential. This relationship has been referred to as the "core relationship" of learning: the roles of teachers and students, the subject matter, and their interaction in the classroom.

Furthermore, she notes that certain behaviors and instructional strategies enable teachers to build a stronger teaching/learning relationship with their culturally diverse students. Many of these behaviors and strategies exemplify standard practices of good teaching, and others are specific to working with students from diverse cultures.

Teacher Behaviors
1. Appreciate and accommodate the similarities and differences among the students' cultures.
2. Build relationships with students.
3. Focus on the ways students learn and observe students identifying their task orientation.
4. Teach students to match their behaviors to the setting.

Instructional Strategies
1. Use a variety of instructional strategies and learning activities.
2. Consider students' culture and language skills when developing learning objectives and instructional activities.
3. Incorporate objectives for affective and personal development.
4. Communicate expectations.
5. Provide rationales.
6. Use advance- and postorganizers.
7. Provide frequent reviews of the content learned.
8. Facilitate independence in thinking and action.
9. Promote student on-task behavior.

Patterns of behavior in underachievement must also be studied in working with diverse gifted learners. Once this is understood, teachers can target achievement motivation and capitalize on the idea that successful gifted students from disadvantaged populations are highly motivated.

Parent Involvement and Working With Other Stakeholders

As part of Palm Beach County's commitment to include more historically underrepresented students in gifted education, a brochure and letter outlining procedures for nomination, screening, and eligibility was sent to all parents of students in kindergarten through eighth grade (100,000). The brochure and letter were translated into Spanish, Creole, and Portuguese. As a result, the district's gifted education administrative team fielded phone calls and other correspondences conducted or sent in other languages, in record numbers. Information is power. Gifted education personnel noted that once parents received the information referrals and nominations increased across the district, including those communities where the gifted pilot models were located. The number of phone calls and inquiries from non-English speaking parents also increased.

In the gifted pilot schools a special effort was made to incorporate the participation of parents or guardians. If a child is to have a positive experience in the newly formed gifted program, parent involvement was going to be important, especially considering the social and personal realities of the children's everyday life. Teachers needed to understand the family patterns contributing to the home, school, and community connection. They include unstable families; lower-socioeconomic status, single-parent households; families with limited social/educational opportunities; inconsistent parenting; and the lack of appropriate behavior modeling for educational attainment. And for at least two of the participating schools, geographic isolation was an issue. In every school, however, teachers tried to stress the role of the parent as an encourager.

The Results: Is There a Difference?

The process for admission into a program for the gifted is a complex one at best. Across the United States, theories, approaches, guidelines, and plans vary, but as more poor, minority, and other culturally and linguistically diverse students enter the schools, it is imperative to have programs in place to identify and educate the most gifted, or those that demonstrate the strongest potential. If this does not happen, the personal and human loss as so many fail to realize their talents is both a sad indictment of educators' shortcomings and the impetus needed to double efforts to provide everyone a chance to excel. This is particularly true for students found in the most poverty stricken and economically deprived communities, such as those found in the pilot schools.

Most of the students found in the participating pilot schools share a background that is in vast contrast to those white, middle- or upper-middle-class students. This does not necessarily mean that they are not eligible for public school programs serving gifted students. We have proven that in our efforts to include more underrepresented students in our own gifted programs. The numbers in Table 10.4 demonstrate that hard work and commitment to equity and access had paid off. More than 400 students have gone through a comprehensive nomination, screening, and testing process to become eligible for gifted education.

It is very likely that these students would have never had the opportunity if not for the decision to impact those participating schools. The gifted programs have transformed the schools themselves, moving from the stereotype of having students who cannot learn, to the reality of having a program that offers hope and encouragement to the most able students.

Summary and Conclusion

If giftedness is to be nurtured, then schools must create a climate for excellence for all, one in which a variety of outstanding talents are understood, valued, and rewarded. Moreover, the affective aspects of talent development must be assigned a high priority in planning and implementation. This requires greater sensitivity to the cultural context of teaching and learning (Passow, 1991).

TABLE 10.4   Students Eligible and Served in Gifted Education by Pilot School, 2000–2001

	African Americans	Haitians/ Haitian Americans	Hispanics	Whites	Other	F/R Lunch	LEP Students	Total
Plumosa Elementary	7	3	10	5	0	16	0	25
Rolling Green Elementary	15	10	13	5	0	31	2	43
Barton Elementary	14	21	9	4	1	49	0	49
Palmetto Elementary	4	0	75	13	3	86	38	95
Westward Elementary	25	8	5	4	2	21	15	44
Pahokee Elementary	23	0	9	0	0	30	1	32
Rosenwald Elementary	12	0	5	0	3	20	0	20
Lake Park Elementary	22	8	0	9	3	40	0	42
West Riviera Elementary	61	2	1	1	4	61	0	69
								419
	183	52	127	41	16	354	56	
	419	419	419	419	419	419	419	
	44%	12%	30%	10%	4%	84%	13%	

Note: Forest Park Elementary School was dropped as a pilot school in the fall of 2000.
Unduplicated counts appear in white cells.

It is often said that youth is the greatest natural resource of a great nation. Through the gifted program the preparation of youth as productive citizens and critical thinkers ensures that the future of the United States is in good hands. Times are changing. Educators are beginning to realize that the collaboration and promotion of inclusionary identification practices in gifted education results in a win–win situation. No other program is best suited to represent diversity in terms of socioeconomic status, intelligence, language, and ethnicity than gifted education.

REFERENCES

Burnette, J. (1999, November). *Critical behaviors and strategies for teaching culturally diverse students.* ERIC Digest: ERIC Clearinghouse on Disabilities and Gifted Education. EDO-99-12. Reston, VA: The Council for Exceptional Children.

Castellano, J. A. (1998). *Identifying and assessing gifted and talented bilingual Hispanic students.* (ERIC Document Reproduction Service No. Ed 423 104). Reston, VA: ERIC Clearing House on Disabilities and Gifted Education.

Coleman, L. J., & Cross, T. L. (2001). *Being gifted in school: An introduction to development, guidance, and teaching.* Waco, TX: Prufrock Press.

Davis, G. A., & Rimm, S. B. (1998). *Education of the gifted and talented.* Boston: Allyn & Bacon.

HEW Urban Education Task Force. (1970). *Urban school crisis: The problems and solutions.* Washington, DC: Washington Monitoring Service.

National Coalition of Advocates for Students. (1998). *A gathering storm: How Palm Beach county schools fail poor and minority students.* Boston: Palm Beach County Community Reporting Initiative.

Passow, A. H. (1991). Educational programs for minority/disadvantaged gifted students. In R. Jenkins-Friedman, E. S. Richert, & J. F. Feldhusen (Eds.), *Special populations of gifted learners: A book of readings* (pp. 1–19). Unionville, NY: Trillium Press.

Resnick, D., & Goodman, M. (1997, Fall). *Northwest education.* Portland, OR: Northwest Education Laboratory Resources.

Stephens, K. R., & Karnes, F. A. (2000). State definitions for the gifted and talented revisited. *Exceptional Children, 66*(2), 219–238.

VanTassel-Baska, J., Olszewski-Kubilius, P., & Kulieke, M. (1994). A study of self-concept and social support in advantaged and disadvantaged seventh and eighth grade gifted students. *Roeper Review, 16,* 186–191.

11 When the Gifts Are Camouflaged by Disability

Identifying and Developing the Talent in Gifted Students with Disabilities

TERRY NEU

Our perceptions or expectations of gifted students can sometimes hide or camouflage the above-average abilities of students in U.S. classrooms. For instance, how can a student be gifted when she or he has difficulty achieving or behaving in the classroom? Stereotypically, the gifted child is seen by many as the perfect student whose talents are easily recognized. This isn't always the case because of a myriad of factors that affect giftedness.

Further complicating the issue of giftedness is attempting to identify gifted students with disabilities. On close examination and under the appropriate conditions, many traits and characteristics describing gifted students are readily apparent in students with disabilities. For instance, Carl is described by his English teacher as a class clown, below grade level in reading, never on task, and disturbing others in class. However, in a different environment, such as a classroom in which the instruction is not in direct conflict with Carl's learning disability, different behaviors are evidenced. Carl's science teachers describe him as a student who asks probing questions, readily takes on any experiment, and is a voracious consumer of knowledge. Students such as Carl demonstrate both gifted behaviors—keen interests, high levels of creativity, superior abilities in abstract thinking, and high problem-solving ability—and learning problems because of physical, cognitive, or behavioral deficits (Baum, Cooper, & Neu, 2001; National Association for Gifted Children [NAGC], 1998).

Too often schools focus on the disability because teachers have seen the students only in a restricted environment where their gifts were camouflaged. These students are often removed from mainstream educational settings and placed in special classes or special schools in which the students have limited, if any, access to existing gifted education programs. Even in school systems with a liberal definition of giftedness, identification of students who exhibit both gifted behaviors and special needs is a rarity (Baum, Owen, & Dixon, 1991; Davis & Rimm, 1989; Neu, 1993).

In studies that have investigated this camouflaged population of learners a theme does emerge: Programmatic interventions suggest the importance of providing these students with a curriculum that accommodates their unique gifts and talents while simultaneously allowing the students to compensate for problematic weaknesses (Baldwin & Gargiulo, 1983; Baum & Owen, 1988; Olenchak, 1994; Reis & Neu, 1994; Whitmore & Maker, 1985).

To address this dilemma of identification, the highlights of four case studies are presented. Each of these individuals was first identified for his or her disability, and only later were these students' demonstrated gifted behaviors recognized. Their gifted behaviors are presented first so that the effect of the camouflaging behaviors can be better understood.

Jason: Gifted and Deaf

Jason is a blond-haired teen, full of energy and quick with a smile. He is an expert mime, and his facial expressions can turn an entire room of students to laughing. He is an accomplished artist and enjoys directing others in painting murals or backdrops of sets for school productions.

Jason's real passion is acting, however. When faced with an environmental problem on his school's campus, Jason formed a group to create a videotaped infomercial to describe the devastating effects of pollutants in the pond. Jason himself took on the role of narrator, portraying the spirit of the water. He introduced viewers to other students portraying life-forms as they told their story of the hardships of living in a polluted pond. The video was shown to the school board as part of a presentation of the pond problem. Jason's group plan was accepted and implemented on a limited financial scale.

In viewing the video one might wonder what is unusual about the narrator. Jason is deaf, and reading and writing are a struggle for him. Jason's exceptional abilities are unknown to his teachers; these abilities are camouflaged by his deafness and learning disability. Unfortunately, in teacher interviews, their comments about Jason centered on his inability to stay on task, his below-grade-level reading skills, and his behaviors that could be indicators of attention deficit disorder.

John: Gifted and Oppositional Defiant

John typically finished his math worksheets earlier than his classmates did. On one occasion he finished a ditto of 30 math problems and proceeded to take his paper to the teacher's desk. John was making strategic stops along the way, picking up materials. On reaching the teacher's desk, he deposited the worksheet without the teacher's looking up and continued his meandering journey through the classroom in search of supplies.

The sixth-grade class had been studying the Middle Ages, and John had become fascinated with catapults. He decided to build one. John had spied the bits of string, a pencil, paper clips, electrical wire, and popsicle sticks that had been lying around the room. He drew a crude blueprint based on the available parts. After procuring them, he set about constructing his private siege engine while his classmates continued working on the math worksheet. As his classmates were turning in their seatwork, John's teacher began to grade the worksheets. Meanwhile, John had completed his catapult and proceeded to fire paper wads at his classmates, an activity not observed by his teacher.

Although John had been identified for the gifted and talented education program for his above-average mathematical abilities and his artistic talent, which had already been recognized in several local art competitions, he had never been placed in the program. After all, John acted out in class. At one point in the semester he threw a desk across the room. His disruptive behaviors continually cast a cloud hiding his gifted behaviors. John had been identified with oppositional defiant disorder, which school personnel chose to address. His giftedness had been ignored completely.

Darla: Gifted and Dyslexic

Darla is an amazing athlete, leading her school in several sports. She is also clever with her hands—whether in art class or helping her father in his wood shop. Darla found a special challenge in engineering. She loved to build with Legos and even took apart all the locks on the doors of her house and reassembled them in perfect working order.

When given the opportunity to try out for the Odyssey of the Mind (OM) team, Darla amazed teachers with her solutions to spontaneous problems. She chose to work on an OM problem involving building a 10-inch tower of balsa wood sticks that would support as much weight as possible. At the state OM competition Darla's team finished in second place. Their structure, which weighed less than 40 grams, held more than 116 pounds before it finally collapsed.

Diagnosed with dyslexia, Darla struggled through the academic part of school. Her mother expressed her frustration with the education system this way:

> They said that she was working up to the best of her ability; that was the biggest phrase I have heard all through school. You have no idea how frustrating that can be with a child who appears bright, but you can't get any help for them.

While she was a leader on the sport field and the OM team, Darla deliberately tried to disappear in the classroom. Years of academic failure had trained her not to participate and to keep the attention away from a public presentation of her disability.

Donna: Gifted and Pervasive Developmental Disorder not Otherwise Specified (PDDNOS)

Donna has shoulder-length brown hair and a light complexion. She wears glasses and appears shy at first observation. Once one is able to engage her in conversation, the extent of her advanced vocabulary becomes evident. She was nominated in second grade for the gifted and talented education program, based on testing results of a full scale IQ of 142.

Donna finished the *Lord of the Rings Trilogy* in the third grade and made a 15-minute claymation video summarizing *The Hobbit*. In seventh grade she completed an 8-week study of captive cheetahs in a local zoo and placed third in her district's science fair, the only middle school student to advance to that level of competition.

This student is in a special pull-out program that serves five special needs students at the middle school level. This class arrangement allows the classroom teacher and her aide more time to work one on one with these students. Donna can prove to be quite a challenge; her vocabulary is extensive but her social skills are very poor. She requires an aide to escort her down the hall when the bell rings because she often becomes disoriented in large crowds and starts to lash out at others. Despite her high IQ, she has been classified as having pervasive developmental disorder not otherwise specified and is receiving special education services to address this condition. Donna's gifts, however, are *not* being addressed.

Talent Discovery: Exposure and Identification

With these camouflaging conditions in mind, one may ask how instruction can be provided that will enable educators to glimpse the possibly hidden talents. In 1993, with funding from Jacob K. Javits Gifted and Talented Student Education Act grant, research began to uncover an answer to this perplexing question. To reveal the gifted abilities of students with disabilities project High Hopes, a Javits Act project, developed a series of activities based on research that had identified two domains in which high-ability individuals with disabilities were pursuing successful careers. The first area the research identified was in the sciences and engineering. According to a position paper published in 1984 by the National Science Teachers Association, "the exclusion of any group or persons from access to science education…is an unnecessary and undesirable waste of human potential," Coble (1998). The importance of identifying science potential in the disabled is underscored by the prevalence of disabled intellectually gifted individuals who have succeeded in the sciences, such as Thomas Edison, Albert Einstein, Stephen Hawking, and John Horner.

The other productive field that research identified for disabled gifted individuals was in the arts. In project Search, for example, researchers Hokanson and Jospe (1976) found that students with disabilities identified as talented in the arts were meeting with success in a state-funded program. Further, Baum, Emerick, Herman, and Dixon (1989) discovered that gifted learning-disabled students demonstrated their exceptional abilities in visual, spatial, and dramatic arts. Today, for example, the John F. Kennedy Center for the Performing Arts in Washington, DC, recognizing that individuals with disabilities can be highly gifted in visual and performing arts, funds a special art gallery where many outstanding works are displayed. Another example of achievement by individuals with disabilities is the National Theater for the Deaf, a leading showcase of dramatic ability for the talented hearing impaired.

The Talent Discovery Assessment Process (TDAP)

Taking into consideration the needs of gifted students with disabilities, project High Hopes researchers realized that traditional testing procedures inhibited the opportunities for some of these students to display gifted behaviors. Influenced by Gardner's (1983, 1993) work on multiple intelligences and developmental identification (Baum et al., 1991; Karnes & Johnson, 1991), the talent discovery assessment process (TDAP) was designed to assess potential talent in the arts and sciences for special needs students in grades 5 through 8. It was based on the philosophy that potential talent is most accurately predicted by observations of behaviors over time when students are engaged in authentic activities within specific domains.

In the first year of project High Hopes students in these settings were screened for talent in the arts or sciences. Content specialists chosen from botany, dramatic arts, drawing, engineering/design, physics, sculpture, and zoology generated lists of behaviors that, when observed, indicated interest with each domain and across domains as well.

Early on, research showed that the targeted behaviors indicating domain-specific talents corresponded to Renzulli's (1977) three-ring conception of giftedness—above-average ability, creativity, and task commitment brought to bear on an area of a student's interest. Identified by the TDAP were domain-specific, observable behaviors of these traits as they related to engineering, dramatic arts, physical and life sciences, and the visual arts referred to previously and displayed in Table 11.1.

The project High Hopes identification process consisted of activities within each domain purposely designed to elicit these behaviors, which could then be observed and documented. These activities, conducted by content specialists in each domain, were administered during eight 90-minute sessions to groups of 10 or fewer students. Two specially trained observers documented and recorded instances or occurrences of the behaviors as individual students manifested them.

TABLE 11.1 Sample Behaviors Indicating Talent Potential

Engineering	Performing Arts	Science	Visual Arts
Actively manipulates materials	Uses expressive voice	Displays curiosity by asking relevant questions	Achieves balance in artwork
Explains the logic of alternate solutions	Shows clear communication of intent	Systematically tests hypotheses	Uses form (dimensionality) and design to produce the desired effect
Puts materials together in a unique way	Creates elaborate movements, characters, or skits	Tries to predict outcomes	Combines disparate parts to create a unique solution

Setting the Learning Environment

The first step in talent assessment is the creation of an appropriate environment in which to conduct these activities. Merely conducting these activities is not sufficient to identify student talent. The teacher must first organize the learning environment for maximal results. The following questions were helpful in achieving this goal:

- What is the appropriate physical arrangement of desks, tables, chairs, stools, and so on, to give each student ample space in which to work at an activity?
- What is the optimal group size for the activity?
- How have students been prepared emotionally for this activity?
- In what ways have students who may be somewhat apprehensive about the activity been encouraged to participate and assured of teacher understanding.
- To what degree is the climate for this activity calm, safe, and inviting?

These environmental conditions are essential—not only for the success of the activity but for student productivity as well. Hence, careful attention needed to be paid to the organization of the learning environment in which a particular identification activity was being conducted. These environmental conditions were precursors to those conditions created by the content specialist as the talent discovery session proceeded. To engage these students the content specialist did the following:

- Arranged the physical space to help students focus on the task.
- Maintained a small group size to encourage one-on-one participation.

- Eliminated the emphasis on reading and writing.
- Acted as a guide, not an instructor.
- Used experiential activities that promoted problem solving.
- Used visual cues.
- Promoted opportunities for lively discussion.

In order for domain-specific talents to emerge the learning environment needed to differ from what the student might have perceived as the regular classroom environment. The traditional classroom setting has long neglected common characteristics of students who are learning disabled, have emotional or behavioral disorders (EBD), attention deficit disorders, or are hearing impaired and, in so doing, has denied these gifted students with special needs the opportunities they required to display gifted behaviors. The intent of creating the optimal talent discovery environment was to ensure that, by employing appropriate techniques to enhance the expression of talent in specific domains, teachers circumvented problematic areas of the students' weaknesses.

As an example, during the biology observation session Donna was filled with awe. She and her classmates were presented with six different living specimens of local reptiles and amphibians. The content specialist presented the specimens with some guidance on scientific observation and encouraged the students to record their findings in words and, especially, in drawings.

Donna went to work immediately noticing the shape of the lizard's head, the movement of its eyes, and the scales around its jaws. Although her fine-motor skills were poor, she began to sketch her observations of the lizard's head but stopped when she noticed the work of a fellow student who was an accomplished artist. When Donna told the content specialist that she was only going to write about her observations, the specialist patiently showed Donna some field sketches of practicing herpetologists. Gradually, she reassured Donna that the art itself was not as important as capturing the data of the observation. This made sense to Donna, so she began to count the scales from nostril to eye, then to draw a corresponding sketch. What Donna had discovered was a common technique for classifying reptiles by counting scales. Donna was subsequently recognized for her ability in biology, but her teachers reported that they rarely had time for science because of repetition and desired mastery of basic skills. Donna's gifts were ignored as a result.

A second example illustrates John's gift in engineering. To identify students' abilities in this arena specialists presented them with an authentic problem of constructing paper towers. Using 20 sheets of 8 × 11 inch paper and a roll of Scotch tape, students attempted to complete a structure 11 inches tall, free standing, and whose base did not exceed the 8 × 11 inch sheet of paper. When the structure was finished, the students' next test was to place as many encyclopedia volumes as they could on top of the structure.

When John approached this project, he chose three classmates he knew he could work with effectively. He organized his group and drew a blueprint that was clear and understandable to all in his group. By rolling sheets of paper into columns and connecting them with tape his group constructed a structure in 12 minutes. John directed his fellow students as they carefully placed 48 encyclopedia volumes on the structure. Through the camouflage of disability, gifted behaviors of a practicing engineer emerged.

Dual Differentiation

In no way can this chapter address in depth all the complex and unique needs of gifted students who are deaf, have emotional or behavioral disorders, or are plagued by learning disabilities. However, by cross-referencing the known needs and characteristics of gifted students with these disabilities, recommendations can be made that apply to the amalgamation of these populations. Specifically, project High Hopes, in which these various disabilities were represented, provided a unique classroom laboratory.

Students such as Jason, John, Darla, and Donna require a challenging curriculum that considers the unique duality that each student represents—a strange mix of advanced abilities and academic limitations. Designing these kinds of learning experiences depends on creating *dual differentiation* (Neu, 1996) in their educational setting. This term refers to meeting the needs of students who exhibit two contradictory sets of learning characteristics by creating a balance between nurturing the students' strengths and compensating for their learning deficits.

The characteristics of gifted students are well documented in the literature (Renzulli, 1978; VanTassel-Baska, 1992; Whitmore, 1980). They include the following:

- A propensity for advanced-level content.
- A desire to create original products.
- A facility with and enjoyment of abstract concepts.
- A need to use nonlinear learning styles.
- Task commitment in areas of talent and interest.
- An identification with others of similar interests and talents.
- A heightened sensitivity to failure or injustice.

As sophisticated as these traits are, they may be offset or complicated by deficits typically impeding the success of students with learning disabilities. The most common reported problems include poor reading and math skills, problems in spelling and handwriting, difficulties with expressive language, lack of organizational skills, inability to focus and sustain attention, limited capacity for social interaction, and poor self-efficacy and esteem (Baum, Cooper, & Neu, 1996; Reis, Neu, & McGuire, 1995).

Because of the concern for addressing (remediating) a student's disabilities, well-intentioned teachers and specialists often ignore particular strengths and talents of gifted students with disabilities. Moreover, because the remediation techniques teachers use lack the very characteristics gifted students require for successful learning, many remedial attempts have been unsuccessful (Baum et al., 1991). The key, then, is to use instructional strategies that accommodate both sets of characteristics to (1) create the appropriate balance between attention to strengths and compensating for weaknesses and (2) infuse these strategies into challenging curriculum. (See Table 11.2.)

Examples of Dual Differentiation

A dually differentiated curriculum represents the synthesis of the need and strength to provide an appropriate curricular accommodation for students with gifts as well as disabilities. Donna was diagnosed with dyslexia, and her reading skills remained a major hurdle for her. Yet, she tenaciously pursued her passion of photography into advanced areas. Because of her reading limitations, Donna had to discover alternate means of accessing information, turning to graphic tutorials and workshops led by a professional photographer, who became her mentor.

TABLE 11.2   Duality of Learning Characteristics and Appropriate Curricular Modifications

Problems Associated With Students With Special Needs	Characteristics of Gifted Students	Curricular Accommodations
Limited reading skills	Propensity for advanced-level content to accommodate the gift or talent	Alternate means to access information
Difficulty with spelling and handwriting	Need to communicate creative ideas and knowledge through authentic products	Alternate ways to express ideas and create products
Language deficits in verbal communication and conceptualization	Facility with and enjoyment of abstract concepts	Visual and kinesthetic experiences to convey abstract ideas concretely
Poor organization	Often demonstrate creative nonlinear learning styles of thinking and learning	Visual organization schemes, such as timelines, flowcharts, webbing
Problems with sustaining attention and focus	Need intellectual challenge based on individual talents and interests	Interest-based authentic curriculum
Inappropriate social interaction	Need to identify with others of similar talents and interests	Group identity based on talent or ability
Low self-efficacy and esteem	Heightened sensitivity to failure	Recognition for accomplishment

Using other ways to obtain information, Donna averted her reading disability and was able to pursue advanced techniques used by professionals in her field of interest and talent.

What can be done for students with difficulty in spelling and writing? In the case of Jason, his drive to produce a creative solution to the real-world problem of a polluted pond on the school property propelled him to take action. Instead of writing a report about the need for a clean pond on campus, Jason and his fellow students decided to convey their message in a videotape. Although they did take written notes for their script, spelling was not an issue. The alternative product, the video, was very powerful and helped persuade the school board to address the pond problem as the students had suggested.

A third example of dual differentiation at work deals with engineering. In many cases, concepts of engineering are abstract and require advanced verbal communication skills to describe and conceptualize. However, the practicing engineer works in a concrete world of models that portray abstract concepts in ways that often need few words.

Engineers who worked with project High Hopes students were expert at circumventing words or communication deficits and, instead, creating visual or kinesthetic experiences to convey abstract ideas. For instance, one engineer used a colander to show the relationship of three dimensions in a topography lesson. Another engineer simply modeled assembly procedures, invited students to test the construction, and then asked them simple questions to propel them into their own investigations.

One of the most frequent teacher complaints concerning gifted students with learning disabilities or EBD is their difficulty with organization. Typically, students with a set of contradictory learning characteristics, as described in this chapter, are often nonlinear, or random (Gregorc, 1982), in their learning styles. Because many teachers have linear styles, they often fail to understand these students who learn best when they use their natural random styles.

In project High Hopes classes it was not uncommon to see entire chalkboards covered in a web of ideas. Additionally, Darla and Donna preferred the computer and date books for maintaining important information, whereas Jason and John used multicolored markers to highlight ideas, check off items completed, and draw attention to the next step to be accomplished. These visual organizers helped the students organize their work.

Throughout the project, researchers documented case after case of students whom classroom teachers had reported being constantly off task and not paying attention in the regular classroom environment. Yet, when presented with activities that challenged their interests and abilities, these same students were focused and even willing to stay after class to achieve their goals. As mentioned earlier, too often the curriculum presented in special education programs is remedial with little, if any, provision for pursuing intellectual curiosity. In project High Hopes activities, stimulating material based on student interests and with real-world application kept students engaged.

John spent his class period fascinated with the dissection of an owl pellet. Owl pellets are wads of fur and mouse bones that are not digested but are collected in the owl's stomach. The owl simply spits out the bones when the digested meat begins to move through the digestive track. Pellets the students used had been cleaned and provided a wonderfully realistic insight on a day in an owl's life. John went the extra mile with his activity; he asked to take the identified bones home with him. He returned the next day with a reconstructed mouse skeleton. Using modeled clay and wire he had painstakingly attached the bones in the fashion in which most dinosaur skeletons are exhibited in museums. This challenge had not only put John on task but also sustained his undivided attention for an unprecedented period of time!

Donna's weak social skills were also transformed through the dual differentiation approach to curriculum and instruction. Although the countless hours of direct social skill training the school had provided for her had produced no recognizable progress, when confronted by female biologists whom she worked with for almost two years, Donna began to practice these skills in a real-world context. For her, to see professional women in science who share with her a similar interest and ability made the difference. She realized, through challenging curriculum and instruction that considered her disabilities, that professionals do have expectations in the way they act and talk with others. In her school environment other students noticed the change, and Donna started making new friends who recognized and valued her abilities for the first time.

Summary and Conclusion

For the gifted student with a disability there are few opportunities for positive recognition. Typically, these students have a heightened sensitivity to failure from years of frustration with the undifferentiated curriculum. In project High Hopes students were identified for their strengths rather than for their weaknesses. They received specialized training in their areas of interest and became experts in specific domains. For these students to receive positive recognition, they engaged in working on genuine solutions to real-world problems, learning to use advanced-level techniques and sophisticated materials that professionals employ in their respective areas of interest. In essence their gifts were emphasized rather than their special education need, or disability.

REFERENCES

Baldwin, L. J., & Gargiulo, D. A. (1983). A model program for elementary-age learning disabled/gifted youngsters. In L. H. Fox, L. Brody, & D. Tobin (Eds.), *Learning-disabled/gifted children: Identification and programming* (pp. 207–221). Baltimore: University Park Press.

Baum, S., Cooper, C. R., & Neu, T. W. (1996, Spring). Project High Hopes: Identifying and nurturing talent in students with special needs. *TAG Update,* 7–8.

Baum, S. M., Cooper, C. R., & Neu, T. W. (2001). Dual differentiation: An approach for meeting the curricular needs of gifted students with learning disabilities. *Psychology in the Schools, 38*(5), 156–165.

Baum, S., Emerick L., Herman, G., & Dixon, J. (1989). Identification, programs, and enrichment for gifted learning disabled youth. *Roeper Review, 12*(1), 49–53.

Baum, S., & Owen, S. V. (1988). High ability/learning disabled students: How are they different? *Gifted Child Quarterly, 32*(3), 321–326.

Baum, S., Owen, S. V., & Dixon, J. (1991). *To be gifted and learning disabled: From definitions to practical intervention strategies.* Mansfield Center, CT: Creative Learning Press.

Coble, C. R. (1998). *Science for learning disabled students.* (ERIC Document Reproduction Service No. ED 258 803)

Davis, G. A., & Rimm, S. B. (1989). *Education of the gifted and talented* (2nd ed.). Englewood Cliffs, NJ: Prentice Hall.

Gardner, H. (1983). *Frames of mind: The theory of multiple intelligences.* New York: Basic Books.

Gardner, H. (1993). *Multiple intelligence: The theory in practice.* New York: Basic Books.

Gregorc, A. F. (1982). *An adult's guide to style.* Columbia, CT: Gregorc Associates.

Hokanson, D. T., & Jospe, M. (1976). *The search for cognitive giftedness in exceptional children.* Hartford: Connecticut State Department of Education.

Karnes, M., & Johnson, L. (1991). Gifted handicapped. In N. Colangelo & G. Davis (Eds.), *Handbook of gifted education.* Needham Heights, MA: Allyn & Bacon.

National Association for Gifted Children (NAGC). (1998). *Students with concomitant gifts and learning disabilities.* Position paper, Washington, DC.

Neu, T. W. (1993). *Case studies of gifted students with emotional/behavioral disorders.* Unpublished dissertation, University of Connecticut.

Neu, T. W. (1996, April). *The dually-differentiated curriculum: Key to meeting the educational needs of gifted learning disabled students.* Paper presented at the annual meeting of the Association for the Education of Gifted Underachieving Students, Denver, CO.

Olenchak, F. R. (1994, Spring). Talent development: Accommodating the social and emotional needs of secondary gifted learning disabled students. *The Journal of Secondary Gifted Education, 5*(3), 40–52.

Reis, S. M., & Neu, T. W. (1994). Factors involved in the academic success of high ability university students with learning disabilities. *The Journal of Secondary Gifted Education, 5*(3), 60–74.

Reis, S. M., Neu, T. W., & McGuire, J. (1995). *Talent in two places: Case studies of high ability students with learning disabilities who have achieved* (Research Monograph No. 95114). Storrs: University of Connecticut.

Renzulli, J. S. (1977). *The enrichment triad model: A guide for developing defensible programs for the gifted and talented.* Mansfield Center, CT: Creative Learning Press.

Renzulli, J. S. (1978). What makes giftedness? Re-examining a definition. *Phi Delta Kappan, 60,* 180–184, 261.

VanTassel-Baska, J. (1992). *Planning effective curriculum for gifted learners.* Denver, CO: Love Publications.

Whitmore, J. R. (1980). *Giftedness, conflict, and underachievement.* Boston: Allyn & Bacon.

Whitmore, J. R., & Maker, C. J. (1985). *Intellectual giftedness in disabled persons.* Rockville, MD: Aspen.

12 Gifted Education in Rural Schools

CLAR BALDUS

With regard to gifted students, "luck" of geography should not dictate the opportunities to identify and enhance talent.
—Dr. Nicholas Colangelo, Director, Belin-Blank
Center for Gifted Education and Talent
Development Keynote Presentation at the
Wallace Family National Conference on
Gifted Education in Rural Schools, 2001

The educational opportunities of gifted and talented young people living in rural areas and small towns in the United States should be of concern and interest to U.S. educators. These students are everywhere: Every state has rural areas and rural schools: Fifty percent of all public schools in the United States are in small towns and rural areas, and 39 percent of all public school students—nearly 17,500,000—live in small towns and rural areas (National Center for Education Statistics [NCES], 1998). This chapter focuses on issues of the convergence of two national issues: ruralness and giftedness. Whereas the issue of gifted education in rural schools is a new topic, ironically, the pioneers of gifted education were individuals from rural areas. (For a historical timeline on gifted education and gifted education in rural schools, see Colangelo, Assouline, & New, *Gifted Education in Rural Schools: A National Assessment*, 1999.)

This chapter first discusses rural education within a context of community issues, including an operational definition of "rural and small-town." Issues of gifted education in rural schools is covered, including challenges and benefits associated with being a gifted student in a rural school.

Rural Communities and Rural Education

Definition of Rural. Establishing a definition of *rural* sounds simple enough. However, it is a rather complicated task. Most reports on rural issues contain an explanation of how the authors grappled with this definition. Even the federal government and its myriad of offices—which has set a precedent—does not use a single definition. Rather, respective federal offices use multiple meanings and often eschew the term altogether in favor of the more homogenous *nonmetropolitan*. Instead of defining what rural is, this latter term lumps together everything it is *not*. Thus, our frustration over the elusive nature of this word puts us in good company.

According to *The American Heritage College Dictionary*'s entry, one common element to the definition of rural is that it is "of the country" and "relating to farming; agriculture." Although the word commonly connotes a tractor in a field, equally deserving of the moniker are New England's fishing villages, logging towns of the Pacific Northwest, and the Southwest's desert region populated by Native American and Mexican American communities. Each of these is a rural area, albeit nonfarming in nature. Each plays a significant role in the national heritage of the United States.

Federal Definitions.   Among the federal offices that have definitions of *rural*, the two definitions of the U.S. Bureau of the Census are the most commonly used. In its decennial survey (1990), the bureau defines *rural* as a residual category of places "outside urbanized areas in open country, or in communities with less than 2,500 inhabitants," with a population density of "less than 1,000 inhabitants per square mile" (Stern, 1994, p. 4). In its monthly household sample surveys, however, the Census Bureau uses the term *nonmetropolitan* instead of *rural*. Nonmetropolitan refers to counties "outside of, or not integrated with, large population concentrations of 50,000 or more."

Another federal office, the Economic Research Service (ERS) of the U.S. Department of Agriculture, organizes its classification by counties. There are 10 ERS categories, ranging from the central areas of very large cities at 0 to "completely rural" areas that are not adjacent to any sort of town or city at 9.

The NCES (1998) provides yet another definition and perhaps the one most relevant to educational researchers. Differentiating by community type the NCES has a five-level chart moving from central city to rural. Each community type is defined, in part, by its relation to a metropolitan statistical area.

Operational Definition.   According to Daryl Hobbs (1994), "The term nonmetropolitan is a residual; it is what is left over after the metropolitan areas have been taken out.... The concept of rurality once had significant economic, social, and political associations, but the nonmetropolitan concept that replaced it is primarily, though perhaps not totally, geographic." (p. 5) This chapter concerns that more traditional concept of rurality. This concept still has currency. This operational definition is pliable and inclusive, allowing the investigation of the nature of schools in a variety of rural settings, each with its own unique economic, social, and political characteristics.

It is important to remember that each of the four previous definitions was developed to fit the specific needs and purposes of the respective governmental offices (i.e., the NCES). They also reflect the considerable resources available to such offices for data collection. For the purpose of this chapter school districts having 2,000 or fewer students are defined as "rural and small schools."

Demographics

Many facets of rural life impinge on schools. In terms of demographics, the number of people who live in rural areas has been shrinking since the nineteenth century. During the Civil War, for example, four of five U.S. citizens lived in communities of 2,500 or less. Today, more than three quarters of the population live in metro areas, and fewer than one fourth live in rural places.

Another imbalance exists within the rural population itself, this one in terms of age. The number of working adults and children is proportionately smaller in rural areas, whereas the rural elderly population is increasing. This is partly a result of the increase in retirement communities, which will grow as the baby boom generation ages. The equation of a shrinking population on one end of the age spectrum and a growing one on the other end does not bode well for rural schools because education funds are often linked to enrollment, and older voters are not always avid supporters of education. In addition, recently arrived retirees are even less vested in local schools, having no personal memories of or connections to the schools via their own experiences or through those of children and grandchildren.

Economics

The economies of rural communities also impact schools. No longer based on agriculture or other natural resources, such as logging or oil, rural economies have been radically altered after decades of little change. In the 1990s, for example, farming employed fewer than one in ten rural workers; at the same time, the manufacturing and service industries have expanded significantly in rural locales. Assumptions can no longer be made about the income of a rural community, and yet to understand the state of a community's schools and its children it must be understood from where its money comes. According to Hobbs (1994), "A community's economic base affects its social organization, social class structure, demographic composition, leadership, wealth, and more" (p. 7–8). And all of this affects children and the schools.

One thing that has not changed for rural economies is that they remain dependent on a single industry, although the industry may have shifted from mining to manufacturing, or from fishing to retirement service. Any study of an industry that goes from boom to bust illustrates the devastating effects that a lack of economic diversity can have on a community. Take, for example, the bleak depression that surrounded many small communities in the Midwest following the farm crisis of the 1980s. Or the widespread unemployment that hit parts of the Northwest after environmental concern triggered cutbacks in the timber industry in the early 1990s.

Although poverty's hold on the rural United States has gradually loosened during the past century, rural children continue to bear the brunt of it. And every farm crisis or timber cutback is especially hard on this segment of the population. In 1993, for example, more than one third of rural U.S. citizens who were in poverty were children under the age of 18. This is partly because of the instability of employment in rural areas, a situation which is not significantly better than that found in many inner cities. Although overall unemployment is lower in rural areas than in inner cities, jobs are often short term, seasonal, and part time in nature. Such work not only undermines stability but it also limits a family's benefits, including health insurance for children, access to unemployment compensation, and retraining programs. As with inner cities, the jobs that exist in rural locales are usually low paying and are increasingly often service related (e.g., restaurants, motels, retail). There are far fewer managerial, professional, and technical jobs in rural areas than in metropolitan areas.

This trend reflects the migration of more highly skilled and educated residents who leave small communities in search of higher-paying jobs. Every out migration of a talented young person is the loss of a community's investment in education. When the would-be doctors, teachers, and entrepreneurs move away, they take with them both their promise for the future and 12 year's worth of education. For rural schools, where the price-per-pupil expenditure is often higher than in metropolitan schools (partly because of the greater cost of transportation) and where few new people migrate *to* the community, this is a significant loss.

Education

These economic conditions impact children and their schools, as is reflected in the differences between rural and metropolitan in a number of statistics. Rural students, for example, do not earn college degrees at the same rate as their metropolitan peers (Stern, 1994). Although the high school completion rate of rural students has gradually risen during the past several decades, the gap between rural and metropolitan students for college completion has grown larger. In 1960, the discrepancy of the completion rate for these two groups was 3.4 percent; by 1990 it was 9.5 percent.

Although some studies show that rural students are not as well prepared for college as their metropolitan peers, their success in higher education and, later, in the work world are linked closely to the climate of their community. "Expectations for students and teachers will vary widely from one type of rural community to the next," writes Paul Nachtigal (1994, p. 25). "The standards for those expectations are most likely tied to the experience of the adults. If there are few professional role models and if most of the adults are first generation high school graduates, the expectations will be very different than those in a community where, because of culture or location, high percentages of adults have some college or post-high school education" (Nachtigal, 1994, p. 27). This is not promising news for communities that are losing their most talented residents.

Schools

Rural schools have a complex history. For many small and isolated communities they have been a focal point of activity, serving not only as a place for the education of children but also as a meeting space for political and social affairs. Townships have traditionally taken pride and ownership in their schools, viewing them as a defining and shared centerpiece. Like many facets of education, rural schools have been victim to cyclical schools of thought. At the end of the twentieth century, for example, many of the mainstays of small schools were being heralded by the education establishment: smaller class size, mixed grades, and the community as classroom are all popular methods today. At other times, however, small and rural schools have been under attack, accused of being backward and insufficiently rigorous. In the name of modernization and industrialization, many rural schools have been closed in favor of larger, consolidated systems. Although critics have sometimes been right about the deficiencies of rural schools, they have more often been shortsighted and unconcerned with the best form of education for rural students.

In conjunction with consolidation, standardization became a central tenet of education reformers. As students, especially in large, urban schools, were more frequently grouped by age and ability rather than taught together in multiage groupings, it became necessary to formalize a set curriculum. The central principle of standardization was that a single curriculum should be presented to same-age students working at the same pace with a qualified teacher. Because smaller schools had neither sufficient numbers of students of the same age or ability level nor more than a couple of teachers, at most, consolidation was necessary to achieve the reformists' goals. The advent of school buses made the movement of students over great distances more practical than it had been previously. Across the United States, schools from neighboring townships joined together to form larger institutions. In the process, at least one school became extinct for each consolidation.

The march for "bigger, better" schools has continued throughout the twentieth and twenty-first centuries. In 1930, for example, there were about 128,000 school districts in the United States; in 1996 there were only 14,883 districts. Between 1940 and 1990, the total number of public elementary schools declined 69 percent—from approximately 200,000 to 62,037—despite a 70 percent increase in the U.S. population (NCES, 1998). Even today, when many people—both experts and lay people—understand the damage that can be done to a community when it loses its school, closings still occur. The impetus for consolidation is now more often financial than curricular related. In West Virginia, for example, 258 of the state's kindergarten through twelfth-grade public schools, or 26 percent, closed between 1990 and 1998. Many of those closings were the result of a requirement by the state's School Building Authority that schools meet minimum size criteria before qualifying for construction funding. Today, small schools and districts continue to fight consolidation, though paradoxically, they sometimes rely on it as the only way to exist.

Consolidation continues despite convincing evidence that (1) small school size is associated with lower high school dropout rates, (2) socioeconomically disadvantaged students perform better in small schools, and (3) student participation is dramatically higher in small schools. Ironically, consolidation continues at the same time that large urban districts are increasingly interested in creating schools within schools and finding other creative ways of forming smaller educational communities.

Qualities of Rural Schools

Many analysts have commented on how the cultural gap between rural and metropolitan areas has diminished as a result of such factors as commuting, cable television, and regional shopping malls (see Hobbs [1994], for example). Still, schools in rural areas possess some unique qualities. For example, they are relatively isolated, situated geographically far apart from resources, such as cultural centers, universities, large libraries, and even other schools. Teachers in these buildings do not have ready access to materials to augment their training, nor are materials easily available to research or expand curriculum. Students have less exposure to a range of professions than their suburban peers. Being part of small classes also limits the chance that a student with special needs will have a classmate with similar aptitude or interests. These and related challenges are revisited in the discussion of gifted education in rural schools.

Benefits of Rural Education

Although it is important to realize the many deficits under which rural schools operate, it is equally key to remember the many benefits they offer. Positive components of rural schools include mixed-age classrooms, schools within schools, and community service. Indeed, urban schools are now copying some of the most successful elements of their rural counterparts. Ironically, many of these positive features were diminished by consolidation, a process that forced rural schools to grow bigger and to lose community ties.

A survey of rural educators yielded many responses demonstrating the benefits of small schools (Colangelo et al., 1999). Teachers, superintendents, parents, students, and association presidents all stressed the following benefits of small schools:

- A higher level of child–adult contact.
- More individualized learning.
- Learning through community involvement.
- Participation in multiple-school events.

These benefits are the norm, not the exception. There is greater opportunity (and need) for students in small schools to participate on teams, serve in student government, and play active parts in clubs.

Students in smaller schools also have an increased sense of belonging. Many teachers and administrators have commented on the ease with which they discuss a particular students' progress and needs with other faculty, sometimes creating individualized plans for students with special needs and interests. Such spontaneous and flexible planning is not as possible in a larger school where the bureaucracy is usually more rigid and the larger enrollment simply means less time per student.

Gifted Education

Like trends in rural education, gifted education has experienced a see-saw effect of interest and disinterest in the educational establishment. Whether seen as an invaluable commodity to be well funded and nourished or as an elitist group draining money from more worthwhile projects, there has often been a strong reaction to gifted education in the United States. Over the years, various research has served to increase the awareness of and interest in gifted education. However, arriving at a definition for "gifted" has been as perplexing as defining rural or small schools. (See Colangelo et al., *Gifted Education in Rural Schools: A National Assessment* [1999], for a more complete discussion of this topic.)

A Crossroads

Similar to rural education, gifted education has not always benefited from reform policies. Notably, the recent move toward detracking (abolishing accelerated and advanced courses) and the increased use of cooperative learning have been considered hindrances to gifted students by many experts in the field. These trends are coupled with the ever-present concern regarding elitism. In attempts to give everyone a fair chance, or to level the playing field, U.S. schools are often guilty of ignoring the talents and needs of their most able students. Some critics go so far as to argue that U.S. schools are markedly anti-intellectual. In their book *Out of Our Minds* (1995), Craig Howley, Aimee Howley, and Edwina Pendarvis say that "the dark side of society's commitment to provide everyone with a standard, functional schooling…[is] the destruction of talent, and not only (or even principally) among the gifted" (p. 142). Gifted students are expected to succeed, whatever the obstacles, without the benefits of "special" help. They, along with their parents and teachers, are often accused of being elitist and of pilfering resources from students who have greater needs.

The State of Gifted Education in Rural and Small Schools

When examining rural education side by side with gifted education, some striking similarities appear. Both have borne the brunt of educational fads, and both have received relatively little funding and national attention. Today, there is a much better idea of what is happening to serve the most able inner-city students, and there are models of successful programming for these students. Nothing on a similar scale, however, is available for those parents and educators working to improve the schooling experience of gifted rural students. Although rural schools are dedicated to helping gifted students, there has been little attempt at providing ample assistance or developing a national network to serve these students.

Schools in rural areas and small towns also have many advantages that provide benefits that small schools provide to *all* students. The advantages most frequently mentioned include considerable individualized attention, familiarity and trust among members of the school community, opportunities for involvement in a large range of activities despite skill level (e.g., the school newspaper, sports teams, and student council), and participation and commitment from parents and community members.

Many gifted students comment on the benefits of both a small school and a small town. Will Nedved, from small-town, Garner, Iowa, said that his senior year independent study project on opera was possible because all of the teachers in the building knew and trusted him. "I set up a plan for my project and presented it to my teachers," said Will. "Because they knew I could work well on my own, they didn't hesitate to let me go for it. It was the most exciting, challenging thing I did in high school." Nedved eventually won a $5,000 Scholastic Art and Writing Award and was invited to Washington, DC, to present his opera. Likewise, Tom Skuzinski, a National Merit Finalist from Reed City, Michigan, said that he really appreciated the support and security offered by his small community: "I sometimes received congratulatory notes from people in town who I didn't even know," he recalled fondly. Although these students may have profited from a wider range of peers and greater academic offerings in a larger school, they clearly enjoyed the advantages of their small schools.

In rural schools, the immediate impact for gifted students depends on changes within the rural schools. In recognizing this, the focus is not to urbanize, or suburbanize, rural schools in the name of gifted education but to advocate educational opportunities for gifted students while preserving the integrity of rural schools.

Literature on Gifted and Rural Education

The Belin–Blank Center at The University of Iowa in Iowa City, Iowa, has produced two extensive reports focusing on issues of gifted students in rural schools: *Gifted Education in Rural Schools: A National Assessment* (Colangelo et al., 1999) and *Gifted Voices From Rural America* (Colangelo, Assouline, & New, 2001). However, these are exceptions and recent undertakings. Unlike the comprehensive reports and histories that have been written separately about gifted education and rural education, there are generally no other such road maps to follow on the topic of how the most academically advantaged and talented students are being served by small and rural schools in the United States. Relatively little has been written on the combined topics. In 1976, T. Ernest Newland allotted one chapter in his text, *The Gifted in Socio-educational Perspective,* to the obstacles of providing challenges to gifted students in rural areas and outlined some alternatives. Almost two decades later, Jane Piirto (1994) also briefly addressed the needs of rural and gifted youth, very much echoing the observations of Newland, her earlier colleague; the only significant difference between the two is the increased attention to technology as a potential delivery system by the latter author.

Indeed, technology is one of the two main themes that recurs in articles addressing the gifted in rural areas. Increasingly, authors are interested in describing methods of delivering advanced materials to isolated gifted students via the Internet, teleconferencing, or other means. The other common theme falls under the heading of a profile article—that is an article outlining the challenges that face both gifted students and those adults involved in their education, often focusing on the progress of an individual or program.

As regards the technology-centered article, the ideas therein are often quickly outdated, like the programs and hardware they describe. Although technology in general is increasingly a popular method for serving rural gifted students, the various methods for transmitting information and course work is ever changing, creating a unique set of challenges. The fast-paced nature of technology, including the spread of the Internet and the advancement of hardware, makes it a difficult topic to cover in any writing that will have more than a year's staying power.

The issue of timeliness also affects the second group of articles, those that profile specific programs. As researchers (Colangelo et al., 1999) who tried to contact gifted programs that had been mentioned in an earlier report on gifted education described, "None of the respondents had anything to report. Every school had long since dropped its programs, usually because the key people responsible for inspiring and directing them had long since departed from the scene, as had the funds needed for the extra support" (p. 24).

Challenges

As mentioned, the Belin–Blank Center is producing a series of reports examining how gifted students are served in rural schools. *Gifted Education in Rural Schools: A National Assessment* (Colangelo et al., 1999) provides an overview of both gifted and rural education and describes how the two have interacted and overlapped. Some of these issues are noted in this chapter. In addition, the 1999 report presents a series of charts and statistics highlighting conditions affecting schools and youths in the 20 most rural states. As part of the report, a survey of rural educators was conducted to better understand the quality of life in rural schools as it pertains to giftedness. As indicated in the 1999 report, the challenges faced today by rural schools attempting to serve their gifted and talented students are numerous. Few of the 50 schools surveyed for the 1999 report had either gifted programs or, in the case of high schools, advanced placement courses. In many instances, students were identified as gifted, often because of state laws requiring such identification, but little or no programming was available. Many students indicated that the services they were offered seemed appended to their regular schedules and were perceived more as excuses to get out of class than as positive, worthwhile opportunities. Teachers, administrators, students, and government statistics report that the following are among the most common challenges:

- Lack of community resources, such as museums, libraries, and professional mentors, with which to augment school resources and facilities.
- Lack of a sizeable peer base for gifted students.
- Lack of time for student involvement in additional programming, such as community college courses.
- Difficulties in hiring teachers, especially those with advanced training and experience.
- Lack of advanced placement classes and an overemphasis on community college classes for gifted students.
- Lack of training for teachers and administrators on issues of gifted education.
- Limited curricula because of small student populations and the need for remedial courses that compete for teacher time and resources.
- Accusations of "elitism" by community members.
- A sense of isolation for teachers dedicated to trying new methods or serving gifted and talented students.

Overcoming the Challenges: Rural Gifted Voices of Success

Gifted Voices From Rural America (Colangelo et al., 2001), the second report prepared by the Belin–Blank Center, focuses on unique schools and educators who creatively faced challenges commonly experienced by rural and small-town schools but effectively developed programs to serve their gifted and talented students while maintaining their rural identity. Six schools from across the United States were included in these profiles: Jackson River Governor's School, Virginia; Kenai Peninsula Borough School District, Alaska; Native American Preparatory School, New Mexico; Nevada School of the Arts, California; Idalia High School, Colorado; and Akron-Westfield Community School District, Iowa. What do these success stories have in common?

- A teacher or administrator with vision and tremendous personal commitment.
- Programs that provided standards and flexibility for the development of exceptional talent.
- Students who were exceptional and needed the special programs.

■ Rural or small-town areas with limited options.

It must be noted, though, that these schools do not serve *all* students and *all* forms of giftedness. Given their size and limited resources, each of these educational communities has chosen its niche. Often there is a special teacher who leads the way, and his or her talents serve as a base for a program. In other cases, the unique nature and background of the local community decides the direction and needs of a school. The results are wonderful and applause worthy, and yet students in the school with the strong writing program, for example, have few outlets for math and science, whereas students in the districts that have banded together to create a science and technology academy often do not have a similar special program for the arts.

Summary and Conclusion

There is still much work to be accomplished as in trying to build better programs to serve the most able students in rural places in the United States. As challenges are identified and rural and small schools continue to creatively serve their gifted students, the goal becomes more attainable. To help achieve this goal Table 12.1 lists available resources targeting small and rural school districts for the reader.

TABLE 12.1   Rural Education Resources

American Council on Rural Special Education
Kansas State University
2323 Anderson Avenue, Suite 226
Manhattan, KS 66502
(785) 532-2737
www.ksu.edu/acres

ERIC Clearinghouse on Rural Education
Appalachia Educational Laboratory
P.O. Box 1348
Charleston, WV 25325-1348
(800) 624-9120
www.ael.org/eric

National Center for Education Statistics
Navigating Resources for Rural Schools
1990 K. Street, NW
Washington, DC 20006
(202) 502-7300
www.nces.ed.gov/surveys/ruraled/
    TextIndex.asp

National Education Association NEA
Topic Legislative Action Center: Rural Schools
1201 16th Street, NW
Washington, DC 20036
(202) 833-4000
www.nea.org/schools/rural

National Rural Education Association (NREA)
246 Education Building
Colorado State University
Fort Collins, CO 80523-1588
(970) 491-7022
www.nrea.colostate.edu

North Central Regional Educational Laboratory
1120 East Diehl Road, Suite 200
Naperville, IL 60563-1486
www.ncrel.org/rural
Pulling Together R & D Resources for Rural
    Schools

(continued)

TABLE 12.1   Continued

Northwest Regional Educational Laboratory
Rural Education
101 SW Main Street, Suite 500
Portland, OR 97204-3297
(503) 275-9500
www.nwrel.org/ruraled

Organizations Concerned About Rural
  Education (OCRE)
1201 16th Street, NW, Suite 510
Washington, DC 20036
(202) 822-7638
www.ruralschools.org

The Rural School and Community Trust
1825 K Street, NW, Suite 703
Washington, DC 20006
(202) 955-7177
www.ruraledu.org

Rural Education Achievement Program (REAP)
Maine Department of Education
23 State House Station
Augusta, ME 04333-0023
(207) 624-6791
www.state.me.us/education/reap/
  REAP_Home.htm

College for Rural Education and Small Schools
College of Education
1100 Mid-Campus Drive
124 Bluemont Hall
Manhattan, KS 66506
(785) 532-5886
coe.ksu.edu/cress

Rural Sites Network
Hosted by National Writing Project
University of California
2105 Bancroft, #1042
Berkeley, CA 94720-1042
(510) 642-0963
www.writingproject.org/Programs/rsn/
  index.htlm

State Web Sites

Montana Rural Education Association (MREA)
1134½ Butte Avenue
Helena, MT 59601
(406) 443-2629
www.mrea-mt.org/about.html

Pennsylvania Association of Rural and Small
  Schools
212 Locust Street, Suite 400
Harrisburg, PA 17101
(717) 236-7180
www.parss.org/about.asp

Southern Rural Development Center (SRDC)
Box 9656
410 Bost Extension Building
Mississippi State, MS 39762
(662) 325-3207
www.ext.msstate.edu/srdc

South Carolina Association for Rural Education
Department of Education
306-G Tillman Hall
Clemson University
500 Ridge Street
St. George, SC 29477
(864) 656-5988
www.scruraleducation.org

Rural School Program: State of New York
11114 Kennedy Hall
Cornell University
Ithaca, NY 14853
(607) 255-8056
www.education.cornell.edu/rsp

The Pacers Small Group Cooperative
University of Alabama
Program for Rural Services and Research
P.O. Box 870372
Tuscaloosa, AL 35487-0372
(205) 348-6432
www.pacers.org

Organization of Rural Oklahoma Schools
Route 1, Box 68B
Caney, OK 74533
(580) 889-7172
www.orosok.org

Indiana Small and Rural Schools Association
Indiana Department of Education
Room 229
State House, IN 46204-2798
(371) 232-0808
www.siec.k12.in.us/sr

Friends of Rural Education Data Center
2031 Rose Road
Elba, NE 68835
fred.bloomnet.com

Alabama's Rural Schools of Yesterday
  and Today
Alabama Department of Archives and History
624 Washington Avenue
Montgomery, AL 36130-0100
(334) 242-4435
www.archives.state.al.us/tours/rural/
  rural.html

Journals

Journal of Research in Rural Education
Theodore Coladarci, Editor
College of Education and Human Development
University of Maine
5766 Shibles Hall
Orono, ME 04469-5766
(207) 581-2761
www.ume.maine.edu/~cofed/research/jrre/
  index.htm

The Rural Educator
Hosted by NREA
Bob Mooneyham
820 Van Vleet Oral, Room 227
University of Oklahoma
Norman, OK 73019
(405) 325-7959
www.nrea.colostate.edu/RuralEducator

Rural Development News
North Central Regional Center for Rural
  Development
Iowa State University
108 Curtiss Hall
Ames, IA 50011-1050
(515) 294-3180
www.ag.iastate.edu/centers/rdev/rdn/html

REFERENCES

Colangelo, N., Assouline, S., & New, J. (1999). *Gifted education in rural schools: A national assessment.* Iowa City: The Connie Belin & Jacqueline N. Blank International Center for Gifted Education and Talent Development, The University of Iowa.

Colangelo, N., Assouline, S., & New, J. (2001). *Gifted voices from rural America.* Iowa City: The Connie Belin & Jacqueline N. Blank International Center for Gifted Education and Talent Development, The University of Iowa.

Hobbs, D. (1994). The rural context for education: Adjusting the images. In G. Karim and N. Weate (Eds.), *Toward the twenty-first century: A rural education anthology. Rural school development outreach project* (Vol. 1, pp. 5–22). (ERIC Document No.: ED 401 073). Oak Brook, IL: NCREL.

Howley, C., Howley, A., & Pendarvis, E. (1995). *Out of our minds: Anti-intellectualism and talent development in American schooling.* New York: Teachers College Press.

Nachtigal, P. (1994). Rural education in a period of transition: Are the public schools up to the task? In G. Karim and N. Weate (Eds.), *Toward the twenty-first century: A rural education anthology. Rural school development outreach project* (Vol. 1, pp. 23–35). (ERIC Document No.: ED 401 073). Oak Brook, IL: NCREL.

National Center for Education Statistics (NCES). (1998). *The schools and staffing survey (SASS) and teacher follow-up survey (TFS) CD-ROM: Electronic codebook and public-use data for three cycles of SASS and TFS*. Washington, DC: U.S. Department of Education, Office of Educational Research and Improvement.

Newland, T. E. (1976). *The gifted in socio-educational perspective*. Englewood Cliffs, NJ: Prentice-Hall.

Piirto, J. (1994). *Talented children and adults: Their development and education*. New York: Macmillan.

Stern, J. (Ed.). (1994). *The condition of education in rural schools*. Washington, DC: U.S. Department of Education Office of Educational Research and Improvement.

U.S. Bureau of the Census. (1990). *1990 Census of population and housing*. Washington, DC: U.S. Department of Commerce, Economics, and Statistics.

13 Evaluating Progress toward Equitable Representation of Historically Underserved Groups in Gifted and Talented Programs

ERNESTO BERNAL

About 30 years ago the movement to achieve an equitable representation of gifted and talented (GT) students from nondominant ethnic groups began in earnest (Bernal, 1974; Torrance, 1973). During the 1980s there were numerous attempts to motivate programs for the GT in the public schools to include greater numbers of the underserved populations. The 1990s saw hundreds of special workshops sponsored by national organizations (such as The Association for the Gifted [TAG]), state organizations (such as the California Association for the Gifted [CAG] and the Texas Association for the Gifted and Talented [TAGT]), state departments of education, regional service centers, and individual school districts to help identify or select more of the children whose gifts so often go unrecognized and undeveloped by GT programs. These underserved populations include gifted children in special education categories that do not necessarily imply an intractable cognitive deficit (e.g., learning disabled gifted, paraplegic gifted); gifted children from most of the nondominant ethnic groups; and gifted English language learners, or, more accurately, children who have not yet mastered the English language to an academic level of proficiency.

What has not been done to date is to determine if any of these efforts are having an effect, that is, if GT programs generally are actually serving more of these populations. It has, of course, been recognized for some time that traditional program evaluation procedures that rely on statistical analyses of large numbers (N) of students (such as those served through compensatory education) do not work very well for GT programs, where small numbers and proportions are the rule (Bernal, 1986; Callaghan, 1983; Carter & Hamilton, 1985). In most cases, the proportions of underserved GT populations are even smaller. This chapter presents a way to identify the need to service one or more of these groups and, by extension, to monitor a school district's progress toward meeting these professional obligations. Quantitative analyses alone, of course, cannot explain any school district's success in working with the underserved populations or its failure to do so. However, having conducted a manageable needs analysis and targeted one or more of these traditionally underserved groups for inclusion, how can a GT program coordinator or director document the effects of these efforts in a practical, quantitative way and improve the GT program's impact on these groups over the years?

A Question of Standards

For all the training that has occurred on behalf of the underserved gifted, it seems that no one has proffered a goal. Obviously, the basic idea implies some type of "improvement," but administrators and evaluators both know just how slippery a general expectation such as this can be. The achievement of this goal also involves the notions of equity and qualification, so for progress to be made and accountability to have meaning among GT educators, some reasonable, specific, and measurable standard needs to be established, a target or an objective that a GT administrator can try to "hit" or accomplish.

A good way to establish a standard is to use a district's current performance as a baseline, particularly for GT programs that have not been able to do much for the underserved gifted. Districts with no or extremely low numbers of children in one or another of these underserved categories cannot use simple statistics to measure progress, at least not in an inferential sense, because statistics require variance, and zero or near zero counts all but rule out these methods of comparison. Small districts or, more generally, districts with zeros or very small numbers of children from an underserved group *currently in the GT program* would do well to establish a simple numerical goal as a first step during the first year of this inclusionary plan. If your district, for example, has 300 or 400 students who are labeled LD, but not one of them is selected for the GT program, a simple but smart numerical goal could be to find two or three students among these who are also GT as the objective for the first school year of your plan's operation. If, however, your district has an adequate database that will permit cross-tabulations of student categories, which is called a relational database, you may be able to locate children who are already GT and members of the targeted, underserved group. These would provide your initial counts.

Next, contact the district administrator to whom the GT program is responsible. Sometimes this person will also be in charge of the program that serves the target group, as would happen when the district administrator has a title that involves "special populations." Then get together with the director or coordinator of the target group, say migrant students, explain your purpose, and secure that person's cooperation. Start with a survey of GT teachers and the teachers who usually serve the targeted group to find out if there are any students within the targeted group who have already been identified or who might qualify for the GT program. Teachers and coordinators can check their students' records, for example. Some special education children have IQ tests on file, and others have the results of achievement tests in their folders—data that could help start a pool from which to nominate in order to reach a modest predetermined goal. Suggestions from the appropriate chapters in this book can be quite helpful in formulating a tentative plan.

Then the two coordinators can pick a few principals and a few teachers who can be approached to hear the issue, discuss the tentative strategy, and suggest other ways to increase the representation of this group of children in the GT program. Under good circumstances the effort will involve the coordinators, the campus administrators, and the teachers in a truly professional learning experience.

Monitor this special project during the year and document both implementation and the outcomes. How many students were nominated? How many were selected? What problems were encountered in the selection process? How can the entire process be improved as a result of this experience? The result of this small, manageable, documented project will likely be a strategy that works on several campuses and that can be adapted for other schools as well.

As progress is achieved, the GT coordinator can (and should) switch to another type of numerical goal, perhaps one that is normative in nature: to do as well as others do, or better yet, to do at least a little better than most, but without having to go into direct competition with other districts. Two touchstones come immediately to mind, the state and the substate region in which the district is located. In Texas and Ohio, for example, there are regional service centers that are the state department of education's service and training link to the schools. In California, the county offices of education serve a similar function. The point is that regional agencies often maintain their own databases and that sources of information for comparative purposes are possible to access by making a few contacts. Larger, more progressive districts with their own research and evaluation (R&E) departments are especially adept at unlocking these sources, but do not be discouraged. A phone call can help.

The participation rates of underserved populations reported by state and regional entities is often higher than that of many districts because of the outstanding work being done by a few districts or even schools that are committed to serving all of their very able learners, regardless of their ethnic or first-language backgrounds, at-risk status, or handicapping conditions. Statewide or regional reports, especially if they are on a relational database, can provide counts or averages, and the regional or statewide average can become the standard for programs that are on their way to achieving equity.

Districts that are the leaders in equitable representation may wish to examine yet other activities. Districts with average or better performance, but who have not quite achieved parity for the nondominant ethnic groups or for students who are limited English proficient (LEP), should seek to define more ambitious goals. For example, ask, "Could we not increase minority participation in our GT program by 1 percent a year for the next x years? What would we have to do to achieve this? Is nomination the key, or do we need to assess the identification and selection process as a whole in the light of new models of intelligence?" To reach more of the GT special education students, ask, "How many of the special ed children are cognitively unimpaired? Of these, could we not find ways to attend to, say, 2 percent?"

Districts that achieve parity should try to disseminate their knowledge of the practices and policies that made parity possible. In addition to publishing in professional journals, one of the most effective means of disseminating information about these successful practices is at local, regional, or state conferences on GT education. Teachers and administrators in particular should be featured speakers in sessions that stress praxis. If the targeted group of students also has conferences—such as migrant, bilingual, and special educational professional groups—consider presenting at their conferences as well.

User-Friendly Statistics

Using a few relatively user-friendly statistical techniques constitutes the next section of this chapter. Owning a computer that has statistical software is not necessary; a medium quality calculator will do. Note that, in the examples, districts are not compared to each other because these juxtapositions could be considered invidious in nature. Instead, other comparisons that can lead to program improvement are stressed.

First, secure an electronic calculator with at least nine registers on its display. This calculator should also have a memory and a square root function.

Second, request copies of three data sources: one from your own district, one from a regional or county service center (or its equivalent), and one from the state about the target population(s) you want to include in greater numbers. These data need to be cross-tabulated and disaggregated in ways that make sense for your needs analysis. For example, if your target group is GT LD (learning disabled gifted), cross-tabulate both the LD and the GT groups to find the intersection of these sets for your district, the region in which your district is found, and your state. These counts will allow you to compute the *proportions* of these children at all three levels.[1] The question, "What proportion[2] of the GT students is LD (or some other category or group)?" can be answered by taking the total number of GT LD students in the district and dividing it by the number of GT students:

$$\frac{N_{GTLD}}{N_{GT}}.$$

---

[1]Converting raw counts into proportions makes data from the different sources comparable, both statistically and intuitively.

[2]Proportions are expressed as 1.00 or less. To calculate the percentage, multiply the proportion by 100, the same as moving the decimal to the right two places.

And to answer the question, what proportion of LD students is also GT, simply divide the number of GT LD students by the number of LD students.

Comparing your district's proportions to regional and state levels can be an eye-opening experience. You will get an instant picture of where your district stands. If you are working with a relational database, disaggregate the data by socioeconomic status, ethnic group, or gender in order to better see any patterns. You may discover, for example, that all the GT LD students identified so far come from one ethnic group, from the upper middle class, or are almost all of one gender, which would serve to alert you as to the focus that your program ought to take in order to improve the rate of participation of the LD target group in the GT program. Again, if your district has an R&E office, solicit the help of a database manager in obtaining these counts.

Some states may not have a relational database. They may be able to provide raw counts of GT students and special education-LD students, perhaps, but have no way to cross-tabulate the results to give you the number of GT LD. One can only hope that your own district's database is not so limited. If these kinds of limitations arise, however, work around them by keeping your own counts based on the needs assessment survey that you completed. These baseline figures can then be upgraded periodically to ensure current data in the future.

To compute the proportion of GT students who are also members of the target category at each of the three levels, use the following formula: Total GT Target Group/Total GT Students. To compute the proportion of the target group that are GT, use Total GT Target Group/Total Target Group. Both calculations will be revealing, for they yield, respectively, the proportion of the GT program that the target group comprises and the proportion of the target group that has been identified as GT. If the numbers are substantial for your district, you can further disaggregate the latter figure to find how subgroups stand in terms of their representation in the GT program.

Third, secure a copy of a unit-normal curve table, otherwise known as a z table or, simply, the normal curve table. Every book on statistics should have one as an appendix.

Understand that statistics are ordinarily used on samples. If you can get complete, accurate counts of the student groups at the levels you are comparing, you will have parameters, not statistics, and statistical analyses, one could argue, are superfluous because any observed differences in parameters are real differences. However, if your findings are to be used inferentially to determine progress toward your goal, then this author recommends the use of statistics to analyze the "significance" of any differences you might find. The reason is that yearly fluctuations, which inevitably occur in the counts and proportions of small populations, such as the ones that would typically be targeted for inclusion in the GT program, can throw off these parameters and leave you trying to decide how to interpret the changes.

A statistic such as z can come to your rescue in cases such as this. It is the most powerful of the traditional statistics that are commonly used to compare two proportions because it detects even small differences yet allows for a certain "plus or minus" (error) factor in the numbers of students involved in your program at different points in time.

Fourth, compute the necessary z statistic to determine if the observed proportional difference between your district's target population (say, GT special ed) and either the regional or the state's level is significant. Use the following formula:

$$z = \frac{P_h - P_x}{\sqrt{\dfrac{P_x Q_x}{N_x}}}$$

where P_h is the hypothesized proportion, or standard, which corresponds to the proportion of GT in the group to which your group is to be compared, P_x is the proportion of GT in your group (e.g., the proportion of GT special ed in your district), Q_x is equal to $1 - P_x$, and N_x is equal to the number of students in your group[3] (e.g., the number of GT students in your district). Note that in these "vertical" comparisons the groups are correlated, that is, the group at the district level is part of the group at the regional level, which in turn is part of the group at the state level. If two groups are correlated, they have elements—students, in this case—in common.

You can also use this formula for correlated groups to test for a change in proportions from one year to another of students in the same category, a kind of pre-post review. Use the previous proportion as the hypothesized proportion and the current proportion and N to complete the formula. Note that the minimal N that can be used is 10.

Should the two groups being compared be entirely independent of each other, i.e., the two groups have no students in common, then the following formula may be used:

$$z = \frac{P_1 - P_2}{\sqrt{\dfrac{P_1 Q_1}{n_1} + \dfrac{P_2 Q_2}{n_2}}} .$$

In this formula P_1 and P_2 are the proportions found in the two groups being compared, for example, the proportion of white students who are GT versus the proportion of African American students who are GT; Q_1 and Q_2 are, respectively, equal to $1 - P_1$ and $1 - P_2$; and n_1 and n_2 correspond to the total GT for each group, respectively. *Note:* If you work in a very small school district and are not sure that you have enough N in the GT category, the special ed category, or the LEP category to use the z statistic legitimately, consider the following rule: Both n_1 and n_2 must be greater than 5; further, if one or both of these is at least 6 but less than 10,

---

[3]Using the state's proportion as a standard against which to compare allows simplification of the computation, so that only the number for the district is involved in the denominator. For the record, however, there is a way to compare proportions that are weighted by their respective numbers (n).

apply Yates's correction for continuity by reducing the absolute value of the numerator of the preceding formula, $P_1 - P_2$, by $1/2(1/n_1 + 1/n_2)$. The "corrected" formula becomes

$$z_c = \frac{P_1 - P_2 - .5(1/n_1 + 1/n_2)}{\sqrt{\frac{P_1Q_1}{n_1} + \frac{P_2Q_2}{n_2}}}.$$

This adjustment takes out some of the distortion brought about by low numbers in a statistic that assumes a continuous flow of values (Dixon & Massey, 1969). If you have smaller numbers, change your strategy from achieving statistically significant results to achieving simple numerical goals.

Fifth, look up the significance level of the obtained statistic in the unit-normal curve table. I suggest that you set the level of significance (alpha) at .05 for all of these comparisons to reduce the risk of claiming a reliable difference between any two levels if in fact there is none, yet not to be so rigorous as to "load" the study and not find a difference in the proportions, say, between your district's and the region's. As is explained later, the value in the unit-normal curve table that we will look for to achieve significance at this level of alpha is .025 or less.

Because different statistics books use somewhat different notation, a few examples may help you find the right columns and interpret the results correctly. If the obtained z were .60, the probability of a significant effect is .2743, or about .27, which is greater than .025 and thus "not significant." This means that the two proportions compared cannot be said to be reliably different from each other at the .05 (alpha) level of confidence. For the second example, suppose you calculated a z of 1.65. Using a so-called one-tailed test of significance, the tabled value of .0495 would be significant, but because the difference between the two proportions could go either way, positively or negatively, the two-tailed test at the .05 level requires that the tabled value be equal to or less than .025 (McNemar, 1962). An observed z of 1.96 is the minimal indicator of a difference that will satisfy the criterion of .05 that has been set. (Check the table: Note that a z of 1.96 has a probability of .0250.) If the obtained value were -2.02, the second group's proportion is significantly larger than the first's (that is why the sign is negative), and the probability of this occurrence is .0217, which is significant (because it is *less than* .05). Now that you have looked up three values, you know which column in the table to use to find the probability and significance of the calculated z.

Computational Examples

The first analysis to be used is the comparison of a state's proportion of GT special ed students (out of the total GT student body) and the proportion for a particular district. Because the district's figures are a subset of the state's, the two groups are not independent of each other. The first formula will, therefore, be employed, with the state's proportion of GT special ed (.0139) used as the hypothesized proportion

(P_h). The district, by comparison, had a total of 1,638 GT students, only 12 of whom were also classified as special ed, that is, as GT special ed. The proportion of the district's GT students who were GT special ed, then was .0073.

$$ z = \frac{.0139 - .0073}{\sqrt{\dfrac{(.0073)(1 - .0073)}{1638}}} \qquad = \frac{.0066}{.0021} \qquad = 3.143, \qquad \begin{aligned} p &= (.008 \times 2), \\ \text{or } p &\approx .002 < .05^4 \end{aligned} $$

The result shows that the state's proportion of GT children with special ed backgrounds is significantly greater than that of the school district. In terms of practical significance (effect size [Cohen, 1969]), however, the difference, .0066, which is less than 1 percent, is very small, so one must be prudent in making a recommendation. It would be concluded that the school district could profitably invest some internal communication and training or technical assistance toward the end of increasing the nomination and assessment of special ed children who might be GT.

The second comparison is between the state and district with respect to GT LEP, another historically underserved population. In this example, the state's total GT population and the state's total number of GT who are LEP are used to compute the state's proportion of GT who are LEP. The district's proportion is similarly calculated: Total GT LEP/Total GT. Note that the district's total GT is used in the denominator for the computation of the z statistic.

$$ z = \frac{.0340 - .0627}{\sqrt{\dfrac{(.0627)(1 - .0627)}{1638}}} \qquad = \frac{.0287}{.0060} \qquad = -4.783, \qquad p < .00001 \times 2 < .00002 $$

Because a z of −4.22 has a probability (p) of occurring by chance alone that is less than .00002, and because this number is less than the selected alpha level of .05, one can confidently conclude that the state's proportion of GT LEP students is significantly smaller (note minus sign) than the proportion found in the district (or that the proportion in the district is considerably larger than the proportion statewide). And although the difference of −.0287 between the two proportions— about 3 percent—is a small effect size (Cohen, 1969), a GT LEP student is 1.84 times as likely to be identified in this district than in the state as a whole.

Expressing the result in terms of odds can be quite useful. The odds of finding a GT LEP in this district, it was stated, are 1.84 times as likely as statewide. This figure is readily computed by taking the district's proportion (.0627) and dividing it by the state's proportion (.0340).[5] Odds make a lot of sense to people

---

[4]Note that $N = 1{,}638$, the number of GT students in the district, and that the result, .012, is less than the specified alpha, .05, so that the difference is statistically significant.

[5]If the results had been opposite, then the odds would be that LEP GT children in the district would be only about half as likely (.54) to be identified and served as they would be statewide.

(Huck, 2000) and can be used to express a result and as bases for making recommendations. Weak odds suggest that the comparison is about on par. Odds much less than 1.0 suggest that strong corrective action is needed because the standard was not met. The odds in this example, which are positive, suggest that the state GT office would be well advised to discover what this school district is doing to select and, perhaps more importantly, to service these GT LEP children. Furthermore, because the district's proportion of GT LEP students served is greater than the state's average, the district appears to be one of the leaders in identifying GT LEP. As such it should undertake more ambitious goals for its GT program's personnel, such as publicizing its results and describing the means it used for the benefit of other practitioners. Presenting at educational conferences and publishing in professional journals with high circulations would be in order.

By extension, the use of the z test can make many useful comparisons between the state or region and an individual school district on many variables, including the proportion of different ethnic groups who are GT, for example, Total White GT/Total White versus Total African American GT/Total African American, in order to assess program needs.

This final computational example involves the formula for independent groups. Suppose that a district had 2,000 white students and that 8 percent of them, or 160, were in the GT program; suppose, too, that the district has 1,000 LEP students and that 3 percent of them, or 30, were in the GT program. Then the statistic for these two independent groups is

$$z = \frac{.08 - .03}{\sqrt{\frac{.08(.92)}{2000} + \frac{.03(.97)}{1000}}} = \frac{.05}{.0081} = -6.159$$

$$p = .000001 \times 2 = .000002.$$

Here the result is very significant and the effect size, while small, is worthy of notice. The difference of 5 percent in the proportion of students identified indicates that whites are 2.67 times more likely to be selected for the GT program than are LEPs ($.08/.03 = 2.67$). In this instance, the district may have to allocate resources to achieve greater equity without compromising the rigor and quality of the GT program.

Summary and Conclusion

Districts that are very small—for example, districts that have less than 100 students—may find that they have too few students to conduct a statistical analysis of one category or another of underserved gifted and should, instead, make achieving a small number per category a priority.

Those districts that have the requisite Ns, but whose record of service to these populations is below average, should make their region or the state their touchstone, using the more attainable proportion as their initial objective, then graduating to the more difficult objective once the first one is attained.

Testing for these proportional differences in correlated and independent groups permits the identification of differences that are more likely to be stable and meaningful, and less subject to the vagaries associated with yearly fluctuations. If the representation of, say, white students from year to year is relatively stable—that is, no significant differences in proportion—while the proportion of the targeted group keeps growing—that is, shows significant increases—then the gap between these two groups is diminishing. Keeping track of significant differences, furthermore, facilitates plotting the course of the effects of the efforts to increase the representation of the selected, historically underserved group(s) in the district on a simple, but effective, chart.

One of the better prospects for serving very able learners from nondominant ethnic groups, of course, is to attract teachers from these groups into the ranks of GT teachers (Bernal, 2002). For the GT LEP students, bilingually credentialed teachers would be appropriate to recruit and prepare as GT teachers (Bernal, 1998). With greater representation of people of color among the GT teachers, many of the other problems associated with selection and service of these underserved populations would probably start to take care of themselves. Without the presence of minority teachers and minority students in the GT program.... Well, go figure!

REFERENCES

Bernal, E. M. (1974). Gifted Mexican American children: An ethno-scientific perspective. *California Journal of Educational Research, 25*, 261–273.

Bernal, E. M. (1986). Evaluation of programs for the gifted and talented. In J. Gallagher & R. D. Courtright (Eds.), *The World Council's annotated bibliography of gifted education* (pp. 65–72). New York: Trillium Press.

Bernal, E. M. (1998). Could gifted English-language learners save gifted and talented programs in an age of reform and inclusion? Texas Association for the Gifted and Talented. *Tempo, 18*(1), 11–14.

Bernal, E. M. (2002). Recruiting teachers for bilingual gifted and talented programs. In J. Castellano & E. Díaz (Eds.), *Reaching new horizons: Gifted and talented education for culturally and linguistically diverse students* (pp. 237–249). Boston: Allyn & Bacon.

Callaghan, C. M. (1983). Issues in evaluating programs for the gifted. *Gifted Child Quarterly, 27*(1), 3–7.

Carter, K. R., & Hamilton, W. (1985). Formative evaluation of gifted programs: A process and model. *Gifted Child Quarterly, 29*(1), 5–11.

Cohen, J. (1965). Some statistical issues in psychological research. In B. B. Wolman (Ed.), *Handbook of clinical psychology* (pp. 95–120). New York: McGraw-Hill.

Cohen, J. (1969). *Statistical power analysis for the behavioral sciences.* New York: Academic.

Dixon, W. J., & Massey, F. J., Jr. (1969). *Introduction to statistical analysis.* New York: McGraw-Hill.

Huck, S. W. (2000). *Reading statistics and research* (3rd ed.). New York: Addison Wesley Longman.

McNemar, Q. (1962). *Psychological statistics* (3rd ed.). New York: John Wiley and Sons.

Torrance, E. P. (1973, September). *Emergent concepts concerning culturally different gifted children.* Paper presented for the Work Conference on the Culturally Different Gifted Child, Rougemont, NC.

INDEX

Acculturation
  of bilingual/bicultural gifted
    students, 5, 13
  of biracial/bicultural gifted
    students, 85, 86–87, 88
Adderholdt-Elliot, M., 51
African American gifted students,
    45–61. *See also* Haitian gifted
    students
  assessment of, 59
  curriculum for, 55
  cyclical action research and, 47–48
  desegregation of schools and,
    45–46, 53–60
  as economically disadvantaged,
    82, 136, 137, 138, 139, 148
  identification of, 56–57, 59
  instruction of, 55
  parent involvement and, 58
  poverty of, 82
  professional development and
    training of teachers, 57
  underrepresentation in gifted
    programs, 45–46, 48–59
African Americans (general)
  drop out rates, 92
  intermarriage rate, 91
  school enrollment, 89–90
Aguirre, Nilda, 17–27, 70
Algozinne, B., 51
Algozzine, K., 51
Allen, S., 52
Amabile, T., 104
American Association of University
    Women (AAUW), 99, 101
American Psychiatric Association, 124
Arnold, K. D., 100, 101, 106–107
Asian/Pacific Islanders
  demographic data on, 88–89
  drop out rates, 92
  female gifted students, 100
  intermarriage rate, 90, 91
  school enrollment, 89–90
Assessment
  of African American gifted
    students, 59
  bias of instruments, 7, 18–19, 21, 68
  of bilingual/bicultural gifted
    students, 12

of economically disadvantaged
    gifted students, 141–144
  of female gifted students, 102–103
  of gifted students with
    disabilities, 155–158
  of Haitian gifted students, 68
  of Hispanic gifted students, 31, 33–39
  of Native American gifted
    students, 116–119
Association for the Gifted, The
    (TAG), 177
Assouline, S., 163, 168–172
Austin, S., 103
Austin (Texas) Independent School
    District, 9
"Awakening experience," 93

Baldus, Claire, 163–176
Baldwin, A. Y., 51
Baldwin, L. J., 152
Banks, J., 114
Barkan, J. H., 2–3, 14
Barr, M., 52
Baum, S., 151, 152, 155, 158, 159
Baytops, J. L., 51
Bean, F. D., 32
Beatty, W., 127
Belin-Blank Center, University of
    Iowa, 170–173
Benbow, C., 126–127
Bernal, Ernesto M., 2–3, 7, 14, 32,
    177–186
Bias, of assessment instruments, 7,
    18–19, 21, 68
Bilingual/bicultural gifted students,
    1–15. *See also* Haitian gifted
    students; Hispanic gifted
    students
  assessment of, 12
  characteristics of, 3–5
  creativity and, 4, 12–13
  curriculum for, 11–12
  history of education, 1–3
  identification recommendations
    for, 5–11
  instruction of, 12
  poverty of, 5, 8
  social and emotional needs of, 13–14
Bilingual Education Act (1968), 1

Bilingual Verbal Abilities Test, 9
Biracial/bicultural gifted students,
    79–95
  contexts for learning and
    development, 79–81
  drop out rates, 92
  family environment and, 83–86,
    90–92
  home-language use, 86–88
  intermarriage rate, 90–92
  mainstream school culture and,
    88–92
  poverty and, 82–85
  role of language and, 86–93
  teachers as cultural mediators
    and mentors, 81, 93–94
Black gifted students. *See* African
    American gifted students
Bowman, D., 123
Bradley, C., 114, 116
Bransford, J., 132
Brierly, H., 127
Brody, L., 126
Broward County (Florida) school
    district, 65–66, 71–73
Brown, A., 132
Brown, D., 114, 115
Brown, L. M., 101
Brown v. Topeka Board of Education, 45
Brumberg, S. F., 11
Brusca-Vega, R., 89, 93
Bureau of Indian Affairs (BIA), 115–116
Burnette, J., 35, 145
Bush, George W., 29–30

California Association for the Gifted
    (CAG), 177
Callahan, C. M., 101–103, 105, 108,
    118–119, 177
Cantu, L., 30
Carpenter, T. P., 99
Carta, J., 85
Carter, K. R., 123, 177
Case study approach
  for gifted students with
    disabilities, 152–154, 157–161
  for Haitian gifted students, 66–67
  for identifying bilingual/
    bicultural gifted students, 8–9